AMERICANA LIBRARY

ROBERT E. BURKE, EDITOR

The Revolt of Modern Youth

By

Judge Ben B. Lindsey

and

Wainwright Evans

Introduction by
Charles E. Larsen

UNIVERSITY OF WASHINGTON PRESS
SEATTLE AND LONDON

Library of Congress Cataloging in Publication Data

Lindsey, Benjamin Barr, 1869-1943.
The revolt of modern youth.

(Americana library, AL-28)
Reprint of the ed. published by Boni & Liveright,
New York; with new introd.
Includes bibliographical references.
1. Juvenile delinquency. 2. Sexual ethics.
3. Denver. Juvenile Court of the City and County
of Denver. I. Evans, Wainwright, joint author.
II. Title.
HV9094.D4L5   1973   301.43'15   73-8818
ISBN 0-295-95298-9

PREFACE

In The Revolt of Modern Youth *I have attempted, with the collaboration of Wainwright Evans, to present a truthful picture of certain aspects of American social life, as they have consistently and continually revealed themselves to me in the Juvenile and Family Court of Denver. This Court has dealt with both children and adults since it was organized under our first Juvenile Court Law of April 12, 1899.*

This is similar to the task I undertook more than a decade ago, when, with the collaboration of Harvey O'Higgins, I produced The Beast, *and pictured therein a cross section of American politics. At that time I also presided in a Court having jurisdiction of cases growing out of the political turmoils of a growing American city. These cases tried by me involved crookedness of public officials and frauds and corruption in important elections, such as contests over the election of the mayor of the city and the very important elections in which the granting or refusing of monopolistic franchises to such utility corporations as the City Railroad, the Gas, Electric, Power and Water Companies, were concerned. In these contests powerful business interests were seeking special privileges and were not particular how they got them. This brought me into intimate, personal contact with the truth about the political life of our cities.*

In both instances, Denver has been my laboratory; but the conditions I portray are not peculiar to Denver. They hold even more true for every city and town in the United States.

v

Like The Beast, The Revolt of Modern Youth *is based
on things which have actually happened. It is not academic; it is not a swivel-chair product.*

*The many stories, scattered through its pages, I told
or dictated to Mr. Evans through weeks and months of
almost daily conference. We would work through an
evening, after he had spent the day watching my Court
at work, talking personally with boys and girls or adults
who, at my request, gave him the confidences they had
imparted to me. Whenever it was possible, he would
be present at my less confidential interviews with persons who had come to me for help.*

*Along with the telling of the stories, I would set forth,
through hours of extended discussion with Mr. Evans,
the inferences which seemed to me to be indicated by
the facts I had been relating. With these inferences, as
it happily turned out, he found himself strongly in agreement. Thus we came to understand each other perfectly
on many matters which we had no opportunity to discuss in detail; and a mere hint would suffice, without
extended talk, to open up connotations and conclusions
which were evident to both of us.*

*Part of the time it was my custom to dictate at length
important material; at other times I simply talked, trusting with perfect safety, as I found, to Mr. Evans's almost
uncanny ability to "get me"—a thing which he has done
with a fidelity and cleverness in adaptation which seems
to me truly marvelous. With this keen, sympathetic
understanding of my thought, he has combined a fine
clarity of style. The result has been a collaboration which
is a source of great satisfaction to me.*

This book, like The Beast, *is the product of first-
hand, intimate experiences with people, and it expresses
convictions which have slowly and irresistibly forced*

*themselves upon me because they are an integral and nec-
essary part of that experience. As a Judge, I cannot form
conclusions in my own private mind and stop there. I am
obliged by my office to express those conclusions in
terms of action and by official verdict.—Sometimes this
has meant taking my reputation in one hand, my courage
in the other, and simply plowing through. This book is
the fruit of all of that. To me, the pages of it seem alive,
like the living reality from which they have sprung.—
As I read them over, I venture to hope that they may
convey to the American people more than a hint of the
stark realities with which I know life to be filled, because I have wrestled with them since, over twenty-six
years ago, under our first Juvenile Court Law of April
12, 1899, I became identified with the Juvenile and Family Court of Denver.*

BEN B. LINDSEY.

*Juvenile and Family Court
of Denver—Aug. 20, 1925.*

CONTENTS

CHAPTER 4

THE KEY TO FOLLY LANE

CHAPTER 5

CRUMPET MUNCHERS, BUTTON SHINING, AND LETTING THEM BOIL

CHAPTER 6

THE HIGH SCHOOL BOY

CHAPTER 7

THE THREE AGES IN GIRLHOOD

CHAPTER 8

CULTURE AND MORALS

CHAPTER 9

THE SCREEN OF SECRET WISHES

CHAPTER 10

"PLEASE DON'T TALK ABOUT SEX"

CHAPTER 11

THE DOMAIN OF GOOD TASTE

CHAPTER 12

CRUDITY, CULTURE AND LOVE

CHAPTER 13

OUR EXPURGATED PHYSIOLOGIES

CHAPTER 14

THE COMPULSIONS OF AN ENLIGHTENED
FREEDOM

CHAPTER 15

CENSORSHIP, THE CREATOR OF A WET-DISHRAG MORALITY

CHAPTER 16

"HANDFASTING"

CHAPTER 17

THE MARITAL FREEDOM THAT BINDS WITH HOOPS OF STEEL

CHAPTER 18

BIRTH CONTROL IN ITS RELATION TO LOVE AND MARRIAGE

CHAPTER 19

THE FRUIT OF THE MARRIAGE TREE

CHAPTER 20

THE RIGHTS OF THE UNBORN CHILD

CHAPTER 21

A JUDGMENT OF SOLOMON

CHAPTER 22

CONCERNING "THE WILL OF GOD"

CHAPTER 23

A HE-MAN IN ACTION

CHAPTER 24

MAMMY FINK AND A TRIBAL TABOO

CHAPTER 28

THE LADDER OF YEA AND NAY

CHAPTER 29

WASHING BEHIND ONE'S EARS

CHAPTER 30

SKINNY, THE JUDGE AND THE COP

CHAPTER 31

A PLEA FOR GLASS PRISONS

CHAPTER 32

ON THE SALUTARY RESULTS OF TERROR

CHAPTER 33

THE RADICALS OF HUMAN LIFE

THE REVOLT OF
MODERN YOUTH

INTRODUCTION

When *The Revolt of Modern Youth* was published in 1925, Judge Ben Lindsey (1869-1943) was already well known to the American public. As early as 1914, a poll in Hearst's *American Magazine* declared that Lindsey had tied with Andrew Carnegie and Billy Sunday for eighth place as "greatest living American." In October, 1910, the daughter of Senator Robert M. LaFollette had written to Lindsey after one of her speaking engagements on behalf of woman suffrage:

> I don't suppose you're conscious of the deep personal feeling that people have for you all over the country, whether in little out of town villages or in the poor congested quarters of the big cities, or in the leisurely homes of the more well-to-do. No name that I ever mention in speaking gets the same quick warm response. And no one that I quote from carries the same finality of conviction.[1]

A decade earlier, Ben Lindsey was unknown outside of Denver. In 1900, he had been given an interim appointment to fill an unexpired term in a small court in his adopted city. The "temporary" appointment was a turning point in the young lawyer's career. In the years that followed, Lindsey's court evolved into the Juvenile and Family Court of Denver, the best known court of its kind in the world. Concurrently, Lindsey was assiduously cre-

1. Fola LaFollette to Lindsey, October 2, 1910, in Ben B. Lindsey Collection (MSS in the Manuscript Division, Library of Congress), cited hereafter as Lindsey Collection.

1

ating a charismatic image of himself in Chautauqua lectures and journalistic interviews. The measure of his success is accurately reflected in Fola LaFollette's comments.[2]

The Lindsey story, which the Judge never tired of telling, had an irresistible appeal. It was the odyssey of a young boy who had spent his earliest years on his grandfather's farm in Tennessee, listening to his father's derring-do accounts of his services in "the War between the States." It was a tale of religious bigotry, when bickering among relatives over Ben's father's conversion to Catholicism influenced the father's decision to move his family to Denver. It was a story of struggle when Ben, a teenager and the eldest of four children, assumed the role of breadwinner following his father's untimely death. It was a melodrama in which young Ben, in a crisis of confidence over his chances of ever making a successful career for himself, attempted to commit suicide and was foiled only because the revolver he used failed to function. Finally, it was a success story of a self-made lawyer who entered the legal profession by clerking in a law office and eventually rose to such prominence as a judge that he was invited by the President of the United States to visit the White House and describe the remarkable court he had created to give other poor boys a chance.

Lindsey's reputation, based chiefly on his role as a juvenile court judge in Denver, was never confined exclusively to his activities on behalf of children in that city. The Judge became the leading propagandist for the burgeoning juvenile court movement, addressing numerous state legislatures and even the Canadian Parliament and

2. For a full-length biography of Lindsey, see Charles E. Larsen, *The Good Fight: The Life and Times of Ben B. Lindsey* (New York: Quadrangle, 1972).

helping to draft statutes in all part of the country dealing with juvenile delinquency and dependency. Since Lindsey considered "the problem of the children" integrally related to other problems in American society that needed the attention of reformers, he soon became part of a growing national network of progressive politicians and exchanged political intelligence, as well as endorsements, with leaders such as Theodore Roosevelt, Robert La-Follette, Joseph W. Folk, Hiram Johnson, Brand Whitlock, and Tom Johnson. In 1909, Judge Lindsey prepared a series of articles for *Everybody's Magazine* exposing the corrupt influence of utilities companies on Colorado politics. The articles were published a year later in book form as *The Beast*. Lindsey thus added a new dimension, that of muckraker, to his national reputation.[3] In 1915, he attracted national attention again when he sailed on Henry Ford's *Peace Ship* in a quixotic effort to end World War I through mediation.

With the publication of *The Revolt of Modern Youth*, Lindsey took on a new role as a leading spokesman, at least on the popular culture level, of the so-called sexual revolution. The genesis of Lindsey's new role lay partly in the work of his court, which had jurisdiction over domestic relations cases as well as juvenile delinquency and afforded the Judge unusual opportunities for observing some of the inadequacies of social and legal institutions in dealing with a wide range of family problems, including their sexual aspects. Although Lindsey's role as a spokesman for the sexual revolution has understandably been associated chiefly with the 1920s, it was actually anticipated more than a decade earlier.

3. Ben B. Lindsey and Harvey J. O'Higgins, *The Beast,* with an Introduction by Charles Larsen (Seattle and London: University of Washington Press, 1970).

As early as 1909, Lindsey had written an article for the *Ladies' Home Journal* entitled "Why Girls Go Wrong." Although the language of the article was often as Victorian as the title, it contained in embryonic form some of the ideas the Judge was to expand upon in the twenties. Its main theme was the role that ignorance in sexual matters played in "the great mass of social ills which infest society." The reluctance of prudish parents to discuss the "facts of life" openly with their children, particularly with their daughters, was the chief contributing factor to the situation, according to Lindsey. In 1909, the Judge was willing to confine himself to urging parents to give such guidance to their children. By the 1920s, he was more inclined to emphasize that some of the parents would have to be educated first.

Although it was not Lindsey's style to discuss in academic fashion the intellectual sources that may have influenced him, at least two writers apparently had some effect. The first was Havelock Ellis, whose *Sex in Relation to Society* (1910), with its emphasis on the need for sexual education and the importance of birth control, was endorsed in a dust-jacket blurb that Lindsey wrote for Ellis' publisher. Another was Walter Lippmann, whose first book, *A Preface to Politics* (1913), caused the Judge to write a six page letter to the young journalist, praising the book for its psychological insights and suggesting his own interest in writing a book to be called *Sex and Sin,* which would deal with some of the absurdities of the criminal law regarding sexual offenses. Lippmann encouraged Lindsey to write the book, but the Judge's energies were diverted for a decade by political battles in Denver and two trips to Europe.[4]

4. Lindsey to Walter Lippmann, November 10, 1913; Lippmann to Lindsey, November 20, 1913. Lindsey Collection.

On a more personal level, Harvey O'Higgins may have given Lindsey the greatest impetus to become a crusader against American "Puritanism." A popular writer and sometime muckraker, O'Higgins had been Lindsey's literary collaborator in the writing of *The Beast.* The collaboration led to an enduring personal friendship. Following American entry into World War I, George Creel, also a close friend of Lindsey since Denver reform days, brought O'Higgins to Washington to serve as a vice-chairman of the Committee on Public Information, which Creel headed. In 1918, Lindsey made a short trip to Europe at Creel's invitation. The assignment led to a second Lindsey-O'Higgins collaboration, a series of articles for *Colliers* that were eventually published as a small book called *The Doughboy's Religion* (1920). O'Higgins was already strongly attracted by the writings of Freud and was soon to join the attack on American "hypocrisy" about sex, a stock-in-trade of contemporary popularizers of Freud. *The Doughboy's Religion* was basically a political propaganda tract, but it also directed a few barbed remarks at the excessive preoccupation with sexual immorality that allegedly characterized Y.M.-C.A. representatives concerned with the welfare of American servicemen in Europe. Although it is not certain whether these criticisms were included at O'Higgins instigation or Lindsey's, they became a dominant theme in Lindsey's two major works on the sexual revolution of the twenties, *The Revolt of Modern Youth* and *The Companionate Marriage* (1927).

In January, 1924, Lindsey, on a lecture tour in New York City, consulted O'Higgins and Creel about the possibility of writing some articles on his courtroom experiences, with particular emphasis on the sexual attitudes of the younger generation. His two friends suggested that Bernarr Macfadden, head of a publishing empire which included magazines such as *Physical Culture, True Story,* and *True Romances,* would be the most promising candidate as a publisher. The advice proved sound and led to the Lindsey-Evans collaboration, which eventually produced the writings that gave Lindsey his popular identification with the sexual revolution. Since Wainwright Evans, then a staff writer for Macfadden Publications, did all of the writing of the articles which first appeared in *Physical Culture* and later in book form as *The Revolt of Modern Youth* under the auspices of the avant-garde publishing house of Boni and Liveright, the Lindsey-Evans collaboration deserves a brief description.

All of Lindsey's major books were done by literary collaborators. A self-made man with a modest formal education, the Judge did not feel capable of writing a book himself. He had much to say, however, and his publishers recognized that any articles or books carrying his name would attract a large audience. The pattern followed with all of his major collaborators was always the same. Judge Lindsey, by a combination of correspondence and conversations in Denver and New York, would supply the collaborator with an account of his personal experiences as well as his observations on them, and the collaborator would prepare a manuscript. The Judge would then make any minor alterations he felt necessary. Technically, the works were not "ghosted" since the literary collaborator was always given credit as junior author. The narrative was always written in the first person singular, however, since the stories derived their importance entirely from the Judge's reputation and activities. Lindsey was fortunate in finding collaborators whose ideas were very much in tune with his

INTRODUCTION 7

own. Evans, the sole survivor among them by the 1970s,
frequently affirmed to the present writer that Lindsey
provided all of the substance just as he provided all of
the form.[5]

The middle twenties was an opportune time for the
Judge to begin his book. On the level of popular culture,
the movies, Sunday supplements, and women's magazines
were publicizing the presence of a new mood that was
abroad in the land. It was variously attributed to the late
war, the growing number of automobiles, the greater
economic independence of women, or the influence of a
Viennese doctor whose terminology could be glibly repeated even when his works were not read. *The Revolt of
Modern Youth* added little that was new to these popular
accounts except that, on this occasion, the "case histories," as Lindsey called them, were not merely jour-
nalists' gossip but had the authority that derived from
their author's status as a judge who had personally confronted the young people whose sexual encounters and
attitudes he described. The book had two other features
that appealed to a wide audience. For those who enjoyed
an iconoclastic assault on antediluvian clergymen, sadis-
tic school administrators, and all others who, in Lindsey's
phrase, wanted "to terrorize people into being good," the
book had a pleasing Menckenesque quality of belaboring
the "boobs" while giving the reader a vicarious feeling of
being a part of the avant-garde. Finally, as several reviewers noted, the main character in the book—the Judge
himself—was a wise and compassionate man whose
empathy for the younger generation would attract a
large number of readers. The appeal of the book was

5. Conversations with Wainwright Evans, April, 1968, and August,
1970. For this reason and because the book used the first person
singular, I refer to it hereafter as Lindsey's book.

attested by its status as a minor best-seller. A year after its publication, it had sold over eight thousand copies in the United States and was translated into German, Dutch, Danish, Swedish, and Japanese. It was also separately printed in London for distribution in the British Empire. For better or worse, the Judge's reputation as chief popularizer of the sexual revolution in the United States was made.[6]

What may be said of the substantive significance of the book? In many ways *The Revolt of Modern Youth* reveals the strongest and weakest points of Lindsey's whole personality. The Judge succeeded in projecting a warm and, on the whole, convincing image of himself as a friend of youth. At the anecdotal level, his stories had the ring of authenticity, an authenticity which no reader of his private correspondence with Wainwright Evans about the actual cases will doubt. When he expressed his indignation at cruel or narrow parents or teachers, he was convincing. He was a man ahead of his times in criticizing repressive laws that hampered the distribution of information about family planning in an era when birth control clinics were still sometimes raided by the police. He was, of course, not unique in taking these stands or in speaking out on other controversial topics, but as an elective official, particularly in a state where the Ku Klux Klan was riding high, it took a special kind of courage to challenge the old orthodoxies so belligerently.

The book, like its author, had some flaws. A successful popularizer of current trends, Lindsey sometimes demonstrated a characteristic weakness of popularizers—a glibness that did not conceal the absence of any careful

6. Exact sales figures are not available. See Walker Gilmer, *Horace Liveright: Publisher of the Twenties* (New York: David Lewis, 1969), p. 239. The figure of 8,000 was reported to Lindsey by Horace Liveright, July 8, 1926. Lindsey Collection.

research or sustained analysis. It was easy to advocate the desirability of sex education, for example, but once the Judge went beyond the inclusion of the mechanics of contraception and the prevention of venereal disease, he became hopelessly vague and general about the actual content of the "new education." Similarly, while Lindsey's statement that "an illegitimate baby is one conceived by parents who are biologically unfit" was praised by several reviewers, they failed to point out that Lindsey had not made it clear what he meant by biological unfitness. Similarly, the Judge's weakness for going along with current trends rather uncritically was reflected in his somewhat naïve comments about eugenics and "a dominant racial strain" that hopefully might be developed in the United States. In fairness to Lindsey, it should be pointed out that he sometimes evinced a desire to be accurate. For example, he might have become even more infatuated with eugenics if it had not been for a particular fortuitous circumstance. In March, 1925, in a private letter to Wainwright Evans, he mentioned that they must not become dogmatic about eugenics because Clarence Darrow had pointed out to him a few evenings ago that stupid parents sometimes have highly intelligent children, and vice versa.[7]

There was an aftermath to *The Revolt of Youth* that requires a factual *addendum*. After the 1924 election, in which the Judge seemingly emerged the victor in the Ku Klux Klan's campaign to take away his judgeship, the Supreme Court of Colorado invalidated the vote in a precinct where Lindsey's margin had tipped the balance to give him his county-wide victory. Two years later, in 1929, he was disbarred. The history of these events is

7. Lindsey to Wainwright Evans, March 6, 1925, personal letter loaned to the present writer by Evans.

beyond the scope of this essay, but a few surviving foes, as well as friends, of the Judge still believe that the "radicalism" of his two books contributed to his vulnerability.

In the early 1930s, Judge Lindsey and his family moved to California. In 1935, he resumed a judicial career after winning an impressive victory in a contest for a Los Angeles county judgeship. In the same year, the Supreme Court of Colorado reinstated him as a member of the Colorado Bar. The Judge stayed in California, however, where he succeeded, in 1939, in having the California Legislature establish "the Children's Court of Conciliation," a formalized effort to prevent divorce through marriage counseling. He presided over this court in Los Angeles until his death.

CHARLES E. LARSEN

Oakland, California
March 1973

THE REVOLT OF
MODERN YOUTH

CHAPTER 1

The world has been hearing lately from a painter who explores submarine landscapes, studies submarine life in its native haunts, and paints pictures of that watery world.

His name is Zarh H. Pritchard.

When Mr. Pritchard first entered upon his curious vocation he used to dive to the ocean bottom with the help of weights. There, holding his breath, he would paint for a precious three-quarters of a minute. Then he would look about him in desperate haste, get an eyeful, so to speak, and come to the surface to finish his work from memory while the remembering was good. Later he rigged a special diving outfit, and thenceforth made his pictures under water with more satisfactory results.

Having had his vision at first hand, Mr. Pritchard, presumably, is not wholly satisfied with the work of his brush. No artist ever is. And yet his pictures are adequate; for they serve to convey to mankind a valid, even though faint, conception of the incredible, the unpaintable reality; and they do somewhat shatter our rooted notion that a world so alien to our common experience must smack more of death than of intense and swarming life.—He who would see the thing itself, let him learn to dive.

11

As Judge of the Juvenile and Family Court of Denver I feel a sense of kinship with that artist. My work is like that. It is delicate, it is an artistry—a *human artistry*— wrought upon material inconceivably fine; and it goes on in strange regions of the human spirit, far below the visible surfaces of life.

I range daily through an underworld of human thought and action whose way is hid, and whose very existence is not quite believed in by workaday, matter-of-fact persons, even though they could find it all beneath the choppy surfaces of their own existences if they would but take an honest look. There, by long experience, I have learned how I may breathe and move freely in sympathetic communion with life that is beautiful, shy, abundant, and often savagely primitive.

One picks one's way through an unearthly, sometimes a terrifying, twilight. One wanders down long vistas, shadowy and lovely, that are the inner lives of people. It is holy ground. Here dwells in naked beauty the human spirit, stripped of the masks, the clothes, the appearances, the conventions, the hypocrisies, and the shams of life. Here, freed from many illusions, one takes the shoes from off one's feet as in the presence of God. Here one moves softly and alone.

Ways of judgment are different in this dreamlike country of my explorations. Even though one be a "Judge" he does not, as in our outer, superficial world, say glibly of This, "It is good," and of That, "It is bad." I have learned, I think, not to judge anybody any more for anything, and to call nothing common or unclean. I claim no special virtue in this. When one discovers at first hand the truth about people, one has no choice. The human spirit is beyond human judgment.

And yet it is not an easy lesson, this lesson of charity.

The appearance of evil in human conduct is an over-powering and convincing thing; and part of this hidden world is a mystic mid-region of Weir more bizarre, more incredible to the eye and ear, than anything ever dreamed by Poe or painted by Doré.

There are blasted places hideous with volcanic scars, overlaid with black lava, cold and dead; places drained by filthy and sullen rivers fringed by the cypress. And by these and many other signs one may know how terrible is the might of the human soul when our so-called civilization goads it into ways of evil.

Here strange monsters make slimy trails, and you look into eyes that are like the eyes of dead men. Here hands, trembling and cold with Fear, reach out for help; here the physically and spiritually sick and crippled ask dumbly for compassion. From beyond, rising like a foul mist, comes sound of strife——

"And we are here as on a darkling plain,
Swept with confused alarms of struggle and flight,
Where ignorant armies clash by night."

There are times, indeed, when the apparently resistless might and supremacy of evil in some lives, and in the very constitution of human society itself, overwhelms one with convinced despair, like a black flood; and then the devils that dwell within these waters come upon one like so many cuttlefish, which one must fight as one may.

But happily that is only one corner of the picture, and a lesser part at that. For the most part my entrance into people's lives takes me through regions of beauty, where youth is lovely, plastic, radiant, and charming even in its blunders and mistakes.

It is on this that I would dwell as much as I may

without distorting the picture. For twenty-five years, through more than ten of which I have had the sympathetic coöperation of my wife, whose desk is next to mine, and who there shares my confidences with youth, it has been my privilege and my delight to work in the midst of eternal childhood. Here, despite moments of blackness, the wind still blows in the willows, Pan still pipes in the springtime, and the very sky takes on a deeper azure from the long, long thoughts of Youth.

I think that if the world better knew those thoughts and motives, how guileless and natural they are, how *naïve*, how holy in their unstudied honesty and simplicity even when they are most unwise, society might recover its sanity, healed as by a touch—such sanity as Christ was thinking of, when out of his fathomless insight into good and evil he said, "Suffer the little children to come unto me, and forbid them not; for of such is the Kingdom of Heaven."

Little children! But what about the big ones? There are no big ones. We are a race of children. Childhood lasts from the cradle to the grave; and it is by no will of my own that they are defined by law in my court, as persons under twenty-one. Still, I have this consolation; while they are young they are plastic, divinely plastic. They bend without breaking; they mend with miraculous vitality; and about them still float those trailing clouds of glory, tenuous yet indestructible, which are the heritage of childhood—and, let us hope, the ultimate inheritance of the human race.

I am going to say some things about certain of our social institutions which will often sound harshly critical, negative, and destructive. When I daily see young children, adolescents, and adults crushed and crippled by the machinery of life as we live it, I find restraint difficult and moderation of statement nearly impossible. And yet I would have the effect a constructive one. Painful as are the diseases that afflict human society today I have faith that they are really the discomforts of a change now visibly under way; and part of my purpose in pointing out the facts is the hope that by intelligently understanding the truth we may so hasten our social evolution that swift decades rather than slow, circling centuries will suffice for some of the changes at least.

I am not attempting to offer solutions. I have no panacea. But I believe that if human society can ever be brought to diagnose its own case, and to understand clearly some of the things that are the matter with it, our national mind—or whatever you choose to call the entity—will work the matter out to a reasonable solution.

As a nation we need to be psycho-analyzed. Modern psychology, within the last quarter of a century, has more and more assumed the aspects of an exact science; and so practical is it becoming that it has begun, slowly but surely, to bring the art of self knowledge to the American people. I do not see how such knowledge can fail to bear fruit, nor how the truth, once known, can finally fail to make us free.

To foreshadow the future and to forecast the changes it may bring to human society in a time perhaps not far distant, it is of first importance that we should know the truth about society *as it is*. With the help of such knowledge it is well within our power to hasten the outcome; whereas if we continue fatuously to wallow in our ignorance of the truth, we shall certainly delay our own evolution, and needlessly stretch the span of human misery. Even to know and admit the truth about things is curative. Let us then candidly do that.

But to know and admit the truth, it is needful to look

beneath as well as above the surfaces of life. That is what I have tried to do in the chapters of this book; and I realize with regret that I have had to tell a story which will be shocking to a great many persons. Of these some will shut their eyes to the facts; others will flatly and angrily deny them; and a saving remnant will look upon them without fear and find good in them. It is for these last that I write.

Shocks are needed now and then to rouse us from our lethargy and complacency. Conservative and conventional people relish them as little as they do the first shock of a cold bath. They want to be comfortable; and if silence and hypocrisy will make them comfortable, then they are for that.

But if the Truth hurts most of us so badly that we don't want it told, it hurts even more grievously those who dare to tell it. It is a two-edged sword, often deadly dangerous to the user. I learned this more than ten years ago, when, in "The Beast and the Jungle" I told the truth about politics in the City of Denver and successfully challenged all America to deny that it was the truth about all cities. I am crippled in my work to this day by the bitter enmities aroused through that book; but though it saddens me to have had to pay such a price, yet I do not grudge it. Who am I to complain? Has not that always been the price? Of those who read this tale of the revolt of modern youth I do not necessarily ask for complete agreement with my views; but I do ask that they will believe in my sincerity.

What I am pleading for in this book is justice, the justice so long denied mankind, particularly the women and children part of it. The injustices I have seen in my long career on the bench have filled me with an indignation that can no longer be silent.

In crying out against these injustices I have found the utmost plainness of speech necessary; and I have resorted to it even though I know it will often create the impression that I have wantonly and unnecessarily flouted many vital standards and conventions. But that interpretation of my attitude, I want, as far as possible, to prevent. Let me say here, then, with the utmost emphasis, that when I criticise many of our present standards and conventions it is not because I do not favor them, because I do favor them. Rather it is because they have become so involved in superstition and ignorance, and have often become so stale and thoroughly second hand, that they have in a large measure ceased to function. As a race we have lost sight of the ideals and practical purposes that originally inspired them. Having accepted them without putting them to the test of reason and common-sense with a view to their revision, we have misinterpreted them. Consequently we have come to regard them as ends in themselves, as so many formulas in magic; and instead of carrying out the ideals that once lay back of them, we are in a large measure unconsciously frustrating those ideals. Thus many of our most important conventions make today for immorality, though their original aim was morality. And by the same token, our social tree bears the bitter fruit of injustice instead of wholesome fruit of justice.

It is hard to write of these things and at the same time cling firmly to the understatement; but I think I have done it. Also it is hard to write about these wrongs without a mounting indignation which is undesirable in such a book as this because it tends to alienate the reader. This I have tried to avoid also. But if at times I have not succeeded, I hope I have at least made it clear that I am as much in favor of our necessary tradi-

tions and conventions as anybody. I am as much for
what is *really* meant by marriage, virtue, chastity, and so
on, as anyone could be. It is in that sense that I speak
of them; and it is for that reason that I reject many of
the shams that are offered us in their place under similar
names.

Thus we come first of all to the need for an honest
statement of the nature of *Human Society As Is,* and a
rejection of those deceiving appearances which we find
it comfortable, in our fool's paradise, to accept as the
reality. This involves an account of the growing signs
of rebellion on the part of modern youth; a rebellion
which is youth's instinctive reaction against our system
of taboos, tribal superstitions, intolerances and hypocrisies. These things contain within themselves the seeds of
their own destruction; and that destruction will finally
prove medicinal, bitter to the mouth but sweet to the belly.

Because of my faith in the final outcome of these
changes I discuss with charity and sympathy the signs
that forecast them. But this does not mean that I
necessarily approve of all that is happening, or that I
would not have it otherwise if I could. Doubtless there
is much lost motion in these natural changes, and doubtless the application of reason in human affairs can save
us much disaster and delay. Hence this book. It is a
plea for the use of reason about things toward which
most of our present reactions are blindly habitual.

For instance, take the institution of marriage, the most
fundamental institution in the world, the instrument
whose intelligent use can regenerate and save the race.
What a world tragedy it is that such an institution should
be permitted to grow untended, like a rank weed in a
neglected garden! To protest against this neglect of it

is surely not to condemn it, but rather to register a profound faith in its possibilities.

The Youth of today is tampering extensively with the
institution of marriage. Some of the tampering is unwise.
But what is the remedy? And how can Youth be persuaded to caution amid these dangers? Can it be done
by assuming toward Youth an attitude of pharisaical
hostility and fierce intolerance? No,—these are capable
of producing nothing but defiance and more intolerance
from Youth. Or is the remedy rather to discuss in the
open, to advise, to counsel, to sympathize? Surely there
is no room for a difference here.

Some may consider this merely a pretty theory, formulated by a sentimentalist. But I have the advantage of
them there; because I have set down in this book nothing
that has not been proved by the test of use. On just that
basis I have for twenty-five years had conspicuous success·
in dealing with individuals; a success which the voters of
Denver have recognized by returning me to office through
nine or ten elections, not including primaries, in the face
of bitter opposition from forces whose sole purpose was
to exploit those voters.

Let me ask, then, but one thing of the reader; that he
will accept what I have written both as the fruit of long
experience, and also as a pledge of my abiding faith in
the ultimate and inherent goodness of mankind and in
a divine destiny for the human race.

CHAPTER 2

A suave young man, grave of face, subdued of manner, modish of dress, stepped from a rakish and shining blue roadster, entered the door of one of Denver's most important schools, and asked for the Principal, whose name, let us say, was Miss Jackson.

That lady received him in her office. —She was all that a guardian of the minds and morals of our younger generation is supposed to be. She was counted a first-rate disciplinarian and a good administrator. In her day she had been an exceptional teacher. As head of a large school, she was watchful over the girls in her charge; and whatever there was to know about girls—and boys too, for that matter—she was supposed to know it. In this day of unheard of freedom in the thought and conduct of the young, she surveyed her domain with an eagle eye that appeared to see everything. As one of her flapper charges put it, "She was the cat's ears; and her optics were the cat's pajamas."

As for the youth who now stood respectfully before her with his cap in his hand, he impressed her favorably; for, as I say, she knew all about young people. He had about him a look of responsibility of which she approved. His restraint, his poise, his grace, were all just right; and he spoke now in a refined and modulated voice.

"I am the brother of Helen Jones, of the sophomore class," he began, looking at her the while with frank and ingenuous eyes. "Mother is very ill; and I have come to drive Helen home, if you will excuse her."

"Certainly," said the Lady Principal—"I will send for her."

She pressed a button. "Please bring Helen Jones to my office," she said to her secretary.

Then, while they waited for Helen, she asked with genuine concern about the condition of Mrs. Jones. What was the trouble?

Young Mr. Jones was not certain. He indicated with a delicate mid-Victorian gesture that he wasn't supposed to be certain. But he looked urgently at the clock, which was pointing to two.

Helen entered. Helen was just fifteen. Helen was the type of girl Miss Jackson was accustomed mentally to label "nice." She had dreamy blue eyes, golden hair that curled all over the top of her pretty head, and a face of delicate, ethereal beauty. The delicacy, the divinity, of developing womanhood hung about her like gossamer. To Miss Jackson's experienced and appraising eyes, Helen and her brother were fit fruit to have come from such a strictly correct home as she knew the Jones home to be.

"Helen," said Miss Jackson, "your brother tells me your mother is ill. He has come to take you home. But before you go, I'll telephone to find out how she is. I do hope it isn't serious. Why only last week I saw her down town, and she looked unusually well!"

As her hand went out to the telephone the girl flashed one look of stony amazement at the youth, who was nervously fingering his cap. "I don't know this boy," she blurted. "And you needn't telephone, because Mother isn't sick at all."

Miss Jackson, being a woman of poise, didn't have hysterics; but so far as the general wisdom of her conduct from that moment was concerned, a fit of hysterics would have been infinitely better. First, in a deep and awful voice, she questioned the boy. He, finding himself in a corner, admitted that he was not Helen's brother. But beyond that he shut his lips completely. Not a word of explanation could Miss Jackson get from him. As for Helen, she knew nothing at all about it—and her frigid dignity of manner was at absolute zero,—particularly when she looked scornfully at the boy, who, when he wasn't staring out of the window was speculatively eying the door.

"Very well," said Miss Jackson at last; "this matter will have to go to the Juvenile Court."—Whereupon she called me by telephone, and explained her conviction that this boy was a representative of the white slave industry, and that he had come to *her* school, of all places, to drive his nefarious trade, and drag Helen Jones, a girl from one of the first families of Denver, to her ruin.

In due time thereafter the boy, the girl, the infuriated Mr. and Mrs. Jones, and the still palpitating Miss Jackson appeared before me. The Parents and the Principal were united in their demand that the predatory male receive a penitentiary sentence; they regretted that the law wouldn't permit hanging him. There was every evidence, indeed, that if I didn't deal out something rough and raw to that boy, not one of them, except the boy—and maybe the girl—would ever vote for me at future elections.

I let them talk—such being the custom in the Juvenile Court of Denver. As soon as I thought they had it all off their chests and were feeling better, I got rid of them, and had a talk with Helen, and with the boy who wasn't her brother. I talked to them together, and then I talked to them separately.

What I learned about the boy, so soon as I had convinced him that neither Miss Jones nor anybody else would be permitted to broil him for dinner, was that he was just a boy, that he was scared to death, that he hadn't meant to be particularly wicked, and that he was glad to find that I was human. He had refused to talk to Miss Jackson for fear her wrath would spill, like vicious acid, upon Helen Jones, whom he had never seen before, he admitted, and who had never seen him before.

As for Helen's end of the story, that explained the whole thing. Helen had always encountered severe discipline and old-fashioned restraint at home. Her parents disapproved of boys, of automobile rides, of parties, of dances—particularly the new dances—and of most other things that enter today into the lives of young people.

Helen must be protected from life till she had some sense, or at least till she was safely married. She must not go near the water till she had learned to swim. They were concerned that her mind remain a virgin piece of white paper, unsullied by knowledge or experience. They did not want that she should be sophisticated and chaste; they wanted that she should be ignorant and innocent. They were afraid she knew where babies came from, but they were not sure.—In short, they were the Joneses. You know them.—I feel perfectly safe in making these comments about them because your name, Dear Reader, is doubtless Brown.

But in high school Helen naturally met boys. To one of these she frankly intimated that she found the drab innocence of her life oppressive and the even tenor of her way monotonous. She wanted "experience." She thought an auto ride might set her up.

"I'll fix it for you," said the boy. "I know a fellow named Harold Simpson. He has a brand new car, and he drives like a streak and makes love like a demon. I'll speak to him, and he'll take you for a ride."

"But I don't believe I want him to make love to me," she quavered, beginning to weaken.

"Oh, that'll be all right," was the answer. "He's a nice chap, and he'll do things your way. He'll just take you for a ride and make it snappy. When'll he come?"

With that Helen's quick wits rose to the occasion. "Have him call at Stonewall Jackson's office at two to-morrow," she said. "He must say he's my brother, that Mother is ill, and that he has come to take me home. That will give time for a ride, and I'll get home in time for them not to be asking what made me late."

"Will you give him a kiss?"

"Sure—that's a fair price," said Helen.

"He'll do—for a beginning," observed her confederate.

After relating these details to me Helen added, "You see, Judge Lindsey, it was the only way I could get to go riding. The other girls go riding. Why should I have to miss all these things? I want a good time like anyone else. I love to dance; and—and the boys like me, too, don't you think?"

"I am sure of it," I said heartily. "And it is natural and right that they should. But, my dear, that is different from this business of going riding with boys you don't know, and doing it in secret at that. You know things happen on these auto rides that are no part of the original program."

"You mean—love making?" she asked.

"Yes, and drinking. Most of these boys carry booze. I know it, even if you don't, because cases of this sort are always coming before me, and most of them involve the fact that the boy carries a flask. Now you wouldn't want to get drunk, or even tipsy, would you? You surely know that drink breaks down all the other barriers, and causes people to lose their heads."

"Judge," she exclaimed earnestly. "I wouldn't think of such a thing—*at my age*. Why, I'm only fifteen; and you know *eighteen is the age for that!* No indeed; I wouldn't drink; I wouldn't think of such a thing!"

Although I have long been accustomed to these glimpses into the minds of our brisk younger generation, I had to look sharply at the child to see if she was joking. But there could be no doubt of her simple and sincere earnestness, or that she was laying down for my instruction the strenuous, strict, and self-denying conventions of the strange Flapper-Flipper world she lived in,—a world whose ways, customs, purposes, visions, and modes of thought were as unknown to her parents, and apparently to her teachers, as the social customs of Mars; ways which they would certainly pronounce beyond the pale of morality and toleration if they knew about them. Judged by every standard acceptable to them, Helen was *bad*. Judged by dictums of conduct which they considered as simply not open to debate or discussion or question, this child had already so far departed from respectable ways of thought that she was hardly fit to occupy a decent home, and fully merited the social ostracism that would be her portion if the truth were known.

I inquired more particularly. I learned that one could go automobile riding at fifteen; that one could drink freely when one was eighteen; that love making could begin at any time. Kissing, petting, and other tentative excursions into sex experience, provided they were not too pronounced, were taken for granted by this sweet-faced girl as part of what she might properly look forward to long before she should be eighteen—if she could manage not to get found out. Such was her code, and such was the code of her friends and intimates.

As to the question of actual sex experience, she hadn't yet come to definite conclusions, but she had an open mind. She debated this with me at length and with a candor based on her knowledge that confidences imparted in my court are never betrayed. She inclined to the view that promiscuity in sex matters might be wrong, but that there was something to be said for the trial marriage or experimental liaisons, considering that most all the marriages she knew of seemed to be ending in divorce. She wondered if it was not more immoral for a man and woman to live together in marriage when they didn't love each other than it would be for another man and woman to live together, though unmarried, because they did love each other.

"Where do you get these ideas?" I asked. "Where do you learn about such questions?"

"Oh, we girls talk about them; and some of the girls talk about these things with the boys; but I never have done that yet."

Her attitude towards her parents was one of unmitigated fear and distrust. She knew from experience that she could not put her thoughts and problems into language that they would understand; and that had they heard what she was saying to me, they would have gone frantic, either with rage or alarm. She understood perfectly that they had always kept certain of the doors of life shut and locked so far as she was concerned; she knew that they did not trust her judgment, and she resented the fact. So far as they were concerned, her lips were sealed on all vital matters, and she had turned for such information as she wanted to her more sophisticated companions.

Toward the Principal and most of the teachers in her

school, she felt the same. She hated some of them, and feared all of them, and would as soon have thought of stripping the clothes from her body as of baring her mind and heart to their critical and disapproving inspection. As to Miss Jackson, whom she called by a nickname which I have translated into "Stonewall" . . . she was conscious that she could expect neither help, information, nor sympathy from that excellent and conventional lady, who would have considered it immoral for any girl to manifest an interest in such matters, and would be all for stern punishment, exposure, and expulsion for any girl found guilty of a sex offense.

Later, when I talked with Miss Jackson I told her so much of what had happened as I could without violating the girl's confidence. At first the story seemed to stun her. Then she recovered her assurance and her tongue. Helen, I learned, had always deceived her with her refined ways into thinking her a refined and good girl. She was thankful to know the truth about her at last; and was also thankful that such cases were extremely rare in her school.

"Besides," she concluded, "I can't be responsible for what goes on among my students outside of school hours. I know everything that goes on inside of my school; I can read their minds; they can't get around me. But after school, when I can't keep an eye on them, it is up to their parents."

"Don't you think," I ventured, "that watching them is a less effective way to control them than to lay all the cards on the table, and tell them the truth, and get their confidence?"

"It sounds beautiful," she said scornfully. "But it would never work. To bring up such subjects is merely to insure that they will think about them. Why direct their attention to the nasty things of life, when there is so much that is beautiful and wholesome? I don't want to direct their attention to sex. I don't want them thinking about such things."

"And you think you are succeeding in that?"

"I certainly do," she retorted. "But, as I say, I can't control them outside of school. *In* school I'm master of the situation."

No, I didn't argue with her any more. I really didn't have the heart to tell her that the whole conspiracy between Helen Jones and her boy friend had been hatched within ten feet of where she was standing in the halls of her own school; and that the conversation had to be carried on in whispers to keep her keen ears from getting it.

Of course she could not have been expected by any reasonable person to fathom a conspiracy that was being worked out in whispers, even within ten feet of her; and it was certainly silly, or conceited, of her to expect such vigilance from herself. No vigilance, no chaperonage however terrible, mean, and suspicious would have been equal to that.

But just that is the point. That is the one final evidence of the woman's incompetence, and of the incompetence and innate limitations of her kind. The amazing thing, not only about her, but about an unfortunately large portion of the teaching profession, was this belief that the job could be done that way; that people could be managed and controlled that way; and that the thing was actually working, when she could not have made it work if she had had a hundred eyes and five hundred ears, and a corps of trained spies with periscopes and microscopes in every nook and recess of her school. To me such stupidity as that is astounding beyond words.

It seems the more astounding when you link it, as Miss Jackson did, with the notion that adolescent boys and girls, subject to such inevitable tuitions of modern life as the motion picture, magazines, books, newspapers, and the like, can be prevented, by means of a conspiracy of silence, from thinking and talking and speculating about sex. Hundreds and thousands of apparently intelligent adults, with short memories, believe that. It is one of the most dangerous of our many follies.

I rescued Helen Jones from the clutches both of her parents and her teachers. Helen and I had many a long talk; and Helen is now thoroughly able to manage her relations with boys, and is under no delusions about many things which were formerly a complete muddle in her puzzled mind.

When she wants to talk to someone on whose experience and wisdom she relies, she comes to me. But consider the absurdity of the situation. Consider the disaster that nearly overtook this child because her parents had dull, conventional minds, and because they and her teachers all believed that the way to make people be good, and to do this rather than that, is to make them afraid and keep them ignorant. The simple fact was that she was starving, and that they refused her the spiritual nourishment and the intellectual enlightenment she craved and had a right to crave.

Helen's case is one of many hundreds like it that I have dealt with since the founding of the Juvenile Court of Denver twenty-five years ago. It is one of the many complete proofs I have seen that young people are seeking, not evil things but good things in life, and that when they choose an evil thing rather than a good thing it is merely because, in their inexperienced eyes, the evil looks as if it were good.

To my mind the incident proves still another thing. It proves that young people demand to be shown. They demand that they be put in possession of the facts, and that they be permitted to come to their own conclusions about those facts. They regard the assumption of their elders that they are incapable of sound judgment on such matters as an insult; and in that they are perfectly correct. It *is* an insult. Openly to underestimate the intelligence of anybody, be he adult or child, is an open insult. No adult person of any spirit will tamely submit to such treatment from another adult, and if it comes from a child or a youth, he considers it a want of respect for his age. But the same person will, without hesitation, tell a young person to his face that he must not have such and such knowledge because he is not old enough to judge and to act soundly. The truth is—and every child knows it—that children think and act quite as logically, and much more honestly, than adults; and that their mistakes come from their limited knowledge of facts, a limit which leads them frequently into reasoning from wrong or insufficient premises.

Helen Jones reasoned from the facts just as soon as I gave them to her. Why were those facts hidden by her own parents, who loved her and who would have gone to any length and made any sacrifice to have served her best interests in life?

Obviously because, like most of the human race, they were not particularly imaginative or intelligent; and because, like most of us, they were content to act upon a received tradition of which they had never made a critical and candid examination. Thinking is hard work; and breaking trail in new lines of conduct is still harder work. Most persons instinctively steer clear of that kind of thing without really knowing why they do it. Most persons hate to be uncomfortable.

The thought that sometimes makes me despair is that when Helen grows up and has children of her own, it is 99 to 1 that she in her turn will instinctively try to shield them, as her parents tried to shield her, by letting down a curtain of ignorance between them and the Truth, which alone makes people free. I have seen it happen many times. Girls come to me in difficulties precisely similar to the difficulties their own mothers approached me with fifteen and twenty years ago. The mothers succumb, even against their judgment, to the social pressure, the overwhelming and compelling *suggestion* from society that ignorance is the best and easiest way to protect youth from an early arousal of its most powerful instincts.

That the thing does not work makes no difference. They think it *does* work. No amount of talk will convince them to the contrary. Helen's parents were sure it was working with her. They thought they knew all about their daughter; that her mind in adolescence was as much an open book to them as it had been when she was just coming out of infancy, and fearlessly prattled whatever came into her little head,—and continued to prattle till she found for some reason or other she mustn't, and henceforth educated herself in hypocrisy and deceit for her own protection.

Mr. and Mrs. Jones thereafter saw only the surface of Helen's mind—a glazed surface that reflected their own conventional standards like a looking glass. Too many American parents know just that much about what is going on in their children's minds. Of course Helen kept her own counsel. She went about discovering the mysterious truth for herself, in her own way, with the help of companions no wiser than herself; and the result was that she nearly ran upon the rocks that have been the undoing of hundreds of others whose plans for secret automobile rides and the like go through without discovery.

This is why distrust, contempt, and a fiery resentment and self will are so greatly in evidence today in the attitude of many young persons toward their elders, and particularly toward those adults who are supposed to control and guide them, their parents and their teachers. If you want to see what I mean, go into any school today and observe the changes that are evident. Where teachers and pupils are on terms of mutual understanding there may be simply a lack of formality and an air of equality and of independence on the part of the pupil which is devoid of offense. But when, for one reason or another, mutual understanding and tolerance are wanting between these representatives of two generations, then there becomes noticeable in the manners of these children a lack of respect, of spontaneous courtesy, and of the natural and kindly graces of life. Where these conditions of misunderstanding between adults and children prevail one notes on the part of youth a flouting independence, a half-spoken defiance, a tacit hostility, a watchfulness, a quickness to take offense at the least hint of adult advice or interference. It is not so much that such reactions on the part of youth are new as that they are manifesting themselves with an openness, a freedom and degree of success which has never been equaled, I believe, in the past. I may add that in my judgment these things originate mainly in the home; and that it is not reasonable to expect even the wisest teachers to cope with them unaided.

These things are symptoms. Symptoms of what? Why

symptoms of a state of mind which is saying to the whole adult world, "So you think you are so much wiser than we, do you! We are to just take your word for things, are we! You must have one line of behavior and we another! You are old and wise while we are young, foolish, and ignorant!—All right; show us! Produce the truth if you've got it. Meantime, we go our way!"

Thirty, forty years ago, youth couldn't have flung such a challenge with the least hope of success. Today, the day of the automobile, the telephone, speed, good wages, and an unheard of degree of economic independence for everybody, it can.

I really see no remedy for all this, unless we of the adult generation can bring ourselves to treat these boys and girls with some respect, and as equals. By that I don't mean being "pals" with them. Adults as a rule are not pals with children. Their interests are different. Adult interests, and the adult point of view, are different from the interests and the point of view of youngsters; and any adult who tries to palm himself off as "young" in that sense too often fails. What I do mean is sympathy and understanding and tolerance, and a complete willingness to let young people order their own lives *in the light of the facts*. Such a course on the part of any adult instantly wipes out the antagonism, the rudeness, the defiance now so in evidence. It never fails. I have never known it to fail in my twenty-five years of experience in dealing with youth of all sorts and conditions, save in the case of the feeble-minded.

More than that, young people, when treated in that way, become humble, receptive, eager to learn, and perfectly free from the cocksureness which is traditionally supposed to be an attribute of youth. The cocksureness of youth is nothing but a brave effort to cover up its own

doubts and weaknesses from the eyes of an non-under-
standing, unsympathetic adult world. It vanishes at the
first sympathetic touch, and one and all they become little
children, pitifully eager for light and guidance, and
demanding of you only, "When you say that, *Smile!*"

And if you *can't* say it with a smile, God help you;
for savagery, fear, and superstition beget their like, and
you have turned them loose to ravage the soul of your
own child.

Your own children, Sir and Madame, are intelligent,
right minded, and full of fine aspirations and quick sym-
pathies, just as you have always hoped and wanted;
and honesty and kindness touch them where they live.
Believe this of them, and rejoice in your hearts, on com-
paring them with yourselves, that they in the days of
their youth, at least, are an improvement on the rag-
tag and bobtail of adult Puritanism that begot them.

Don't let the stick that has tarred you disfigure them.
Throw it away. They need no beating, either with that
or any other stick. Mentally, save in experience and
knowledge of fact, they are your equals; spiritually they
are often your superiors, particularly in honesty. Treat
their minds with respect, therefore; instruct them; and
then leave the ordering of their lives to them. They will
meet the responsibility with a more generous idealism
than is evident in the lives of most of their elders.

CHAPTER 3

So much for the case of Helen Jones. But after all, one swallow doesn't make a summer; there always have been and there always will be girls like Helen, who mature early and are perhaps a trifle over-sexed, and who are on that account always to be found fluttering around the danger line. And so, why make such a pother over these occasional cases of delinquency? What about the ninety and nine to whom nothing happens?

And when they say ninety and nine, they literally mean it. It isn't so very long since one of the administrators of our Denver schools said in a newspaper interview that he did not believe that one per cent of high-school students go wrong, and that my estimates, running to much higher figures, are gross exaggerations resulting from my constant contact with delinquent cases. In other words the gentleman agrees with Miss Jackson. I may add that his knowledge about high-school students appears to be about commensurate with that of Miss Jackson, and that he evidently believes such things could not go on right under his eyes and he not see them. I find that all too large a portion of the teaching profession has jollied itself into believing that.

But when boys and girls of high-school age get to telling me things, they don't stop with themselves. They tell me about other students who need my help; and I can follow the thread from case to case at any time as far as I may have the time and physical strength to go, and still it travels on and on. I have said many times, and I maintain it now, that from any ordinary case, selected at random, I can uncover a thousand; and that the rate of increase in the revelations will be in an almost geometrical ratio. The ordinary delinquent generally can tell of at least one to two others whose way of thought has been sympathetic to his.

The reason the case of Helen was exceptional was that Helen, by a trick of circumstance, got found out. It is the getting found out that is exceptional. *They don't get found out one time in ten.* Indeed, I regard this estimate as conservative. It is a mystery to me how more than one in fifty ever gets found out—and for all I know to the contrary that might well be the ratio.

I am in constant touch, confidential touch, with scores of these boys and girls; they tell me things; and when I piece together this patchwork of information, coming in constantly from such diverse sources, none of which knows of the others—information all of which has approximately the same import—why I get a picture of the whole which I believe is a true picture. And I have yet to see the parent or teacher that had come within a thousand miles of possessing the same information or of having any way of getting it.

To many this will seem a shocking statement—though it isn't to be compared for shocking power with certain things I shall say presently. Those who are shocked will, of course, reply in the usual way. They will turn the picture I have drawn to face the wall. They will repeat that my contact with delinquents has warped my vision, and that I know nothing of the *wholesome* girls and boys because *these* don't come to my court. In that they are quite wrong. Scores and hundreds of the young people of Denver come to meet me and to watch the Juvenile Court in action not because they have ever been guilty of delinquencies themselves but because they are

interested and want to see what it is all about. And
then we run a Juvenile Employment Agency in connection
with the court. This brings to us many of the finest
and best youth of the city. Many come also to consult
me about friends of theirs who have gotten into trouble
or who need guidance and help. Some come with their
parents. Some are sent by their parents, who wisely
wish them to have some first-hand contact with things as
they are. Thus my contact with wholesome boys and
girls is quite as extensive as my contact with those who,
in the judgment of their adult contemporaries, are not
wholesome.

That method of closing the argument, by maligning the
character of my young friends, is an old story in Denver.
I recall a Denver minister, for instance, who some years
ago publicly denounced me and my warped vision, and
my "libels on American youth." His eloquence was as
great as his indignation, and I don't doubt that many
were convinced by his fiery words. As he spoke those
words, he no doubt had in mind the vision of his own
sweet and beautiful daughter. Perhaps she sat there
listening to his words. How unthinkable that *she,* or that
thousands of other pure young girls in Denver, could
be considered in the same breath with such preposterous
notions. For his premise was that to say or admit that
young people make mistakes, particularly in matters of
sex contact, is to say that they are "immoral," a view
with which I strongly disagree.

Well, at the time those words were uttered, in denunciation of me, that young girl was under my care, and
I was having her treated for an infection by a physician
on whose discretion I could rely. Her father didn't know
it; and he doesn't know it to this day. He would drop
dead if he did. Knowing that he must not be told, she

was forced to come to me for the help, tolerance and loving sympathy she should have been able to seek from him. Tell her father? What a pity she can't. What a pity it is that he would merely mess things up if he knew the truth! What a pity his own intolerance barred her way to his confidence!

That girl was a perfect example of the futility of trying to bring up our young people by methods that have been notoriously ineffective through all the ages, and which today, under modern conditions, are more absurd than ever. She had been carefully guarded. She did not dance, she had never seen a motion-picture show; she didn't play cards because card playing was sinful; and her so-called religion was a system of voodoo worship in the service of a wrathful God, whose chief function was to punish the imperfect creatures he had made, and reward the few who might pull through with his approval.

Such was her training and preparation for the actualities of life. One day she met two soldiers. They took her for a ride in their automobile. Thus her father's good old-fashioned methods were put to the test of modern conditions and the test failed.

And when it did fail, she *couldn't tell him*. I think that was a deeper tragedy, even, than the mistake she made in the depths of the systematic, calculated ignorance into which she had been trained.

And yet he professed to practice as well as preach the precepts of the Man of Nazareth, whose mouthpiece he was supposed to be,—the Man who said to the woman taken in adultery, "Neither do I condemn thee; go, and sin no more."

That, they said, was encouraging immorality. Indeed they said Christ "encouraged immorality" all the time.

That was one reason why eminent clergymen of the Jewish Church in his day couldn't stand for him, and that is the reason why a certain conservative and reactionary element among our Christian clergy still zealously crucify him whenever they get the chance. *They* don't "encourage immorality," thank God; and their own daughters, when ignorance bears fruit, don't dare to ask help of *them*.

They are like the model church members mentioned by Samuel Butler in "The Way of All Flesh," of whom it was said that "they would have been equally horrified at hearing the Christian religion doubted and at seeing it practiced."

Once there was another minister who also spoke against me in a Denver church. I was then helping his daughter out of a sex scrape, but he didn't know it; and like his colleague he was as confident that cases of sex delinquency among the young of our species are exceptional as he was that sex delinquency, when it happens, is a deadly sin rather than a mistake, and that any young person guilty of such sin is a moral leper and utterly "ruined." With such a choice of evils as that, it is no wonder that such men denounce me as a "libeler of youth."

Since I am about to cite other cases involving the children of ministers, let me here make myself clear on one point beyond all possibility of misunderstanding. I do not cite these cases as attacks on the clergy or on the church. Some of the best friends and heartiest sympathizers I have in Denver are ministers for whose sympathetic insight and breadth of vision I have the warmest admiration and to whom I am indebted for helpfulness in my work. My purpose in these references to some of the clergy is to show beyond dispute that many of them do not know the first thing about conditions as they exist, and that their theories, when opposed to mine, are out of court because they are not founded on first-hand information as to the truth concerning modern youth as it is rather than as they think it is. Fatuously ignorant of what is happening to their own flesh and blood, how could ministers of that type know what goes on in lives of which they have no intimate knowledge? In short, what can they know about society as it is?

There was another minister I have in mind, who, like Polonius, had a daughter. One Sunday evening she attended service in a church of her father's faith. Afterward she walked home escorted by a youth who was the son of a man who was prominent in educational circles in Denver. The moon was bright; the summer evening put them under the spell of its witchery.

What followed took place under the steps of the very school which the two of them were accustomed to attend during the day.

As a result of this unfortunate yielding to impulse, the girl became pregnant; and she and the boy came to me in terror. They well knew the disgrace that would follow if the facts were known—not to mention the easily predictable reactions of their parents. Summary expulsion from school would be the least of their troubles; and the girl would be branded for life. As for her child, it would be branded too; disgraced as "illegitimate."

The law of Colorado gives me the power to protect unborn children from that kind of fate. Its purpose is that no child shall suffer because of the sin, poverty, mistakes, or incompetence of its parents. Although it was a peculiarly difficult situation to handle, I arranged things so that the girl had her baby without the facts becoming known. The two families remained entirely ignorant of what had happened, and today both youngsters are going straight, and have turned out well, as most such youngsters do when handled properly. The baby was adopted by a woman who wanted babies and couldn't have any of her own.

The first instinct of the conventional minded is to demand that boys and girls who do such things be punished, both because they deserve punishment and because such punishment would deter others. My answer is that it does not deter others, and never has in the history of the world. Also, that if anybody ought to be punished when such things happen it is, in some cases at least, the parents; and in still others all society itself should be brought before some cosmic bar of justice for punishment. As a matter of fact we do have a law in Colorado which would have permitted me to put the careless parents of such a boy and girl in jail to think things over. Of course I didn't; for I recognize that the parents are only children grown up, and are as much the victims of ignorance as their children. Besides this was a confidential case. But in all such cases the great remedy is real education and real religion rather than vengeance or violence.

I suppose I need hardly point out the crowning absurdity of this situation, consisting in the fact that the Church and the School, as we insist on running Churches and Schools in this age of grace, were both more or less directly and officially represented in these cases. And they both failed, because their methods of handling these questions of sex are methods of hypocrisy, deceit, and fear. The fruits of hypocrisy, deceit, and fear are today just what they always have been and always will be. How strange that we should cling to the notion that the Eternal Verities will become impotent at our bidding!

I am here speaking of conditions and cases that may be regarded as exceptional; but to a greater or less extent such things were undeniably then going on in Denver, *and they are as undeniably still going on in Denver—and in every other town in the United States of America.* Make no mistake about that. And make no mistake about the fact that Denver is no worse, but, I think, a great deal better, than any other city of similar size with similar social problems. It is all the direct fruit of our national conspiracy of silence that treats sex as a shameful and forbidden thing. These young people are *not* bad, and they are *not* as much to blame as some of their elders, themselves the victims of our social system. If society had intended young people to follow such lines of conduct it could hardly have devised a way of treatment more certain to turn them in that direction than that which it follows at present. My justification for bringing these cases so close home to the clergy and the church is that they clearly prove that the church, by its present methods, has been unable to cope with these conditions among modern youth.

And speaking of that "one per cent," I recall another pedagogical authority who happens to be one of my best friends, a man who has unselfishly devoted a lifetime to the service of youth. In a moment of exasperated frankness he told me to my face that he thought I had gone rabid about sex delinquencies on the part of young people as a result of having so many such cases to deal with, and that my vision was evidently distorted because I never came in contact with the big majority of wholesome girls and boys who are free from such obsessions and mistakes. He added that in all his years of teaching, he had only known personally three or four cases of sex delinquency on the part of girls.

I retorted that he would be interested to know that on that very day I had had precisely four such cases, all of them from Denver high schools, and one of them from his own school—a girl he thought he knew and understood very well, a girl he never would have suspected of such an offense if he had been given a year to think it out. There was no reason why he should suspect her, of course, I told him, for he wasn't in her confidence.

He replied that the rule of the School Board was that teachers could not accept from children confidences which they could not at once communicate to their parents. Also that any girl or boy known to be involved in sex delinquencies should at once be expelled—which was, of course, publicly to expose them and destroy their self-respect.

With such rules could anyone be surprised that such schools and teachers know nothing about modern youth?

The type of teacher who is likely to be the most skeptical when confronted with evidence about what is really going on in his own school without his knowledge is the one who has taught for 25 to 30 years, and so began his service in another generation. Here again, however, generalizations are unsafe; for I know several of the older teachers here in Denver to whom this generalization does not apply, and who are as heartily opposed as I am to the rule of the School Board just referred to.

Several months ago, however, I had an encounter with one of the type to whom the generalization does apply. I had been called on to address a group of social workers in a Denver high school. The meeting was interested in questions of health and social hygiene. In the course of my talk I told them that a very lovely, sweet-natured girl of 15, from a Junior high school, had only a few days before come voluntarily to see me regarding a suspected sex difficulty. I found that she had had relations with as many as eight boys. She also gave me a list of several girls who had had an experience similar to her own, at least to the extent of one affair.

At this moment groups of high-school teachers were coming into the room for another meeting which was immediately to follow the one I was addressing; and my wife overheard this man, who was principal of one of the schools, angrily exclaim to a group of teachers gathered around him, "That's a lie!" She heard it because he was sitting directly in front of her. Instantly she challenged his statement. Then she came up to me to have me take up the gentleman's challenge, and show him that he was mistaken; but by the time she had reached me he had disappeared, apparently because he was not prepared to substantiate his charge.

The next day the girl of whom I had spoken came to my chambers. I told her of my experience, and then asked her if she had any objection to taking into her confidence my Chief Probation Officer. She consented to this, and confirmed to the Probation Officer all she had told to me.

I shall never forget how that child smiled both at the ignorance of the principal, and that of high-school teachers generally.

"You see, Judge," she said, "they don't know much about us. They think they do, but they don't and it wouldn't do to tell them!—You know I wouldn't have them know for the world what I have been telling you because all the kids would get expelled."

"Don't you think they might help you?" I asked.

"Help!" she exclaimed with unutterable scorn in her voice. "Help—nothing! Why if they found it out, you'd be just ruined!"

From start to finish that principal's conduct was a perfect example of that stubborn determination *not* to see, and of that vicious enmity toward those who insist on seeing, which constantly reduces the effectiveness of my work in Denver. They don't *want* the truth. And the reason they dread to face it is the terrible interpretation they put upon it, because of their puritanical attitude toward sex. It is my hope that through the machinery we have built up, and through the confidence which Denver youth has in me and my colleagues in this work, the principals and teachers of the Denver schools will, as time goes on, more and more form with Denver youth the same kind of alliance that I have formed, and so bridge the gulf which the blindness and bigotry of our traditions and conventions have fixed between them and their pupils. And why should we not all of us recognize that in our limitations we are simply creatures of the order we have been born into; and that only the exceptional person has the strength, courage and vision to throw off the shackles which modern youth is determined to break— either with or without the help of the adult world? How much better it would be if instead of holding ourselves aloof we would act as sympathetic advisors and counselors, rather than as hostile critics.

CHAPTER 4

In the spring of the presumably enlightened Year of Grace in which this book is written, a woman teacher in a certain Junior High School in Denver found, carelessly left in a text book that had been turned back to the school by a fifteen-year-old girl whom I will call Elizabeth, an unmailed letter to a seventeen year old boy. Here is the letter, with expedient changes in names, etc.

Paul:

I am sorry to say but I think I am going to have a Y. K. W. It sure is yours. I kept it back as long as I could. You needn't think just because it has been about four weeks since we quit that it isn't yours because it sure is. I have done all I could in four weeks to keep it back. Don't think that I have been doing y. k. w. to some other boy and trying to say that it is yours for I haven't. If I do have a y. k. w. it belongs to no one but you. My stepmother don't know what to think about it. I won't be mean enough to tell your girl about it. Because it might cause you and her to fall out. I don't want to see you quit. But if I do have a ———— I expect to see you do your part, and Anna won't have to know it. I don't care if I do have it because school will be out. Don't think that it belongs to some other boy for there's no other boy in Denver that I would let do that to me. I'm not like some girls that do everything boys ask them to do. Because most of these boys here in Denver have some kind of disease. I guess you know what I mean. I would rather have a b—— than

46

the disease. So don't think that it belongs to no other boy but you.

Don't get mad after you read this. It isn't my fault for I did all I could. I won't tell anyone that it belongs to you. It's nobody's business. If you answer this I will know that my stepmother won't have to see your mother. If you don't answer then my stepmother will have to see your mother. If she don't come herself she will send Miss Hughes to see your mother. You know that would be awful. So you can have your choice about it.

From
Elizabeth.

Elizabeth did not mail this letter. As I have said, she left it in a book, where her teacher found it two months after it was written. The teacher hied with it, in a state of pleasant excitement, I presume, to the Principal of the School. Let's call him Pecksniff.

Unfortunately for the girl, Mr. Pecksniff was suffering from an acute case of psychosexual hyperæsthesia. At least that appears to be the only explanation for what follows:

Elizabeth, let me explain, is a very pretty girl, and unusually bright. She had an excellent record in the ———— School, and lacked just one week of graduating from the grammar grades. She was, and is, a perfectly normal, healthy-minded girl. She had, as her letter shows, a normal and womanly instinct for the sacredness of the sex relationship, leaned not at all toward promiscuity, and had given herself to her lover under conditions which were "immoral" in the sense that they violated the social code, but which were, so far as her attitude toward such an intimacy was concerned, morally impeccable. In short, she was crude, with the ignorant crudeness of youth, but her instincts were normal and sound. Every line of her letter shows this, even to her desire not to betray the boy or interfere in his affair with his new sweetheart. Her generosity and her courage are both evident and serve to make it clear that she was abundantly worth saving.

When confronted with the evidence of her letter, she promptly acknowledged it, and told the Principal and his confederate that she had been intimate with the boy on two occasions, and *that she had never had such relations with any other boy,* a fact to which her inquisitors did not attach the importance it deserves.

Nobody knew in the first place about the girl's delinquency except the teacher who found the letter; nobody knew about it now except that teacher and the Principal. It was not a case that had been noised abroad in the school, nor was Elizabeth's observable conduct such that anybody in contact with her could say that she was an evil or contaminating influence among her schoolmates. There was nothing whatever in the situation that could justify these two savages in making an example of her.

Mr. Pecksniff roasted the child roundly, and he told her she was immoral, bad, and a degrading influence not fit for further contact with her schoolmates. Then he expelled her. To her stepmother he sent the following brutal note:

Mrs. ———,
— ——— St.,
Denver, Colorado.
Dear Madam:

For practices of which Elizabeth has been guilty, I find it necessary to suspend her from all the privileges of ——— School.

Miss Hughes will call to see you and explain the whole matter.

It is of such grave, immoral consequences that I do not want Elizabeth ever to return to ——— School; and further, I insist that she shall not be around or near the school at any time.

Respectfully yours,

——— ———.

It is an unlovely letter. It is appalling to think that a thing so callous, and so unfeeling, could have come from a man to whom the People of Denver have for years and years been intrusting the tender minds and hearts of children that they might be guided and trained right in ways of kindness and knowledge.

Was he interested in saving this child who had been under his charge on the supposition that he could correct and modify such mistakes of conduct, and throw a light upon the path ahead for bewildered Youth? He was not. His sole impulse was to strike, savagely, under the pretense that he was upholding the standard of "morality"; and I think he licked his lips when he struck. Had his impulse been one of pity or loving-kindness he could never have written that letter—even though he had felt it necessary to expel the girl.

I found Elizabeth bitter against the Principal, bitter against the woman who had needlessly betrayed her, and bitter generally.

When she came to court she was accompanied by another girl, aged 16, who was also a pupil in Mr. Pecksniff's school, and was "in good standing." This girl confessed to me that she had made precisely the same mistake with another boy in the school.

From Elizabeth I got a list of ten other girls in the

same school who had done what she and her 16-year-old friend had done, and who had gone much further than either of them in such courses. That was as far as their personal knowledge went. The girls they named to me were sufficiently intimate with them to have confided in them. But there were hundreds of other girls in that school who had *not* confided in them; and the sex conduct of those remains a matter of conjecture. But it cannot possibly be supposed that the conditions which had affected Elizabeth and her circle of friends had affected none of the other circles and cliques in that school.

And yet to Mr. Pecksniff Elizabeth was the one case. He was in blissful ignorance of the others; nor was there any way for him to learn about them because he had cut himself off from the one source of information, his pupils. Nothing could have been more evident than that he would punish to the extent of his ability any boy or girl who sought his confidence or confessed to him. He was the one person, aside from their own parents, whom they should have been most able to trust, and from whom they should have been able to expect love and understanding. But it was not there. And so he stands in the public eye, splendid, towering, imposing, outwardly dependable and solid; but inwardly like a tree whose taproot has been severed.

What that man, and what his staff of teachers could do among the pupils who are in their charge, including the ten cases which I learned of so incidentally from this girl because I won her confidence and wanted to help her and them, is obvious. What an opportunity they are throwing away is also obvious. I wish the sheer criminal negligence, the cruel blindness with which they and many of their kind do their work could be comprehended by the public that intrusts its children to their care. What a travesty on teaching! What grossness, coarseness, and hypocrisy masquerading under the cloak of respectability, and wearing the name of a profession that should be a sacred calling. What a want of imagination! What a murderous morality!

If this were just an isolated and exceptional case I would not feel as I do about it. What makes me white hot is that it happens all the time, and that teachers and parents who think and act rationally about these matters are the rare exceptions, not the rule, as they should be.

When I encounter this determined and willful blindness, both in the schools and churches, and among parents, I feel that it is time for at least a temporary change in our national bird. The mighty St. Gaudens eagle is scarcely a symbol of our present social psychology. We had better put the eagle in cold storage for a time and substitute on our escutcheon the rear view of an ostrich hiding its head in the sand of the Great American Desert.

The Desert would come in very well in the design for a reason connected with the present discussion. For Sex is not the only thing that our adolescent children are investigating for themselves in the teeth of the dense silence maintained by their elders on such matters.

Booze is another thing that interests them. No petting party, no road-house toot, no joy ride far from the prying eye of Main Street, is complete unless the boys carry flasks. There are no actual statistics to be had on these matters, but it is very clear in my mind that practically all of the cases where these girls and boys lose their judgment in Folly Lane involve the use of drink.

A few years ago, when these conditions were becoming

most apparent, the principal of the Lawrenceville School, at Lawrenceville, New Jersey, one of the most important boys' preparatory schools in this country, wrote a letter to the parents of all Lawrenceville students calling their attention to the prevalence of drinking among schoolboys everywhere, and asking them individually to warn their boys that this temptation lay before them, and to urge them not to yield to it. This letter was given wide publication in the newspapers.

Likewise, at Phillips Academy, another boys' school of the first rank, it was found necessary a few years back to forbid dancing at the school because of the license that went with it. This incident likewise received wide newspaper publicity. Alfred E. Stearns, Principal of Phillips Academy, said in an article in the *Boston Globe* that measures which had previously been taken had included the appointment of student and faculty committees charged with the following duties:

"1. To serve as police and to remonstrate with, if not actually eject from the floor, couples who dance in an indecent manner.

2. To prevent the admission of girls of questionable character.

3. To prevent drinking, by boys and girls alike, on the floor and elsewhere.

4. To eject those found to be under the influence of liquor and to prevent the admission of those in like condition.

5. To supervise the girls' dressing room for the purpose of preventing extravagant dress and indecent exposure, drinking, and loose talk.

6. To insist that visiting girls should be accompanied

by chaperones; to prevent auto 'joy rides' during the dancing.

7. To prevent the parking of automobiles in close proximity to the dance hall.

8. To prevent other and outside gatherings exempt from the control and supervision of the main dance.

9. To see that girls are promptly and properly returned to their rooms at the close of the dance."

I give this list at length because it leaves no doubt of the sort of conditions that existed in a school second to none in this country for the quality of its students. They are for the most part boys drawn from eastern homes of considerable wealth and culture. They have behind them first-rate traditions and training. And yet such measures, involving both the Sex question and the Booze question, were necessary there; and a later upshot was the temporary abolition of dancing at the school altogether. I understand that the ban was lifted later on, as soon as conditions had come well under control.

To say that that happened when this kind of folly was at its height and that the hysteria has since died down— that it was therefore just a passing brain storm on the part of youth after the war, is nonsense. Concealment today is more skillful and more general, because the thing isn't new any longer; but if the adult population of this country think the relative calm on the surface means that there is nothing happening any more beneath the surface, they are living in a fool's paradise. Youth is shrewder, more sophisticated, more contemptuous of its elders, and more coldly bent on following its own path than it ever was before. Nor does that necessarily imply that it is wholly an evil path, nor that they are all, as the saying goes, hell bent for destruction. It does mean that they are changing our social code; and in my judgment they are going to win through, if not with us, then without us. I shall take up that end of the question later.

For the present I want to make myself very clear on one point. Not only is this revolt from old standards of conduct taking place, but it is unlike any revolt that has ever taken place before. Youth has always been rebellious; youth has always shocked the older generation. That's traditional. The "modern girl," wearing skirts that reached only to her shoe tops, was a "problem" in mid-Victorian England. But this is different. It has the whole weight and momentum of a new scientific and economic order behind it. It has come in an age of speed and science; an age when women vote and can make their own living; an age in which the fear of Hell Fire has lost its hold. In the past the revolt of youth always turned out to be a futile gesture. It never brought much change. But now the gun's loaded. These boys and girls can do what boys and girls never were able to do in the past. They can live up to their manifesto, and nothing can prevent them. The external restraints, economic restraints that were once so potent, have gone never to return; *and the sole question now is how soon and how effectively will the internal restraints of a voluntarily accepted code, which alone can keep people going straight, take their place.* I think this is already happening. I don't think this younger generation is just a blindfolded bull in a china shop. I think, considering the temptations it is under, and considering the folly of the adult portion of the population, that it is relatively the most moral and the most sane younger generation the world has ever seen.

But more of that later.—Just now I want to clinch some

of the statements I have already made about the conditions which exist in our high schools, taking Denver high schools as typical of high schools everywhere, and Denver youth as typical of American youth everywhere, for Denver youth are certainly no worse, and I think they are better.

CHAPTER 5

What I am now about to put down is not primarily my own opinion. Rather it is a message from the youth of Denver, not only to the parents and teachers of Denver but to parents and teachers everywhere. I call it a message from the youth of Denver because hundreds of them—literally hundreds—have from time to time asked me to say in their names what I am now about to say. In other words, it is information from the inside. It is not my testimony but theirs; and for myself I can only say that my own observation and experience tend to corroborate it on every point. Two years ago I published these findings in Denver newspapers for the benefit of Denver parents. I now publish them for the benefit of all parents; for what happens in Denver, you may rest assured, happens in every other city.

The first item in the testimony of these high-school students is that of all the youth who go to parties, attend dances, and ride together in automobiles, more than 90 per cent indulge in hugging and kissing. This does not mean that every girl lets *any* boy hug and kiss her, but that she *is* hugged and kissed. And evidently this 90 per cent estimate does not apply to those of our young people who lack the biological energy and the social urge which leads the most worthwhile portion of our youth to express their natural instincts in these social diversions. Another way of putting it would be to say that what leads these youngsters into trouble is an overflowing of high spirits and abounding energy which only needs more wise direction.

The testimony I receive regarding this estimated 90

per cent is practically unanimous. If it be true, it means that these young people have more or less definitely come to the conclusion that this minor form of sex experience may be legitimately indulged in. Also that a very large number do indulge in it, without permitting the diversion to exceed certain rather clearly defined limits.

Some girls insist on this kind of things from boys they go with, and are as aggressive, in a subtle way, in their search for such thrills as are the boys themselves.

I recall one very beautiful and spirited girl who told me that she had refused to go out with a certain boy because he lacked pep, and didn't know how, as she put it, to "love me up."

"Do all the boys do such things nowadays?" I asked.

"Of course they do," she retorted. "If they don't there is something wrong with them."

That girl represented a type which I shall consider in detail later, the type which matures early, and which feels the urge of sex years before the mind has grown sufficiently mature to cope with it and control it. She wanted thrills.

The Flapper world, however, contains another type of girl who is not necessarily over-sexed at her age, but who nevertheless permits boys to take liberties with her as a kind of reward for dancing with her and showing her what she calls a good time.

I have in mind one of these, now in high school— a girl who has been in the charge of this court for the last two years because her parents have divorced and remarried, and do not properly look after her. She is very cynical and scornful of boys, but she is passionately fond of dancing. She uses boys as dancing partners; and

her use for them stops right there. The dancing interests her; the boys do not. She, however, is enormously attractive to boys; and occasionally, she told me,
she gives one of them a kiss because it's expected.

"But don't you resent the way they dance?" I asked.

"Oh, you mean the button shining?" she asked cas-
ually. "Not at all. Close dancing affects some girls,
I know; but it never has any effect on me. In fact,
I don't think it has on most girls."

"There is a common impression to the contrary," I
observed.

"I know there is," she came back crisply. "All
the old kill-joys and weeping willows in the country
think the dirt that is in their own minds. That's the
way *they'd* feel; so they think that's the way *we* feel;
and how they do envy us the thoughts we don't
think!"

"But—" I began.

"I'm telling you the truth," she went on. *"Most* of
us girls don't get any special thrill out of close dancing.
We do get a thrill out of the dancing itself; and we go
to parties with these young crumpet munchers and snuggle
pups because we like to dance, and for no other reason."

"And the—er—crumpet munchers?" I asked, trying
to snap the words out the way she did.

"They dance for the kick they get out of it," she said
promptly.

"In the dancing?"

"Yes, in the dancing—holding the girl close, you know.
And afterward, in petting, heavy-necking, and other
things, if she'll stand for it. I don't."

"But why do you stand for the close dancing? When
they get a kick out of the dancing, as you put it, don't

you feel that they are taking liberties with your person?
Don't you resent it?"

"What those young fools get out of it is nothing to
me," she replied. "Why should I bother my head about
what *they* think? If they want to make themselves miserable, that's their affair. I should worry. Let them
boil. Don't I get to dance? And after the dance—why
I'm through with them."

In order to keep the record straight, please let me
emphasize that the young women whose opinions I am
recording here are not from the "lower classes." I have,
whenever possible, picked my witnesses from representative homes of reasonable wealth and considerable culture; homes where the entrance of such views as these
are completely revolutionary, or would be so if they were
suspected.

The girl I have just quoted is extraordinarily keen
and intelligent. She is sixteen. In spite of the cynical
vigor of her language, she is refined and well poised of
manner; and I know that none of the adults in her circle
have the slightest inkling of the side of her life and
the point of view which she so freely revealed to me.
They think her a singularly restrained, well-poised girl;
and they would be shocked to know how much more
restrained and well poised she is than they have any
notion of.

So much, then, for the first part of the message from
the youth of Denver.

The second part of the message is this: At least 50
per cent of those who begin with hugging and kissing
do not restrict themselves to that, but go further, and
indulge in other sex liberties which, by all the conventions, are outrageously improper.

I need not say that this is a difficult and dangerous

problem. It is one which cannot be met by denunciation or watchfulness on the part of adults. It can be met only by a voluntarily adopted code of manners—by genuine internal restraints approved and adopted by the young people themselves. Such a code can be called into free and spontaneous action only by education of the frankest and most thorough-going sort. Ignorance and Fear are back of the whole melancholy business.

These familiarities, quite apart from the obvious danger that they will lead to other things, are responsible for much nervous trouble among young girls, and for the prevalence of certain physical ailments which are peculiar to them. Of this fact most parents and teachers are completely ignorant.

Many parents would not impart this important information to their daughters, even if they possessed it. And yet ignorance of the truth is what causes girls to allow that kind of thing.

I am told by eminent physicians that so far as the moral and physical results are concerned, the effect of such half-way improprieties on these young girls is just as dangerous as if they yielded themselves completely. So far as I can see few parents are aware of that fact. All of which goes to show how inherited conventions warp our minds. The parents mean well, they would do anything to save their children from folly and misery; anything but enlighten them. Thus, in spite of their greater years and experience, they remain as much at sea as are their children to whom they so carefully bequeath their own ignorance.

The plain fact is that society has taught girls that they must at all costs avoid the social stigma of an illegitimate pregnancy, because that means getting found out, and therefore social ostracism; and so, being badly edu-

cated in this matter, they conclude that the moral dereliction involved in the sexual act is greater than the
moral dereliction involved in liberties whose only possible justification would be that they sought consumma-
tion in that act.   Evidently the moral dereliction of such
outrages is quite as great as complete, improper yielding
to the normal impulses of sex.   In the judgment of many
physicians, in fact, the effect, mentally and physically,
may be even worse.

But how lamentable that our young people are ridden
by the inherited tradition that there is something shameful and immoral in the sexual act itself, even when
prompted by sincere love and emotional exaltation.   How
unfortunate that they should have been made blind to
the fact that the problem here is not one of outwardly
imposed "morals," but rather of *voluntary internal
restraints on the conduct of individuals that will serve
to maintain human society on a workable basis*—not a
taboo which forbids this or that kind of conduct, but
an enlightened freedom which confers, like a crown of
life, the liberty and the ability to do right.   You can
depend upon it that whenever these youngsters have a
false and rotten idea they have probably inherited it as
one of the superstitions and traditions that enslaved their
elders; and that, as a rule, whenever they have an honest,
candid, clear-thinking moment, they have dug that up
for themselves.

The conclusion I draw from the fact that 50 per cent
of the original 90 per cent indulge in half-way sex intimacies that wreck the health and morals alike, is that
here is an example of the effects on human· life of false
and illogical thinking—or, if you will, logical thinking
based on false premises.   Such is the fruit of some of
the most stubbornly cherished of our puritan traditions,

of our lies, our hypocrisies, our concealments, and our unwillingness to face the facts of Sex and to tell the whole world, young and old, the whole truth about it.

No normal girl would ever submit to these outrages if she knew the truth. A few morons and half-wits might; but not normal girls. That such things are happening seems to me one of the very ugliest facts in our social life today. And nothing but complete confusion of mind, and a terrible want of honesty about questions of right and wrong, and an unconscious hypocrisy that confuses morality with conventionality, could possibly account for it.

So much for that. Now for the third point of the message. It is this: Fifteen to twenty-five per cent of those who begin with the hugging and kissing eventually "go the limit." This does not, in most cases, mean either promiscuity or frequency, but it happens.

To most persons reasonably well acquainted with girls and boys of high-school age, that estimate will doubtless appear excessive. Note the case already mentioned of the school executive who places these figures at one per cent, and who thinks I am rabid on the whole subject.

I can only say that the estimates come from high-school students, and that they are the most conservative estimates I have received from that source. If I should name the figures I get from a majority of my informants they would merely excite incredulity and hostility. The accusation that my opinions about sexual delinquency in young people is a libel on the youth of America is an old story with me. I am used to the charge. Still, it is not my purpose to shock anybody more than I have to. Of course I am not libeling the youth of America.

I am one of its best friends; it is for this reason that I want to protect it with the truth about itself as told by itself. For 25 years I have devoted my life to my young friends, and I have had hundreds of them ask me to do what I am here doing.

Most educational authorities who attempt to make estimates in this matter forget that they have long and consistently cut themselves off from the one authentic source of information, the young people themselves; since boys and girls—particularly girls—in our Denver schools who, through bad management or bad luck, get found out in sexual delinquencies, are summarily expelled, on the theory that they are bad, immoral, and a danger to their fellows—like so many lepers running around loose in a community otherwise free from leprosy! Oh, yes, they really think the community is otherwise free from leprosy!

Only the other day a girl and boy were brought before me. Both of them were twelve years old, and attended a junior high-school. They were precocious youngsters and had gone too far; but they were both of them fine, sweet children, and they were not *bad* by any possible stretch of a sane imagination.

Their teacher insisted that the reform school was the place for both of them. She indignantly informed me so far as the boy was concerned, if I insisted on returning him to the school, she would resign her position.

Such is the point of view by which such teachers cut themselves off from any real knowledge of what is going on right under their noses. But most people are unintelligent about all that concerns conduct, and such teachers are just people. Still—it's too bad.

But are they competent to talk in authoritative percentages on the subject of such delinquency?   I think not.

I have at hand certain figures which indicate with certainty that for every case of sex delinquency discovered, a very large number completely escape detection. For instance, out of 495 girls of high-school age—though not all of them were in high school—who admitted to me that they had had sex experiences with boys, only about 25 became pregnant.   That is about 5 per cent, a ratio of one in twenty.   The others avoided pregnancy, some by luck, others because they had a knowledge of more or less effective contraceptive methods—a knowledge, by the way, which I find to be more common among them than is generally supposed.

Now the point is this: First, that three-fourths of that list of nearly 500 girls came to me of their own accord for one reason or another.   Some were pregnant, some were diseased, some were remorseful, some wanted counsel, and so on.   Second, the thing that always brought them to me was their acute need for help of some kind. Had they not felt that need, they would not have come. For every girl who came for help, there must have been a great many, a majority, who did *not* come because they did not want help, and therefore kept their own counsel.

In other words, that 500—covering a period of less than two years—represented a small group, drawn from all levels of society, that didn't know the ropes, and got into trouble of one kind or another; but there was as certainly a much larger group that did know the ropes, and never came around at all.   My own opinion is that for every girl who comes to me for help because she is pregnant, or diseased, or in need of comfort, there are many more who do not come because they escape scot free of consequences, or else because circumstances are such that they can meet the situation themselves. Hundreds, for instance, resort to the abortionist. I don't guess this, I know it.

CHAPTER 6

I have so far said little of high-school boys. The high-school boy is a much less dramatic figure than the high-school girl. Generally she sets the pace, whatever it is to be, and he dances to her piping. Still, the high-school boy has his own psychology, which I shall come to presently. In the meantime, this is as good a place as any to say something about the percentages. The estimated percentages as to the number of boys in high school who have probably had sex experience ranges from thirty to ninety per cent. I have a letter from one boy, for instance, who was till recently a crack athlete in a Denver high school, and was intimately associated throughout his high-school course with boys who made places for themselves in an athletic way. He says that fully ninety per cent of these boys known by him more or less intimately, have had sex experience by the time they finish school. I give the estimate for what it is worth.

My own opinion is that 50 per cent is a safe and conservative estimate for all classes of high-school boys averaged together. It is the lowest estimate that I find any degree of probability in; and for the most part it would apply to boys in the last two years of the high-school course. Perhaps, among boys of a certain type, and more inclined to independence of action than most of their companions, as in the case of these young athletes, the percentage would run much higher.

Inquiries among both girls and boys seem to show that in former years there was practically as much incontiñonce among boys as there is now, but that it was less apparent because then they sought prostitutes in the red-light districts. Also, that with the breaking up of those districts, they turned to girls of their own class, a thing they had seldom done in the past.

This tendency apparently gained a tremendous impetus when our young men returned from Europe after the war, inoculated with many Continental standards of conduct to which they had formerly been strangers. They urged those standards on their girl friends; it all fitted in with the hysteria for extremes which was a part of the rise of flapperism; and the result we now have on our hands, to make the best of.

Once a "nice" girl would have considered such advances an insult. Now, though she may refuse, she is not so likely to be offended. She is too sophisticated for that, and knows enough about the male animal to understand that his impulse is a normal one. Whether such frankness between boys and girls is a gain or the reverse I shall not try to consider at this point. It is, however, quite in keeping with the very evident determination of these young people to call a spade a spade; and we adults have it to reckon with, whether we like it or not.

Years ago, when the Red Light District was in full blast on Market Street in Denver, I made a somewhat incomplete survey among the boys of two high schools as to sex morality. The survey was made with the help of the Chief of Police, who coöperated with the Juvenile Court in an effort to keep boys away from the then tolerated Red Light District. Even with such help it was very difficult to get many names. A few sufficed, however, for usually, on gaining their confidence, I got, not only their own stories, but information concerning other boys who were following like courses. Some of the boys even brought their chums to see me and talk with me.

The result was that I personally talked with forty-one boys from one certain high school. All but three or four of these had been in the forbidden district. Many of them went there at first from curiosity concerning matters on which they could not obtain information otherwise. Twenty-six of the group had actually been inside the houses, and twenty-two of these had had relations with women and girls living there.

I made a somewhat similar investigation of another high school. I personally talked to about one hundred of these boys. Over half of them admitted to me personally, and of course confidentially, that they had had sex relations with women, mostly on Market Street.

In many of these cases the experience had been only occasional. They were not making a continued practice of it, and curiosity was generally the cause. In some cases lack of sufficient funds for such amusements accounted for their moderation.

Some of the boys told me that they had been disgusted and frightened by their first experience in these places, and were more than willing to promise me that they would "cut it out." Some of them, on the other hand, showed signs of extreme sensuality, and were already regular frequenters of the Red Light District. Two of them were sons of men who were Sunday-school superintendents in two of the largest churches in Denver. Some of the group were diseased, and were either neglecting their condition or resorting to quacks. These I sent to physicians who were ready to coöperate with me in this work.

I had most of these boys sign a personal typewritten pledge that they would henceforth refrain from such conduct and lead continent lives. Years later I came across that bunch of pledges in my files. By that time most of those boys were grown up, married, and apparently doing well. I burned the pledges. I remember, however, that to my disgust, but in the face of my utter helplessness, several of the worst of the group, some of them rotten with disease, married into leading Denver families; and many divorces followed these unions within a year, with broken health for ignorant and trustful wives.

In hardly one of the cases with which I dealt on that occasion did the parents have any idea of the real facts. While all this happened many years ago, still I remember being invited to dinner at the home of the Sunday-school superintendent who was the father of one of these boys. The estimable gentleman and his wife decried "the carelessness of parents" to me while at the very time their son, a high-school boy, was suffering from a terrible case of gonorrhea. So severe was his illness that it would frequently double him up when he was walking; and this he had explained to his father as due to his having been kicked by a horse out at their ranch. The parents accepted his story without suspicion.

And now, while the parents berated the carelessness of other parents, I, being in the boy's confidence, hardly dared to look across the table at his flushed face. That boy was one of the most sensual I have ever had to deal with; but I finally succeeded, I think, in putting him in control of himself. He would never consent to my confiding in his parents.

I was and am strong for the abolition of the Red Light Districts. I do not believe that the toleration of such a district is necessary in any city, or that such toleration is the right way to keep sexual vice under control. It is necessary for me to record here, however, the fact that not one of those boys had had relations, or attempted to have them, with high-school girls—"decent girls," as they called them. And this, as I have already indicated, is in sharp contrast to the conditions which now obtain.

But this fact should be interpreted, not as a reason for "protected" vice in our cities, but rather for sex education of the young, and for a more enlightened application of the principles of toleration and justice in connection with our social conventions.

One high-school boy with whom I recently talked admitted that he had had relations with fifteen girls of high-school age, about half of them still in school. He had chosen them in preference to "chippies," or common street girls. I verified this confession, talked with practically all of these girls, and found that they were good, average girls. His experience with each of them had been on only one or two occasions. The girls, with one or two exceptions, were not given to promiscuity, and I believe most of them have turned out well.

A Red Light District in Denver might have saved those girls from these experiences, but it would not have saved the boy—nor the prostitutes, who have as good a right to be saved as anybody else.

There can be no doubt, I think, that since the Red Light Districts were abolished far more "good" girls than formerly have had sex experiences. But, curious as it may seem, fewer girls have been "ruined" and "lost."

Many a prostitute is lost, not because she is really irredeemable, but because her self-respect is lost. Society has pronounced it lost; ergo, it *is* lost. The social verdict in such cases becomes an anti-social *suggestion*, virtually a *hypnotism*, of the most overwhelming and overpowering sort. It destroys the individual against whom it is directed by arbitrarily, superstitiously, and, as a rule, falsely declaring such a destruction to be an already accomplished fact. Everybody accepts and believes this declaration, including the victim of it. That such a verdict is no more intelligent than so much voodooism makes no difference. It stands.

The prostitute is known—she is promiscuous—she is "different"—she is hopeless; and in the course of time, she becomes all these things, filthy in body and mind, a hideous caricature of womanhood, limned by the society that made her as she is. Even in the first stages of prostitution, before she is set in the hideous and evil travesty she calls "Love," she is not permitted to recover and find herself, even though she often has more of the Other Virtues than some "Good" Women who apparently specialize on the One Virtue of Chastity—which they have not lost, and in some instances cannot lose.

Thus it would seem that the fewer prostitutes we have the fewer lost women we have, in spite of the fact that with open prostitution suppressed there are more girls who occasionally violate our sex conventions. For these girls, happily, are not "lost" and "ruined" in the old sense, both because society sometimes deals more leniently with them than it once did, and also because relatively few of them encounter the exposure which might bring down upon them, and force them to *believe,* the destructive, anti-social suggestion, "You are lost—you can never come back, having stooped to folly."

Some time ago, within a period of a few months, Mrs. Lindsey and I had the pleasant experience of being called on by ten young wives and devoted mothers who proudly brought their babies that we might see them. Every one of these girls, in their high-school days, had, unknown to their teachers and parents, "gone wrong" with boy companions. With the sympathy, compassion, and substantial material aid which the Juvenile Court was empowered by the State secretly to bring into their lives, they had righted themselves, and later became good wives and mothers, even as the boys, on their part, became good husbands and fathers. Through avoidance of exposure, with its consequent "ruin," they had gained for themselves what society so readily conceded to the boys, even though *they* had been found out.

For in the past, notwithstanding the Red Light District and its ruined women, the boys who helped by their patronage to make that District possible stood excellent chances of becoming good citizens, husbands and fathers; but the girl denizens of that world did not. Thus these new conditions, in spite of the increase of sex experiences among girls, as compared with the days of the Red Light District, would seem to have brought with them less that is destructive to womanhood than did the old order with its stricter conventions, its savage punishments, and its hypocritical double standard of "morality." I don't say, mind you, that the new order needs no mending; I merely insist that it contains more essential morality than did the old; and that, all calamity howlers to the contrary notwithstanding, we have *not* gone backward.

I have already been at some pains to make it clear that the presence of any girl or boy in my court room, or their friendship with me, carries with it no implication of wrongdoing on their part.

In fact there are many fine-spirited girls and boys of high character, and of unquestionable poise, who by their presence in my court, or in my company, furnish the camouflage that protects from suspicion other young people whose relations with me are of a different sort because they have come to me voluntarily to be helped out of some difficulty. This circumstance makes it easy for those whose conscience would otherwise make cowards of them to come to me without fear of exposure or loss of self-respect.   They also know that they are further safeguarded by the fact that in such cases no records are made or kept that might ever be used against them. In a sense the Juvenile Court of Denver acts as a kind of impersonal oracle to which these hard-pressed children may come with the certainty that their confessions will not be betrayed, that their point of view will be understood, and that here they will always find sympathy for the sinner though not for the sin.

This is, perhaps, as good a time as any to explain, parenthetically, what are the conditions under which my conferences with girls are conducted.   These conferences are at once absolutely private and absolutely public.   By this I mean that they are held in my judicial chambers behind a closed door which anybody, whether a newspaper reporter, a court official, or a casual and curious visitor, is at liberty to open and walk through at any time.   The rule for reporters, court officials, visitors, and *possible scandalmongers*—of which last there are many on the job—is "Don't knock; open the door and walk right in."

As a further means of protection against enemies who have tried to blacken my name with trumped up stories in the past, and who would welcome the flimsiest pretext to do it again, my wife has her desk in the room next to mine, with only that door between us—the door which, let me repeat it here with emphasis, may be opened by her or by anybody else at any time.

There is hardly a day that some newspaper reporter does not walk in on me, in accord with our established convention about that door—two doors, to be exact. Often he finds me in conference with some boy or girl

who may be in trouble, or who may have come to me
in behalf of a friend who needs help, or who may be
there merely as a visitor, interested in the workings of
the Juvenile Court.

Thus I follow St. Paul's injunction to avoid even the
appearance of evil. The privacy of the conferences protects the self-respect of the unfortunates I deal with and
the publicity of them protects me at the same time
against malicious gossip.

Such precautions are far greater than those adopted in
the office of the average physician, where women and
girls are allowed, by our conventions, to come for professional advice regarding the most private affairs. No
reproach and no breath of mean scandal ordinarily at-
taches to such consultations; and I am sure that there
are few medical men who, under such circumstances,
would violate their responsibilities as men of honor and
priests of the healing art. There are exceptions, of
course. Only within the last few weeks it happened that
a girl came to me with the complaint that a physician
to whom she had gone for treatment of a cold in the
head had barred the door of his office, told her she needn't
think she was any better than the many other women
who conformed to his wishes, and attempted to assault
her. She pretended willingness, got him to unbar the
door, and escaped by a ruse. She came straight to me;
but as she was more than twenty-one years of age I could
only refer her to the city attorney's office.

But in general such things don't happen, and the public
stands ready to believe in the good faith of most medical
men, and to waive the question of conventional pro-
priety.

It is certainly significant of malicious hostility on the
part of somebody, therefore, when not even the extreme

precautions I adopt suffice to protect me from poisonous whisperings and politically manufactured lies.

A physician's office is a kind of hospital; it deals mainly with physical ills. In like manner the Juvenile Court of Denver is a hospital, a moral hospital. It deals with the sick and crippled of spirit. Its function, therefore, is psychologically one of extreme delicacy. People have reservations about any sickness of the soul which they don't have about sicknesses of the body. The only possible way of diagnosing these spiritual ailments is to get the patient to tell the truth without fear; and the only way to remove the spell of fear which gags them and holds them dumb is to create the right protective conditions, the right privacy, and the right sympathy. It can't be done in any other way. Moreover there are many women and girls who, when they are not afraid, will confide to a man things they would ordinarily fear to confide to another woman. If the Juvenile Court of Denver has always had an exceptional insight into the lives of people it is partly because I have been willing to use methods that would work, and in so doing to take the chance of encountering filthy stories and suggestions about myself.

Some of these stories are really believed, I think, by the people who invent and spread them. For the most part they have their source in the minds of unfortunate persons who are the victims of suppressions and complexes that lead them to delight in imaginings which in a measure satisfy impulses within them that have been denied a normal outlet. Among the chief offenders in this respect are certain aggressively respectable and painfully chaste females whose protests on behalf of morality and whose demands for the punishment and exposure of erring girls are delivered with an emphasis that should furnish the judicious with food for thought. Some of them protest too much. One wonders what the Freudian *Wish* may have to do with it.

The same is true, in a lesser degree perhaps, of the people who greedily seize upon and devour such garbage. Curiously enough it appears to be women who most readily accept these tales at their face value. As nearly as I can judge from the reports that come to me, one will hear these stories referred to by women and believed by them in a ratio of about ten to one, as compared with men. There are men in Denver who spread these tales for political reasons, but I think there are relatively few who originate or spread them because they believe them. And yet, it is for the women and children that I have at times all but crucified myself. How strange that the hostility of women should have been one of the chief things that worked against me in the recent election, when I was returned to office, in the teeth of the Ku Klux Klan opposition.

The campaign of 1924, just finished, has been a perfect example of the futility of the precaution of the unlocked door, of my wife's presence in my court, and of every other reasonable guarantee of decency. For example one woman made a political speech against me in which she said, "There must be a change in that court because that man locks himself up in his chambers for three or four hours with young girls when no one can get in; and a condition like that is simply scandalous."

That the statement happened to be patently false did not matter. When such charges, absolutely contradicted by known facts, are made in the heat of a political campaign, many persons believe them. I have no doubt that that libel won many votes for my opponent, and that many persons in Denver believe the charge.

And while I am on this subject, let me refer briefly to one other favorite cry that is often raised against me in Denver. It is to the general effect that I am casting reflections on the morality of the young people of Denver. A Denver minister attacked me on that ground recently. He declared that he resented these imputations and attacks upon our school children "by a well-known judge." He said in effect, "I know they are not true. The children of Denver are the most moral children I have ever known and surely as fine as any children in the country, and we must rebuke the people who asperse the morality of these little ones."

That is plain demagoguery. I have never aspersed the morality of our young people; I have a very high opinion of their morality. But I know—what my clerical friend apparently does not—that they do many unwise and ill-advised things; and that they make *mistakes*. My preacher friend, if he admitted those mistakes, would interpret them as "badness"; but I don't—I call them by their right name. I call them mistakes; and I deny that the children who make them are "immoral." I leave the charge of "immorality" to those painfully moral persons who find their own record so clear that they can follow the bidding of the Master, and, without hesitation, cast the first stone. I can but congratulate these righteous judges of their fellow men on the heights of Christian infallibility to which they have attained.

CHAPTER 7

But to return to the girl question: During the years 1920 and 1921 the Juvenile Court of Denver dealt with 769 delinquent girls of high-school age. We kept a particularly close record of those cases. They ranged in age from 14 to 17 years. Four hundred and sixty-five of them were no longer in school; *304 of them were.*

Three-fourths of these girls came to me of their own accord. The only reason why the number was not very much larger was that it was physically impossible for me and my small staff to follow the thing up from case to case. For let me repeat here what I have already said, that starting with one case, I can uncover a thousand. The clues lead from girl to girl and from boy to boy, straight ahead, criss-cross, and round-about, a chain so extended that I hardly dare hazard a guess at its length and the number of its branches. It includes the schools and extends far beyond them.

For instance, at least 2,000 persons were directly involved in the cases of those 769 girls. For one thing, the boy had to be reckoned with. In addition, the two of them always had a circle of intimates, many of whom were in on the secret, and indulging in the same kind of experiences. So it goes, from one girl to other girls, and from one boy to other boys; and every time I have tried to follow up the many bypaths that present themselves for investigation it has been like exploring the endless passages of a dark cave, whose galleries and secrets lead one beyond the limits of endurance. That is why I have never followed it further than here recorded. There is only one of me; my staff is small; my budget at the time of that research was only $30,000 as compared with the $250,000 budget of the District and Criminal court across the hall; and we handle 12,000 cases of individuals a year as compared with a possible 2,000 handled by the other judicial machine. Our machine is administrative, and concerns the affairs and welfare of human beings rather than their relationships to property or their collisions with the formalities of law and its remedies of vengeance.

On account of these limitations in equipment and personnel, therefore, I have to call a halt somewhere. But if I had the machinery for carrying on this work of straightening out young people and putting their feet on the right paths, I could bring to light facts and figures that would be much more surprising than those here mentioned.

More hidden truth about the minds and conduct of young people comes to the surface in my court, I venture to say, than any place in the world; and yet, even though the light here compares with the knowledge held elsewhere as an arc light compares with a candle, I have been able only to scratch the surface.

Consider, for example, that for every one of those 769 girls of high-school age whom I helped in the biennial period of 1920 and 1921, there was *at least* one other girl whom this court knew nothing about and never reached. That, surely, is as conservative an estimate as could be asked. And yet, conservative as it is, let us see where it leads. It involves a *minimum* of 1,500 girls of high-school age (not necessarily in school) in Denver as having indulged in some kind of sex delinquency. It involves the assumption that 608 of them were actually in school. Assuming that there are about

3,000 girls, then, attending the high schools of Denver, that figure *608* would represent about 20 per cent over the period of two years, or 304 for each year, 10 per cent per annum. It would mean that one high-school girl in every ten, or ten in every hundred in our high schools, have their feet set on more or less perilous paths, are subjecting themselves to regrettable risks, and are in need of guidance and counsel for one reason or another.

Let me repeat that these are minimum figures, and that they include only the ages 14, 15, 16, and 17. They do not include the ages 18, 19, 20, where there is doubtless a larger percentage of such delinquency. Let me remind the reader also of my conviction, already stated, for every sexually delinquent girl we deal with there are an unknown number, possibly a much larger number, who escape our attention.

I have no wish to run these estimates into the ground. Even the minimum figures are shocking. I handled about a hundred cases of illegitimate pregnancy last year; taking care of most of the mothers and the babies, and in most cases adopting the babies out. *With every one of those girls it was a touch-and-go whether to come to me, and arrange to have the baby, or to go to an abortionist and arrange not to have it.*

How many others chose the abortionist and said nothing? How do I know? Do your own figuring. Suppose there were a hundred who chose the abortionist, just as there were a hundred who chose me. That would make a total of two hundred pregnant girls, would it not?— by very moderate figuring indeed!

Very good, we found from our own records that of 495 girls we dealt with who confessed to illicit sex relations only 1 in 20 encountered pregnancy. In that case

100 pregnancies, taken care of by us, implies, on a ratio of 1 to 19, at least 1,900 escapes from pregnancy; and 200 pregnancies would imply 3,800 escapes from pregnancy. *And that among the girls of high-school age, some in school and some out of school, in a city of 300,-000 population!* And these figures, let me say again, represent a *minimum* below the level of probability and common sense. The number of cases is certainly very far above what even these figures indicate.

I am not a statistician; and I confess I put down these estimates with some trepidation. There is a saying that figures don't lie, but that liars will figure; and I've no doubt that some clever statistician could make my logic look sad. But statisticians can do that with anybody's logic. They will figure. I shall therefore maintain, in the teeth of them all, that my deductions have common sense behind them, and are reasonably sound, and as conservative as they are startling—which, as some of my young protégés would put it, is saying a mouthful.

Our records reveal another thing of prime importance. Every girl has three ages. First, she has a chronological age that tells how many years she has lived. Second, she has an intellectual age that gauges her intelligence; which is to say that with a chronological age of 17 she might have an intellectual age of 12; or vice versa. Third, she has a biological age, which means that some girls mature into womanhood very early, say 11, and that others mature very late; and that *girls who mature early, while they are still very young chronologically and intellectually, are the most likely to get into sexual trouble with boys.* Sex overwhelms them before their minds and their powers of restraint and judgment are mature enough to cope with it.

Of the 769 girls of high-school age already mentioned,

we made a special study of 313. We found that 265 of
the 313 had come to physical maturity at 11 and 12 years,
more of them maturing at 11 than at 12. Dividing the
313 girls into two groups, we found that 285 of them
matured at the ages of 11, 12, and 13; and that only
28 of them matured at 14, 15, and 16.

The significance of this is very great. It is perfectly
in line with a fact that I have constantly observed through
the many years I have worked in this field, that girls
who mature early are in much more danger of getting
into sex trouble than those who mature late. For one
thing, they are usually more attractive to boys; and, as
I have already indicated, they are physiologically awake,
with the desires of maturity without the intellectual restraints and sophistication of maturity. They are women
with the minds of little children; and for many of them,
the burden and the responsibility are too much. If we
educated them properly this would not often be the case;
but we give them no hint of their own danger.

Such children, at 11 or 12 years, may have the desires
and physical needs of the girl of 18 and older. Thus
the biological age becomes dangerously preponderant in
the combination. Physical maturity, devastating in its
demands when not controlled, is on them at a time when
it is not fair nor reasonable to expect adult judgment.
But we do expect just that; as we quickly make them
understand when, blindfolded by our conventions, they
fall into the ditch.

Long experience enables me usually to pick these victims of early maturity at sight. There is an indefinable
something in the eye, a something about the mouth, that
tells the tale, particularly when there has been an actual
sex experience. Usually when I see such indications in
children, I talk with them, get their confidence, and find

that I am seldom wrong. I wish it were possible for me at this point to explain with precision how I detect these cases. But I can't. The process is apparently subjective. It is the result of powers of observation sharpened by years of contact with people and experience in discovering that which is instinctively hidden because of the fears I have learned to lift. I am a good deal like a sheepherder I know whom I once saw go into a flock of 5,000 sheep and pick out one which did not belong there. He couldn't tell me how he did it. To him, though not to me, that sheep had stigmata that marked it off from others. So it is with people.

Among the many instances of this sort in my memory, this one will serve. A woman made a complaint against a small boy for stealing the battery of her doorbell. The boy was interested in electricity, and took the most direct way to gratify his wish for some apparatus. He wasn't a thief. He was just a normal, enterprising boy whose courage and independence of mind, rightly directed, will serve him well when he grows up. The woman brought her little girl, a child of eleven, to court with her as a witness against the boy. After the case was disposed of, I asked her if she had ever given much thought to her little girl. She was indignant. What did I mean?

"Send your daughter to me tomorrow," I said. "I want to talk with her."

She finally consented, but left in a huff.

The next morning the child presented herself. She had all the signs, right in her pretty face. And sure enough, when I talked with her, and got her confidence, I learned that she and the boy who had stolen the battery had already had sex relations with each other. *Bad?* Not a bit of it. Simply a case of an innocent, ignorant, blindfolded child, brought up by one more dull, unimaginative, conventional mother who was perfectly sure the great conspiracy of adult silence was working perfectly, and who nearly expired with wrath, humiliation, and open rage at me and the child, when—with the little girl's consent—I told her the truth, and suggested that she had better let me look after Elsie for a few years. She had the good sense to do that, at least. Elsie came up for a chat with me every few weeks, and Elsie is today growing up into as fine a woman as you would want to meet. But that isn't the fault of her foolish mother.

The early coming of maturity in such girls is interpreted by their stupid elders as a kind of sexual obsession. As a matter of fact it is not necessary to interpret it in terms of sex. It may be regarded as maternal, just as the liking of a little girl for dolls may be interpreted as maternal.

A worried mother once came to me for consultation about her 15 year old daughter, in whom she had seen signs of sexual precocity. She happened, in the course of our talk, to mention that the child had lately developed a marked gift for drawing, and that she was making pictures all the time.

"I can tell you something about those drawings," I said to her. "They are not pictures of houses, or landscapes or animals. They are pictures of babies and lovers and the like, are they not?"

She looked at me startled. "How did you guess it?" she exclaimed.

"It's simple," I replied. "That growing artistic instinct in your daughter is as much an expression of her developing sex life and of her yearning for maternity as are those relations she has with boys about which you have come in such alarm to consult me."

I recall another clear cut case. Frances Darley—that,

of course, not being her name—was the daughter of a family living on Capitol Hill, one of our select residential districts. They had money, social standing, and culture. Frances had been for the most part well and carefully brought up, by the usual conventional standards.

She had an older sister who was happily married, and who lived with her husband at the Darley home. And the older sister had a baby, to which Frances, then aged fourteen, was devotedly attached. Till the baby came she had never tired of her dolls. After it came she forgot dolls; and every minute she was permitted with that baby, she took greedily. In fact her devotion was the source of considerable quiet amusement to the rest of the family.

Then came a dark day when the sister and her husband moved to a distant town, taking the baby with them. Frances was inconsolable; but it was just the grief of a child, and nobody paid more than perfunctory attention to it.

It was not long, however, before Frances began to wonder why she could not just as well have a baby of her own. She didn't know where babies came from; and inquiries along that line, she discovered, were not encouraged by her elders. She consulted an older girl, who, as it happened, was adequately informed; and thus she learned all about the way in which babies come.

The story of how she carefully nursed that secret I had later from her own lips. It was very beautiful; and touching beyond my power to convey. She understood that for some reason the whole matter was taboo; but she never wavered from the purpose that gradually formed within her mind. She bided her time, and at last deliberately importuned a good-natured boy, about 16 years old, otherwise as harmless as a Newfoundland dog,

to help her have the baby she was fully resolved to have
for her very own.

In due time she discovered that a marvelous thing had
happened to her; and her delight was so great that she
went to her mother and told her "secret."

Of course the effect on the mother was what might
be expected. She was shocked and horrified beyond
words, not so much at the really difficult problem raised
by the child's conduct, as by the wholly false and superstitious notion that her little girl was "bad," that she had
done an "immoral" thing, and that she was henceforth
smirched, "impure," "ruined," and beyond the pale of
law or decency. She blistered the sensitive and aston-
ished girl with her reproaches, she loaded her with vili-
fication, and she fell only just short of uttering the conventional "never darken my door again."

What she made very plain indeed was the disgrace that
would attend discovery. She didn't *say* that the sin of
sins was getting found out; but every tone of her voice
and manner conveyed it. Her fear was directed toward
the people like herself, whom she herded with,—the social
clique that would judge her and perhaps cut her. Children are not blind; they can see through a millstone when
there is a hole in it. I well recall the frantic fear dis-
played by this woman, when in talking to me she exclaimed over and over, "Oh, what have I done that God
should curse me like this? Haven't *I* been a good woman?
Do I deserve this? Why should I have such a sinful
child?"

"You've got a wonderful child," I said to her. "She
is neither bad nor sinful. She is natural and human and
simply misdirected. It is now up to you either to make a
tragedy of your daughter's life or help her to the maternity she so beautifully yearns for. Stop thinking of your-

self. Think of your child, and the causes of this thing you call her sin.—You should know how to sympathize with and advise your daughter when she most needs your love."

But my advice came too late. Filled with terror and remorse, Frances had already sought other advice—naturally not from her idiotic mother; for she instinctively saw that there was no counsel or wisdom or sanity to be found in the mind of that frantic woman. She went rather to the sophisticated young woman whose information had gotten her into this trouble, and asked to know the way out. She learned that she might still escape "ruin" by getting rid of the unborn child; and she received some general directions as to what to do.

She did it, or at least tried to do it. And then came a revulsion of feeling. She repented. She would have her baby anyway. But she changed her mind too late. Whether because of the injury she had inflicted on herself, or because of the terror and the nervous tension, her child was born prematurely; and her first joy in her new found motherhood was quenched and blackened with the news that her baby was dead.

When things like that happen, they make me see red. But later, when my anger stops boiling, I settle back again to a sad recognition of the fact that we are all, even the mother of Frances, victims of tradition; that no individual is to blame; and that it is for those of us who see more clearly to be patient, do what work of alleviation we may, and look hopefully to the future, now more or less in the hands of a younger generation that, fortunately, has small reverence for certain customs of its fathers. In a rational and critical testing of traditions, to the end that we may determine which are fit to survive and which have served their turn, lies the hope of our civilization.

If the mother of Frances Darley had been able to choose and select in that manner, she would not have ruined, or partly ruined, the life of her own daughter. What she did was not so violent as a Salem witch-hanging or the methods of the Inquisition with heretics, but it was just as intelligent; and the torture was certainly more acute than any agony that can be inflicted on the body. This she did to her own child—in the name of decency and Christian morality. So deep beneath the glittering surface of our lives goes our culture. It is as if a mere sheet of paper separated us from jungles that echo to the tom-tom and the tribal taboos of races whose mental development enables them to count as high as ten.

The thing I particularly want to make clear about this case is that it was not primarily a sex offense; it was the offense of wanting a baby instead of dolls to play with. I commend it to the consideration of some of our lovers of lap dogs—even the unmarried ones.

Frances had a desire for what is genuinely good in life that puts to shame our conventions and our shams; and I think Frances is a touchstone by which many an apparently oversexed and apparently reckless and pleasure-loving little flapper can be judged. There is a delicacy, and fineness, a spirituality, an unearthly sweetness about these young girls that we, their elders, often lose sight of because we see no deeper than the carmined lips, and cheeks that are too pink, and the behavior that is too reckless. They are not fresh bodies offered for the pleasure of men but bodies offered to the agony and bloody sweat of motherhood. That is what it really means with most of them, whether they and we are conscious of it or not. This is as true of them now as it was when they crooned lullabies over their dolls. Let us not, when we look upon them, coarsely leer and smirk. In saying this I am not unmindful that sex plays its part as sex in human life, and is in that sense a thing distinct from procreation and parenthood. But I shall discuss that side of the question later. The separation is more apparent than real.

Another point of interest in the case of Frances is that it tended to support Bernard Shaw's view, developed in "Man and Superman," that contrary to the general view, it is not the male who does the pursuing but the female; and that women universally make men their creatures to the end that they may gratify the maternal urge within them.

I think that even now the public looks upon that notion as a mere bit of Shavian perversity and wit. It apparently occurs to few that Shaw really meant it; and that such a view, coming from the mind of one who is certainly one of the towering geniuses of our age, is entitled to serious respect.

The reason I respect it is that I see it working out right before my eyes all the time. There is no buncombe about it. In the case of Frances you get it reduced absolutely to primitive first biological principles, unclothed in the conventional concealments which ordinarily serve to make the male appear as the predatory aggressor. In a lesser degree, the typical flapper, with her bold meeting of the male half way, illustrates the same point. And now that women are coming to their own in our civilization, it is interesting to speculate on what may be the ultimate outcome.

These girls I deal with have many of them dropped the fiction that a woman must be wooed from any real reluctance. At a meeting of parents which was recently held in Denver to discuss what could be done about the "immorality" existing in a certain school, the principal of the school told the parents that it was the girls who were largely responsible because they pursued the boys.

One father who was present said of his son, who was responsible for the condition of a 16 year old girl in the same school, "I don't know what I can do about his conduct. I have forbidden him to go out at night, but I can't *always* watch him (*sic*)! Every evening the girls come around outside the house and whistle for him."

A high-school boy, in confessing to me his experience with a certain girl said, "I didn't go after her. She used to stop her automobile on the street and ask me to take a ride. I felt like a fool if I said I wouldn't go with her."

Then there was the case of Ellen. Ellen, who is the daughter of a wealthy man in Denver, entered into an agreement with five other girls in the boarding school she attended, that she and they would each contrive to have a sex experience sometime during the summer vacation then approaching, so that they might compare notes in the fall.

Ellen selected a boy, who had no thought of anything of the sort, to take her to dinner in a well-known, questionable restaurant where they obtained a private room. There she seduced him, to his own utter astonishment. The boy was bewildered and amazed at what took place.

Ellen had no notion of any after consequences, because she had been brought up most "properly"; but months later her mother discovered something.

Ellen confessed what had happened. There was a stormy council of the two families, as a result of which the boy's father put the lad out of his home, that being the traditional thing for a right-thinking, conventional father to do.

To her parents Ellen told the story of the compact with her school friends; and then they brought her to me. And her father, in tears, exclaimed to me, "I quit. I guess I don't know anything about kids. You'll have to take charge of this." I concluded that, unlike the boy's father, he was at least capable of learning something from his own mistakes; for he did stand by his daughter handsomely later on.

They were debating the question of an abortion. That is the usual course when fear enters in. Fear, I estimate, is responsible for at least a thousand abortions in Denver every year.

But I dissuaded them from anything so criminal and cowardly as that. I promised them that the future of Ellen's child would be my care; and then we cooked up a plan.

They gave out that Ellen had gone east on a visit. But she hadn't. She was installed in a bedroom in the tower of her home, with a nurse.

Now the waiting list of people who want to adopt babies is always longer than the list of available babies. From my list therefore, I easily chose a well-to-do couple, and told them that I would have a new baby ready for them about a certain date if they would, as the saying is, "stick around." I told them to employ a physician to take charge. They were to trust me as to the child's antecedents, and were not to know where it came from.

One night my telephone rang. Ellen's baby was on the way. I telephoned the foster parents during the hours that followed, keeping them informed of the progress of the case.

"I wish it were over," said the foster father to me. "My wife's so nervous she's gone to bed. You'd think it was she that was having the baby."

Finally it was all over, and the new baby was ready for the transfer. The two physicians met in the darkness on a street corner. Neither of them knew the other or could see the face of the other. Each carried a satchel. The one didn't know where the child was coming from, the other didn't know where it was going. They transferred the baby from one satchel to the other, and parted.

A passing policeman looked at them rather sharply, but fortunately he didn't complicate matters by following up his hunch, if he had one. Presently Ellen's baby was in its new home.

"At least," said the foster mother to me later, "when my baby asks where she came from I can truthfully tell her that the doctor brought her in a bag."

So I saved Ellen from being torn to pieces by our enlightened and moral society. I let her hide behind my judicial chair, so to speak, till the chase should go by. Then she came out into the daylight. Today she isn't "ruined." She is happily married, and has babies of her own, that she can keep. That is better than "ruin," I think.

CHAPTER 8

And now what about the boys and girls who *don't* go wrong! I am conscious that in dealing so extendedly with the problem of those who get into trouble I may have given many a dissenting reader the impression that this younger generation is just a wormy apple; and if I have, I am sorry, and can only refer the reader back to figures and estimates already given. Let me add, however, that I do not admit that we are dealing with a wormy apple, even where the lapses and mistakes of youth are admitted. I do not consent to so negative an interpretation of the facts. People are not necessarily rotten because they make mistakes and have been so trained and educated that they can hardly avoid making them. It is true that disaster overtakes individuals, but looked at in the mass, these changes which are so alarming to most of us are constructive in their nature; and the only really deadly element I find in the whole business is the attitude of mind that tries to make such changes rotten by calling them rotten and thinking of them as rotten. Such a way of thought is hideously destructive.

Just how destructive and terrible it can be is well illustrated today in the crusades of censorship of everything and everybody which have spread over this country like a cancer within the last ten years. Prudes create the very states of mind they say they are trying to get rid of—and which I'll say *they* badly need to get rid of, considering that the mountain of filth which they so eloquently describe is largely contained within the compass of their own minds. A well-meaning minister recently came to me with a bill which he wanted to see introduced into the legislature. Among the things the bill prohibited was the display of women's lingerie in shop windows. It went on from that to take in books containing any reference to sex, movies of the same sort, jazz music, and the dancing that went with it, what he called "pelvic dancing";—a fairly wide field for one bill. Lingerie in shop windows! Now just what sort of a cesspool do you suppose that man's mind contained?

But to come back to the boys and girls who *don't* go wrong. Who are they? Is there a discernible number? Again, I say that I am sorry if I have given the impression that they are only a corporal's guard. The girl who permits a boy to kiss her may not be doing wisely, but she can hardly be described as having gone wrong, can she? Actual sex liberties are another matter; and I have already given estimates on that.

In general I find that there are several types of youth who are unlikely to get into trouble. First, there is the type that lacks energy, self confidence, and initiative. One characteristic of most of the boys and girls who get into difficulties is that they have just those qualities, and are all the more worth saving on that account. It is not always true that the boy or girl who never is willful or troublesome lacks energy and character, but it is quite likely to be so. Consistently high marks in deportment in school, especially for a boy, may merely mean that he lacks courage and energy, and perhaps health, and is restrained, not by morality but by *fear,* for "morality" doesn't play much part in the reactions of the normal lad —not if he is the healthy young animal he should be. He ought to be about as unconscious of his soul as he is of his breathing, or any other vital thing about him.

The second type that does not get into trouble is the kind that has had the *right home training*. I say nothing of the right *school* training, because, except in a few private schools, and the exceptional public schools, right training does not seem to exist where the question of sexual conduct is concerned, however excellent a school training may be available in many other directions.

The home is the very heart of this problem. Well-born young people of good stock who come from a certain type of home are in little danger from the ordinary temptations and freedoms that come their way when they are among their fellows.

Unfortunately there are only a few such homes, even among people of good stock. I am sorry to have to say this. I know we talk a lot of patriotic spread-eagleism about the American home—even when there are nearly as many divorces and separations as marriages in a representative American city like Denver; but I am obliged in honesty to say, that homes in which children can find the right spiritual and intellectual atmosphere are the exception rather than the rule.

Take, for instance, the home of the minister whose daughter got into an intrigue with the son of the man prominently connected with Education. That was supposed to be a very superior sort of home. It had good blood behind it; and it was supposed to have religious atmosphere, and culture also. But of course religion and culture were precisely what that home lacked. It had a puritanical theology and a routine of systematized hypocrisy and cant instead, masquerading as religion and culture. A young plant can't thrive in that kind of acid-soaked soil. The old saying about some ministers' sons and deacons' daughters is as fundamentally true psychology as it ever was.

Again, the parents of Ellen and her young man were both supposed to represent the best we have in morals and in intelligence. And yet, whatever the appearances of surface refinement, and whatever they professed, they were *not* moral because they were not intelligent. They had a bourgeois dullness of mind that was far more to blame for the waywardness of their children than were the children themselves.

It is impossible to be moral and at the same time to be a hypocritical ass. It is impossible to be truthful and yet to hide the truth from people who have a right to it. It is impossible to be intelligent, enlightened and cultured, and yet superstitious, cowardly, unimaginative, and blindly conventional.

The freedom of action you will find in the slums is a better and more genuinely moral thing than such bondage as this bondage of pretense and concealment. It produces less spiritual disease, though it may produce more violations of the social code.

If that sounds extreme, let me say right here that of the hundreds of young boys who are brought before me for theft, I have had comparatively a very few newsboys in the last twenty years; and yet most of our newsboys of the streets come from so-called slum homes, where poverty and the temptations of poverty are rampant, where they don't always wash behind their ears, and where six persons are likely to be using one toothbrush.

Where do an appallingly large proportion of the theft cases come from? Why from our respectable and cultured homes, where Morality glares at you from the windows as you pass, and where Respectability goes around looking like the proverbial undertaker, and where you can find mature and rebellious girls who don't know where babies come from, and are cynically using their wits to find out, and where the whole game of living is "Don't do this; and don't do that; but if you *do* do it, for God's sake *don't get found out; don't get caught.*"

The boys brought before me for theft come for the most part from the best day schools, the best Sunday schools, and many of them from boys' organizations that are nationally known,—agencies, one and all, supposed to make men of them.

Judging by results, I should say that one of the things most lacking in this enlightened culture on which we pride ourselves is enlightenment, and that the other is culture. Those poor kids come out of Main Street. What can you expect of them, either with respect to theft, or to sexual restraint, or anything else—except *keeping up appearances*. They all do that to the best of their ability. If they don't they are "ruined," unless they can beat their parents, their teachers, and the police in a race for my judicial chambers, where I manage to save them by violating most of the judicial traditions that have ever grown out of the black muck of human intolerance.

My observation of children who come from these homes in which money, comfort, and the surface refinements of life play a conspicuous part has now extended over a long period. There is every reason why such homes should as a rule produce children fully equipped, mentally, morally, and physically, to take their places as sane and stable members of society. But only a portion of them do. Of the others many are sending out into the world boys and girls who, in their ignorance and recklessness are as dangerous to themselves and to society as a ten-year-old child toting a loaded gun which he playfully points at all bystanders. That children should be endowed with a greater freedom of action than youth has ever had before is a splendid thing; but that our present way of educating them, both in the home and at school, should fail to train them to use such freedom wisely—this surely is tragic. They may win through; but the process is bound to result in individual disasters beyond computation.

The only ground on which I can account for the failure of many materially complete homes to put sweetness and light into the lives of the children they bring into the world is that they have everything *but* the culture they profess. Judging by their fruits many of them must be the abode of insufferable vulgarians and bigots.

What have such people as these smug and comfortable standpatters to impart to children? What spiritual meat and drink can they offer them? What Religion, pure and undefiled, can they transmit to them? What notion of their duty toward God and their Neighbor can they leave them to be kept forever burning like a flame upon an ancient Altar? And what sweet communion of free spirits can they institute within the sanctity and freedom of the home?

Is it conceivable that such adults as these should deal *respectfully* with children, treating them as equals instead of with careless contempt, like stupid tyrants? Is it conceivable that they should do other than produce after their kind, imparting to their young, so far as they can, the tooth-and-claw philosophy by which they live themselves and which they never acknowledge to themselves? They don't *mean* to—Dear, no! They try to bring the children up in the way they should go, by means of second-hand and hollow exhortations, by stupid commands and by the concealment of every inconvenient truth.

To them the art of hypocrisy has always been as the breath of life. More—it is a cloak which protects their white and tender hides from the gusty winds of Reality.

They can't understand that human beings can live without it. They think pretense is necessary to their authority. Later, when the child discovers the pretense, at just about the time when he is suffering the physical and spiritual growing pains of adolescence, the sham authority crumbles, and he is left with nothing to stand on save what he can fashion for himself. But builded in simple honesty, the foundation would have held, solid as a rock.

The results of this adult folly are visible on every side. Youth is like a boat guided by a pilot who has never learned to "shoot the sun." It can't navigate because it lacks a point of reference. It sails on with no clear-cut purpose. It lives in the present and for the moment, finding no stimulus in the thought of a goal ahead. It is emotionally unbalanced and wanting in nervous and mental stability. Therefore it is crazy for excitement, and averse to disciplined effort; and it automatically and instinctively avoids contacts with life which are not superficial and easy. By the same token it finds, in the vapid, meaningless, purposeless world of jazz, where experiences are valued by the violence of the immediate "kick" they can deliver, little to respect and little to compel either worship or reverence.

This means mischief. And the responsibility for the creation of it rests in just one place, squarely on the shoulders of an adult generation which is still trying to force upon Youth a body of traditions, customs, laws, and forms of authority in which it does not itself any longer believe and by which its own inner life is no longer dominated.

These traditions were once potent. Parents were able to transmit them to their children because they themselves really were compelled by them, and really believed in them with all their strength. It was a vision. They lived by it. But it has vanished like a mirage; and now *something* must come in its place; for when there is no vision the people perish.

In the meantime, how shall the blind lead the blind? The older generation stubbornly affirms that it is still zealous for this body of cant which it hypocritically preaches to Youth and discards in its own life. How is it possible that there should grow up alongside of this dishonesty, this insincerity, this futile cherishing of a thing that's dead, a system of education capable of dealing illuminatingly, convincingly, and inspiringly with the amazing opportunity for spiritual adventure and sheer romance that lies in modern life? About us is a body of newly discovered truth capable of fulfilling and preserving all that was sound and permanent in the traditions and customs bequeathed us by our forefathers—amazing, blinding, beautiful truth, fit, should it touch a dead stone, to turn it into a whizzing meteor, fit to send forth the spirit of Youth into the world of purposed action like a flaming sword. But—how, in the name of the God we so desperately need to find, shall we show them that vision while we stubbornly look back—look back—look back— forgetting Lot's Wife?

We have to make new decisions and new choices in this modern world. Youth has to be taught to make them too. But in what essential respect have we changed our educational methods to suit this need? Hardly at all. Education still remains a process, not of unfoldment or discovery or of original effort, but rather of injecting into the mind a body of crystallized knowledge, supposed to be perfect and final, which a child is to accept and believe without examination or critical scrutiny. Let us not deceive ourselves about this. Any teacher who tried to teach by making his students really do their own think-

ing, particularly in the field of science, religion, political
economy, sociology, economics, and the like, would be
discharged as a dangerous person by the school board at
its next meeting. As for any teacher who dared to ex-
pound some of the things that are going into this book
—well, I hate to think what some irate white-robed mob
might do to him.

The student in the average American school and college
is handed certain "truths" which he is to *believe*. He
must not appraise them, question them or put his own
valuation upon them. His morality, his Americanism, his
sanity, his social fitness, are all called into question if
he does.

What is the result? Does Youth reply by going
spunkily and fearlessly ahead? Does it independently
appraise life in the teeth of these prohibitions? Does it
seriously weigh and consider facts in spite of all obstacles,
and in spite of the want of encouragement and inspiration? Yes, a few strong ones do; and these are the
leaven in the loaf. But the youth who is one of the herd,
with merely average energy of mind, does nothing of the
sort. Something divine within him, that up-reaching,
fresh interest and enthusiasm for fine and true things, has
been ruthlessly crushed. He has done his own superficial
appraising, unhelped by the adult world, and in resentful
independence of it,—and he has done it badly. Suddenly,
as he passes from childhood to adulthood, and through
the impressionable and formative years of adolescence,
he becomes "hard boiled." Overnight as it were, he
loses interest in this whole fascinating and difficult game
of seeking the truth; he turns forthwith to the super-
ficialities and crudities of life. These look like truth to
his inexperienced eyes, and they are, moreover, gaudy,
attractive, and easy of access. Henceforth they take his

attention and sap his energies. While they fill his mind he will submit to no discipline and to no genuine and difficult culture. Thus he easily becomes habituated to the intellectually effortless way of life which thrusts itself upon him as the only apparent alternative to a body of belief and custom which he regards as false and repellent because he perceives it to be out of joint with the times.

The curses which descend upon him as a consequence of his inexperienced choice of one evil for another evil are intellectual mediocrity, vulgarity of manners, an unstable standard of conduct, and a lack of that fine discrimination and power of fastidious judgment which are among the hall-marks of culture.

Our parrot system of education has the additional and dangerous effect of making young people into rubber stamps, slaves of mass sentiment, like their elders. However much youngsters may seem to depart from the old traditions of thought and conduct, they nevertheless do act and think consistently and strictly within the limits of certain shifting codes and traditions which they have created for themselves. They dress alike, look alike so far as they can, and act alike; they dread being different from their fellows; and the pack will set upon any individual in it who does not run true to form. This is as true among our Youth as it is among the older generation. However much Youth may flaunt its independence, therefore, it has little genuine liberty, little real emancipation. By its departures, *en masse,* from ancient standards, it has doubtless achieved some real progress; but its individual members have simply jumped from one form of slavery into another. License is bondage; liberty, on the contrary, is a free obedience to laws more compelling and difficult than human law, and far more exacting. Youth, unhelped by any wisdom but its own, often confuses the two.

Thus does Youth inherit from its elders one of the worst plagues of American life, a compulsion on individuals not to be individual, a compulsion to be standardized and cut-to-pattern. We have effectively taught Youth our own intolerance of freedom because intolerance is one of the things in which we adults so sincerely believe that we consistently and vigorously practice it. Witness, for instance, the growth of the Ku Klux Klan, an organization which, for its own ends, capitalizes and uses this detestable vice as the turbines utilize the power of Niagara.

CHAPTER 9

Unavoidably the mind turns in this connection to the Leopold-Loeb case. Let no parent flatter himself that the Leopold-Loeb case has no lesson for him. Let us all clearly understand that that crime was the fruit of the modern misdirection of youth; that the present drift of our social forces produced it; that the responsibility fastens, not individually on the well-intentioned parents of those unfortunate boys, but on American parenthood in general. It was more than the story of a murder. It was the story of modern youth, of modern parents, of modern economic and social conditions, and of modern education —and this is true even though the event worked out into an extreme and exceptional deed of horror.

I have already dwelt at length on the extremes of unwise conduct to which our young people go, with their joy rides, their ways of dancing, their petting parties, their freedom in sex relations, and the like. I might have gone with some detail also into the domain of actual crime, such as automobile stealing, banditry, burglary and assault committed by mere boys. These things often proceed from conditions similar to those which produced the Leopold-Loeb crime.

These minors, be it remembered, are "children." The law goes even a step further and calls them "infants." Leopold and Loeb were infants in that sense. All the young people I deal with are infants. I do not emphasize this in mitigation of the offenses they commit, and most certainly not in mitigation of the Leopold-Loeb murder, but rather to emphasize that for hundreds of years the law has taken the enlightened view that persons under twenty-one are children, and that they must, for that reason, be dealt with in a way different from that accorded to adults.

What this implies is that persons under 21 years of age are assumed to be inferior to adults in judgment and experience, and in the sense of responsibility which comes with physical and mental maturity. It is for this reason that children cannot, in their own name, and of their own motion, buy and sell property; or marry without the consent of some adult responsible for their welfare; nor operate dangerous machinery; nor use firearms without supervision; nor do many other things without adult sanction. More than that, the State protects them in a degree, however insufficient, from exploitation by adults. Parents are required to send their children to school; children must not be made to work at occupations in which the conditions imperil their health and welfare; children must be protected from adult influences which would "contribute to the delinquency of a child" as the Colorado law puts it. Our laws, particularly with regard to child labor, often fall far short of what they should be; but the tendency of the State to take over a parental supervision of children, in certain cases, under the doctrine of *parens patriae* (the State as a superparent) is becoming more and more marked.

But our logic in this matter does not yet carry us through. It is obvious that if children are to be thus regarded in connection with such economic and social matters as, for instance, the ownership of property, and the making of marriages, it is just as important that they be consistently provided with protection, advice, and guidance in matters having to do with mind and morals. Some such protection is given both by the State and home, but it isn't given energetically; and it is particularly lacking in homes where the restrictions placed on children are in some directions unduly severe.

It is one thing to protect and enlighten; it is quite another thing to restrict, to prohibit, to forbid. The one implies tact, sympathy, and respect; the other implies coercion, flat commands, and no attempt at true enlightenment and education.

And thus, in this business of governing the young, we come to a parting of the ways, the choice between government through reasonable counsel, through conviction, and through the art of imposing responsibility on Youth, and the government through Fear.

Government through Fear produces the impulse to do the other thing—in secret if need be. It rivets a child's whole attention on the negatives of life. It makes of them an overpowering suggestion, it creates an overpowering impulse to turn them into positives, till the "thou shalt not" of tradition becomes the rebellious and unreasoning "I will" of modern youth.

The chain of cause and effect leading to all kinds of youthful delinquency, and to much adult misconduct, can thus usually be traced back to prohibitions and taboos arbitrarily imposed in childhood through the agency of Fear. The child, because of his Fear, may yield an outward obedience to commands which do not seem to him reasonable, because he has never been appealed to as a thinking and reasoning being. Secretly he is thinking other thoughts and harboring other impulses of a contrary and often anti-social kind. These he conceals. *Thus by means of an outward conformity he raises between himself and this adult world which refuses to reason with him an anti-social screen behind which all kinds of dreams, fancies, visions, and half-formed pur-*

poses take shape,—thoughts and wishes that would astound his parents and teachers if they had an inkling of the truth. This tendency becomes intensified in children of certain types. A strong child may harbor a strong resentment; a weak one a consuming and furtive terror. Both bide their time. Later they come in contact with the modern outside world, with its tremendous opportunities for liberty and independent action; and then things, anti-social things, begin to happen. The dreams, the fancies, the secret wishes, the furtive purposes, tend to take the form of action. They are no longer an insubstantial pageant. What some of the possibilities are, the briefest consideration of the conduct of many of our young people shows all too plainly. What the ultimate possibilities are in some extreme and exceptional instances, the story of the Leopold-Loeb case tells in a way that can't be misread.

Please understand my use of the word Fear in this connection. Fear may have many degrees, and it may take the form merely of a dread of social disapproval, and of the expressions that result from that dread. The point is that Fear represents a difference of point of view between child and adult which results in the creation of a kind of silent, ill-defined hostility in the mind of the child—a hostility which is likely to manifest itself in the form of deliberate defiance, aggressive independence, jeering rebellion, and genuinely anti-social conduct later; or such conduct, instead of being open and defiant, may be secret and furtive. It depends on the child. *In either case there is an absence of those internal and voluntary restraints which alone make moral conduct possible.*

My big job in dealing with young people is to create within them, as well as I can, those internal restraints which their childhood training has failed to produce. And since youth is plastic and generous in its impulses, I often succeed in this beyond my hopes.

Leopold and Loeb were both of them brought up in conventional homes. It was, I suppose, taken for granted from the start that they would follow the lines of conduct which were traditional in their homes. They were trained in those lines of conduct by nurses and by teachers and attendants hired for the purpose. This was unfortunate. For, except in rare instances, such hired persons rule children by arbitrary commands which put them into a state of internal rebellion. Often too such persons lack firmness and fail to command respect; and then contempt on the part of the child reinforces the attitude of inner rebellion.

With such a basis as this for conduct, and with this covert hostility toward society, these two boys were turned loose on the world so soon as they emerged from childhood. The presumption was that they had a normal social point of view. The truth was that they had been robbed of it by the money which had cut them off from intimate touch with their parents.

The truth also was that they reasoned from what premises they had with the logical clarity of two lunatics. People in asylums reason more clearly and unswervingly from given premises than other people. That's why they aren't sane. I don't say that these boys were insane, but their way of thought had about it a logic and ruthlessness which certainly was not characteristic of sane thought. For sane thought is adaptable. It temporizes. It demands of its theories that they shall work. No lunatic does that: ideas captivate him, but their results don't concern him.

The irresponsible liberty given these boys in the matter of spending money was a contributing factor in all this.

It gave them a power and an opportunity to follow their impulses which would not have been possible otherwise. But money was not the root cause, nor was idleness. The root cause was Fear, in the sense in which I have defined my use of the word. And Fear is the root cause of the anti-social conduct of all modern Youth today. The difference in the results is a difference of degree. The Leopold-Loeb case, therefore, ought, rightly understood, to serve as the one and only lesson needed to *wake this nation up*.

I suppose it is hardly necessary for me to add to this the corollary that if Fear is the cause of most wrongdoing, it follows that COURAGE is the most fundamental of all the virtues, and is indeed the virtue which makes all other virtues possible. Love, kindness, compassion, generosity, faith, hope—go as far as you like—are impossible to persons who lack courage; and there is nothing in the world that can blast these virtues as Fear can blast them. And yet, in the hope of making noble men and women of our children, we dare to *make them afraid*. This enables us to control them with less trouble to ourselves. It is easy.

The trial of Leopold and Loeb, as conducted by Judge Caverly, seems to me to have set a new precedent, not so much with respect to the verdict rendered as with respect to the spirit of the trial and the purposes and ends of justice which it defined so clearly in the public mind. It was educational. How the calm and true majesty of the law shone out through that ordeal. How impotently the cry of the mob for blood beat against it.

Judge Caverly, in the rendering of his verdict, did two very wise things. He based the verdict itself on a legal precedent which nobody can question, the youth of the defendants. He then called attention to the fact that though it is not at this time apparently possible for science to arrive at accurate conclusions regarding the question of the responsibility of individuals for what they do or do not do, the future may yet bring forth great things when research along such lines has come to a fuller development.   There is implied here a recognition of the fact that mere revenge taken by society upon its offenders is not a solution, and that motives of revenge should have no place in the operations of a criminal court.   It was a great and a wise decision, and it is to be hoped that the whole American nation will learn a lesson from it.

CHAPTER 10

I was once invited to address the students of a certain high school in a large western city. The school superintendent, however, called me by telephone ahead of time, and said the Board of Education requested that in my talk I should not touch on questions of sex, marriage, divorce, and similar topics. He apologetically added that some of the Board were to be there, and that knowing my habit of frank speech, they had been uneasy for fear I might open up subjects about which they did not consider it wise to set young people thinking.

"Far be it from me," I said, "to start anything that might imperil the morals of your young. You may rely on my discretion."

He breathed an audible sigh of relief that made me think he had anticipated there would be trouble when he should try to separate me from a subject so near my heart. "Thank you very much," he said pleasantly; "I'm sure you will have many other interesting things to say."

When I delivered my talk, therefore, I kept off the grass. I skirted the whole sex subject in a discreet and long-skirted manner. I did, however, take the liberty of referring, warningly, to the fact that unchaperoned automobile riding carried with it moral responsibilities equal to the opportunities it might give for irresponsible conduct. And in that connection I quoted to them those fine lines from Richard Lovelace:

> "I could not love thee, Dear, so much,
> Loved I not Honor more."

They got the point. However, that was as near as I came to the forbidden ground. Though my student audience was plainly hungry for some plain speech and some truthful information I couldn't give it to them.

Later I learned that they knew I had been muzzled. At the time, however, it was a surprise to me when, after the members of the Board had left, a group of about sixty senior girls came to me and asked if I would answer some questions.

Considering that this had nothing to do with my speech before the school, I consented; and we had a round-table talk. The questions were too many to put them down here, but I can give a few, to which I listened remembering how the superintendent had told me over the telephone that I must not say anything that would set these young people thinking along forbidden lines. Was it possible, I marveled, that he could be in daily touch with these adolescents and imagine that they were not thinking about such things, and that he could not see that ignorance was their greatest danger?

"Do you believe, Judge Lindsey, that when two persons don't love each other they should be compelled to remain married?"

"Don't you think that for a man and woman to live together when they don't love each other is as sinful as if they were not married at all?"

"Do you think a loveless marriage more sinful and wrong than for unmarried persons to live together because they love each other?"

"Do you believe in a federal marriage and divorce law?"

"Do you think a girl ought to be bawled out in school if she puts too much rouge on her face?"

"Do you think it wrong for a girl to bring her vanity case to school?"

"Is it wrong for a girl to let a boy kiss her; and why is it wrong?"

Poor little starved souls! They wanted knowledge, and facts for the forming of sound judgments on values of life which most concerned them, as future wives, mothers, and citizens. And yet their own parents, teachers, and trustees, charged with the responsibility of preparing them for life, had united, consciously or unconsciously, in a conspiracy of silence, to see that such information was put out of their reach. And so devilishly complete was their system for carrying this out that they had seen to it that I, a possible source of information, should be gagged and muzzled beforehand. The cream of the jest was that they didn't want their "attention directed to such matters." They didn't want them "thinking along those lines." They wanted them thinking about something else.

Consider! Here was a big school, filled with young people in whom the awakening of the sexual life was a biological and psychological *fact,* in many respects the most important fact about them; and they were not to have their already seething attention *directed* to such matters.

The consuming desire to know and understand had long since *directed* the attention of those students toward Sex, and what was keeping their minds unduly *riveted* on the subject was their ungratified curiosity about what had quite needlessly been made to look like a shameful mystery. The way to direct their minds *away* from such matters, and to give them a proper and healthy perspective, was to tell them the truth and let them take Sex as much for granted as the weather.

Under such conditions they would continue to think about it and be concerned with it, I grant you; but the repressions and suppressions that work most of the mischief at present would be done away with, and sound and decent codes of conduct would follow. I don't mean that we would have a Utopia, even at that,—for the enormous mass of our other accepted sex conventions and restraints would still have to be reckoned with; but it would at least be a start, and something rational would come from it.

One of my reasons for thinking that the result would be a greater rationality and restraint than anything we have at present is that girls who have complete information about sex seldom make mistakes in the relations they permit between themselves and boys. Instinctively a sophisticated girl puts up whatever conventional barriers may be necessary to her own defense. It is a simple matter of self preservation and of common sense; for the burden, in these matters, falls on the woman. Hers is the risk because the consequences, if there are any, are hers to reckon with. She has a biological reason for self restraint; and if our volunteer censors of morality think she needs *them* to come to her defense, they flatter themselves. Nature took care of that long ago. Women have ordered and will order the activities of sex, both as to time and occasion, by their own convenience and by their own sense of expediency. But of course this presupposes that they know what they are about, and have the necessary knowledge of fact. An untaught little girl can't exercise such judgment; and she is more likely, on urging from some importunate male, to do things which, in her ignorance, she sees no adequate reason for not doing. And the more independent and alive she is the more likely the thing is to happen; so that the finest and brightest and most worthwhile girls are, as judged by the standards of Mrs. Grundy, most likely to become "immoral"—if they are left in ignorance. And the contrary is true when they know the facts. Then they are the *least* likely to go wrong.

I remember three girls coming to me together. One of them was 17, the other two were 16. All were from good, middle-class homes. They wanted advice. The oldest said she had had sex relations with a boy, and was worried for fear she might be pregnant. I told her that if she cared to she might consult a man or woman doctor on our staff, and that if she should prove to be pregnant, the court would help her, in a legal and proper manner. The second related that she was going with a boy, that he was accustomed to kiss her and take various liberties with her, and that she was afraid she might some time yield to him completely. I told her to warn him that she was under my care, and that no further improper liberties would be tolerated. Also that she had better keep in touch with me, for support. The third was contemplating eloping with a boy of about her own age. She wanted to know what I thought of it. I told her I didn't think well of it, and told her why. One of the reasons was that he was not making a living, and that the coming of a baby would put them up a stump. I gave her other reasons also. She finally agreed that the whole project was foolish, and consented to abandon it.

Every one of those three girls, you see, came to me for information: and the one already in trouble was there because of ignorance, an ignorance which had been laid on all of them, and which was already leading the other two into danger. Fortunately they had come to me in time. But why didn't the Home, the Church, and the School tell them things that would have made such folly unlikely or impossible? Why let them walk blindfold to the very brink of the precipice? All they needed or wanted was the truth. Once they had it they were ready to act on their own responsibility and in their own defense,—for that, I repeat, is a biological instinct common to all normal women.

Years ago I had in my charge a girl of 17 who, when I became acquainted with her five years before, had already had relations with several school boys. Immoral? Bad? Poppycock! She was ignorant. One talk with me ended it; she became one of the finest young women in Denver. No casual male would dare cross her path. She is very beautiful, has a remarkable mind, and some time ago was married to a youth who, I trust, deserves her.

Long before her marriage, and long after I had put an end to the promiscuous intimacies with boys with which she had begun her sexual life, she came to me frankly and told me that she had *one* lover now instead of many; that they intended to marry as soon as he should be in a position to support her, and that in the meantime she was living in "pre-nuptial relations" with him, that being the term used by these young people to indicate such intimacies.

Could I have done anything about that? Conventional-minded people would say, "Certainly. You should not have countenanced it. You should have forbidden it flatly."

Well, I did nothing of the sort. She had been frank
with me; and I didn't violate her confidence by inter-
fering. If I had done so I'd have lost my influence over
her for good. When I found that I could not persuade her
to a more conventional kind of conduct I let her go
her way without interference. Though I expressed strong
disagreement with her course, I condemned her not at
all; and what's the result? Simply that she and her
lover got married in due time, and are now happy in
a way which society would have made impossible if
it had had an opportunity to interfere. Recently a beautiful baby was born to them.

I want to point out in this connection, where the responsibility for this state of affairs really lay. It lay
with the parents, the church, and the teachers, and the
convention of silence which made it possible for that
girl ignorantly to stumble into a sex experience at the
age of twelve. What happened then aroused in that
child impulses which would normally have remained dormant till much later. Her sex life was aroused; it made
her an adult before her time; and now—though I might
talk continence to her till I was blue in the face, I could
not stop her.

But I could make sure that there was no promiscuity
in her relations, and that her intimacy was limited to
the youth she loved and intended to marry. And they
afterwards did marry, and had a big society wedding;
and her mother and her mother's friends wept, as women
have a way of doing at weddings, and no doubt thought
sentimentally how innocent and unprepared she was for
the experience of marriage. How it would interest them
to know that their little girl would by now be a "bad
woman" if I had not gotten her in time. Of course, by

their standards, she is today as "immoral" as ever, or nearly so, because she once lived "in sin" with a man she wasn't married to, a thing that by their code can never be blotted out. She could live with him "in sin" later, after the marriage ceremony, and it would be all right. Where do they get their logic? *Did that relationship really smirch and defile her, or was she at fault simply because she was violating the social code?* The distinction is extremely important. We may admit that she was at fault in her pre-nuptial intimacy; but the fault lay in her violation of a social convention, and not in a mysterious "defilement" conjured up by our tribal superstitions. That "defilement" was as much present after the marriage as before, if by "defilement" is meant the physical and psychological fact of sex-relationship. This is not said, of course, to imply that I justify her course, but simply to show what are the true grounds on which she may be rationally judged; and to show that those grounds do not justify the severity of the condemnation which our superstitions and hypocritical society visits on girls who thus violate the conventions. I am here writing as much in the interests of justice as in the interest of morals.

In relating such incidents as these I am trying to make clear my reasons for thinking that girls would establish their own standards of safety if they were properly and completely informed about sex. They normally turn to the right about when they know the truth; and whenever they get into trouble or into danger, it is invariably for the reason that they have an imperfect comprehension of the facts and significance of sex as these things apply to them.

One evidence of this is that it is the girls rather than

the boys who come to this court for help in sex problems. The same thing is indicated in the fact that it was the girls in that school in the western city—not the boys— who gathered around me and asked questions. Boys would be incapable of it. The young male animal has not matured to the point where such problems strike him as particularly vital or as socially significant. He has, however, quite decisively reached the point where his own aggressive desires are an acute factor in the situation, particularly when he deals with girls who are as ignorant as himself. The young male doesn't think beyond the satisfactions of the moment, particularly where sex is concerned. I see this constantly in my court. The boy, mentally and spiritually, is less mature. And when sex looms into an actuality, it is the girls who come for help and counsel because nature lays on them a responsibility from which the boy is free.

This lack of capacity for positive and constructive thinking on the part of boys comes out in other ways. My files are full of letters which I get from both sexes, and almost invariably those from the boys are childish and ill expressed, in English that is inadequate and incorrect. The girls, on the other hand, express themselves with an ease commensurate with the relative clarity of their thinking. The ability to write or to speak clear, straightforward, understandable English has always seemed to me one of the best single indications of intelligence that I know of; and the lack of such ability is often an indication either of an inactive or an undeveloped mind. And as between girls and boys in a school, the difference is too pronounced to be ignored in such a connection as this.

This will in part explain why I have had so much

more to say about girls than I have about boys. Aside from the fact that the girls' part in such questions is the more dramatic and interesting, it is also a fact that the boy, relatively, doesn't count. You can always tell what he will do, for his sex psychology is relatively direct, simple and uninvolved. But with the girl it is different. Her decisions are important—both for herself and for the race; and this she instinctively knows.

Another point to which I want to direct attention is that the responsible interest taken by girls in such subjects as those broached among those schoolgirls in that western city means that women are going, sooner or later, to come to certain definite conclusions; and that from those conclusions will come a woman-made code of sex morality on which the women of the future will act, for their own protection and for the protection of children— and on which they will therefore require men to act. What that code will be, and how far it will depart from the code of this day, I don't pretend to say. But I am certain that women will create it, and that it will be saner and better than our present code, because its tendency will be to make the marriage contract much more workable and successful than it is at present.

I don't want to be misunderstood here as implying that men will not willingly conform to such a code. Boys and men are alike capable of restraint and judgment in sex matters when they have been properly educated. But the leadership, nevertheless, is not going to come from them; it will come from women because women have more at stake. The issue with them is direct; with men it is indirect. It is a question of concrete morality and concrete results with women; it is a question of abstract morality and of no results in particular with men.

Again, the intent of the questions posed by those high-school girls was not cynical nor sensuous. They were not seeking excuses for lax conduct. The inquiry was spiritual and honest in intent. Those girls were not satisfied with their received traditions, they resented the attempt to muzzle me, and they had a perfectly proper desire to know. They were refusing to be put off. The directness of their methods suggested an intelligence and independence of spirit of which their purblind elders would have done well to take account. The frankness of their speech showed moral health. Everything showed that they were engaged in an honest search for valid principles of conduct *for women*. They were not asking what boys should do. It was plain that they would decide all that for the boys so soon as they had decided on the proper courses for themselves.

Still another thing is evident. This active and aggressively inquiring attitude of mind on the part of girls has of late years become general rather than exceptional. Also, it is more and more unconcealed. The reason is that social and economic conditions have placed these girls more on a level with men. Many of them, when they leave school, take positions in which they make more money than the boys they go with. The result is that many a youth finds himself subject to rather contemptuous inspection by the young woman of his choice.

To many persons this cold sophistication on the part of our girls is shocking. It seems to carry with it implications of evil knowledge gained by evil experience. What I find, however, is that a very large number of the girls who talk most familiarly about sex problems are in reality almost absurdly innocent and touchingly pure of heart. Frequently their appearance of being young in years but old in sin amuses me. There are many of them like little girls strutting about in their mothers' dresses; and I have never been able to see that their knowledge does them any hurt. The evil seems to pass them by, somehow. What they know with their minds does not seem to touch them emotionally. They take no harm; it is as though the angels literally took charge of them.

CHAPTER 11

Sometimes the growing economic independence of girls, combined with their spunky determination to do their own thinking works out in ways that are almost comic reversals of all our old traditions. I remember a typical case that came my way not long ago. A certain girl was having an affair with a youth—an affair so indiscreet that it became the consternation of all her family, who could do anything with her but manage her.

Finally one of her relatives came to me. "Judge," he said, "I'm afraid Mary is booked for a tragedy. I want you to see if you can't straighten her out."

"What's the tragedy?" I asked.

"She is going with Bill Riggs," he replied. "I don't think he amounts to much, but she is crazy about him. Several times the two of them have come to my house when my wife and I were away; and last week my wife came home suddenly and found them there. It was scandalous. In fact, we think the worst has happened.

"It wouldn't be so bad if there were anything to that boy. But he's no good. Sure as shooting, he'll give her a dirty deal. If anything happens, he won't marry her. I'm sure of it. Won't you get hold of her, and make clear to her the kind of tragedy she is facing?"

I promised I would. But before I could send for Mary, she showed up in my court of her own accord. She was about 22 years old; and she was a beauty, with snapping eyes and a manner that didn't lack for assurance. She had graduated from high school, and wound up in a finishing school.

At first I thought she must know about the visit of

her interested relative; but no, her call didn't concern her own affairs. She was worried over a 17-year-old girl friend of hers. Maude, it appeared, was becoming wild. Lately she had shown a shocking preference for petting parties and booze; and wouldn't I take hold of her and see if I couldn't straighten her out and warn her of the tragedy that might result from conduct so ill-advised.

"I'll be glad to do anything I can, Mary," I said. And we then and there concocted a plan of campaign designed to bring Maude back to the straight and narrow path where she belonged.

"Well *Mary*," I said when we were through with that, "what about yourself?"

"Oh," she said, carelessly, "I'm going with Bill Riggs."

"Is Bill your steady?"

"Sure," she said; and then, without any reservations she told me the whole story. It was considerably more scandalous than her interested relative had dreamed. She saw nothing wrong about it. She and Bill, she pointed out, had lived on the square like a true married pair, but this business of promiscuous petting that Maude was going in for was quite another matter. It was shocking. Maude must be made to—

"Well *Mary*," I put in; "why don't you and Bill get married?"

"Married!" she said derisively. "Why Judge, out of ten girls in my set who have gotten married in the last two years more than half are divorced or separated from their husbands. Look at all that scandal. For instance, there was Jenny Strong. She testified in court that her husband didn't want her to have a baby, and had made her go to an abortionist. None of that for me. If Bill and I don't get along, we'll quit without any fuss."

"But what about babies?"

"I haven't thought about that yet much. I'm not sure I want any."

"But suppose you do. That would be a difficult situation, wouldn't it?"

"Oh, no," she said. "Bill would marry me any time. He wants to. He's crazy about me. But I'm not sure I want to marry him. I haven't any too much confidence in Bill's capacity. *Why I'm earning more than he is right now.*"

Well, what could I say? Reprimand her? Impossible. A reprimand wouldn't have changed her view and would merely have deprived me of what hold I had on her.

She didn't know why she wasn't marrying Bill; but she had put her finger, unconsciously, on the economic failure of the institution of marriage as we have always known it. She was earning more than he, and now she was going to look twice at this marriage business before she tried it. It had nothing to do with her three meals a day. She didn't have to marry a meal ticket. She could earn one. She was a free agent. Bill would have to prove himself competent all along the line before she would tie up with him.

I didn't press the question further, and she left. Later, she came from time to time in behalf of Maude, whom I finally got hold of and dissuaded from the line of conduct she had lately adopted.

Mary continued to prosper in business. One day I noticed her out with another boy than Bill. The next time I saw her to talk with her I asked her about it. "You've been going with Bill a year and a half now, Mary," I said. "Why don't you marry him?"

"I'm disgusted with Bill," she said, "and if there is

any one thing I'm glad of it is that I didn't marry him when you suggested it. Why Judge, he's no good. He's been working a long time now, and yet he's only making $80 a month as a soda clerk, while I'm making $150 a month, and without much effort at that.—Marry him? I guess not. Imagine me, on $80 a month, and perhaps with a baby?"

Well, that seemed to be that. But there was more. One day in walked Bill. Bill was swallowing, and he looked as if he were going to cry. "Judge," he said, "I want to talk with you.—You know Mary, don't you?"

"Surely," said I.

"Mary and I have been steadies now nearly two years, and I know she knows you, and I thought—I thought you might help me. Judge, if you'll only help me out— I'll—"

"Glad to do anything I can, Bill. What's the trouble?"

Whereupon poor Bill burst into tears and leaned his head on the table—my shoulder being safely out of his reach. "My God," he cried, "she's ditched me!—She never would marry me, and now she's ditched me."

Poor Bill! She'd ditched him! *That* was the tragedy. Times had changed. In this day and age, apparently, it wasn't the helpless girl that got the worst of it after stooping to folly, it was the fellow.

I wasn't able to do much for Bill. Mary, to the wild consternation of her helpless family, went on an automobile tour with Bill's successor, and is living with him at present. I think she will marry in time, as his income is apparently ample.

No, Mary isn't of the demi-monde. She is the daughter of a prosperous Denver business man, and the granddaughter of another man so distinguished that his reputation is national.   A few of her friends are in on the secret, but not many.

The story of Mary teaches a good many things, including the fact that persons who cry that the youth of this day is marrying in haste don't know what they are shrieking about.   Also that the conspiracy of silence is not working.   Also that we must expect rebellions against the existing code so long as we insist on making that code a matter of legalistic fiat and of rigid moral compulsion, externally applied by authority.

Sex is simply a biological fact.   It is as much so as the appetite for food.   Like the appetite for food it is neither legal nor illegal, moral nor immoral.   To bring Sex under the jurisdiction of law and authority is as impossible as to bring food hunger under such jurisdiction; and we all instinctively recognize that it does not belong there.   That is why, when the law and the prescribed custom run counter to desires which are in themselves natural and normal, people refuse to recognize the authority of law and custom, and secretly or openly give their often ill-considered desires the right of way.   This they will continue to do until Sex can be presented to them in another light, with law and authority as completely eliminated as it is in the case, say, of gluttony.

The crude Sex hunger, like the food hunger, should be governed and controlled, not by legal fiat and moral compulsion, but by the educated wisdom, common sense, self control, and good taste of the individual.   I shall try to show presently that such self control is possible to most persons.   In the meantime it will suffice to emphasize the easily observable fact that since it is extremely easy for anybody to commit sex offenses without getting found out, law and authority haven't a leg to stand on, and must rely for their apparent enforcement on the

voluntary and free conformity of those of us who choose
to conform. Since such intelligent and enlightened conformity is the only thing that really works, why not rely
on that?

There is no law against gluttony, though gluttony is,
I believe, listed among the seven deadly sins, and ranks
therefore with fornication. Not only that, but it comes
under the ban of no social custom masquerading under
the name of "morals." In other words, a man may be
a glutton without being haled into court and without
ostracizing himself from the company of conventional and
respectable persons who would avoid his company if he
were guilty of a sex offense. Gluttony, however regrettable and disastrous a vice it may be, is commonly left
to the individual to control; and if he be properly educated in dietetics, or if he have a reasonably cultured
outlook on life, and a voluntary aversion to piggishness,
he will, of his own accord, avoid gluttony because he
wants to avoid it, and dislikes the effects of it on himself and on others.

Partly from the logic of these considerations, and partly
from my own practical experience and observation, I
conclude that the only thing capable of effectively con-
trolling the sex life, and of making it a reasonable rather
than a crudely instinctive and primitive thing, is an
educated, delicate preference for that sort of conduct
whose actuating, driving *motive* might reasonably be
adopted as a safe rule for universal human conduct.
Note that I emphasize the motive rather than the conduct itself. Conduct allowable in one set of conditions
may not be right in another; but the motive, the accepted
standard, back of either course would be constant, a
point of reference always applicable. In other words
the key to the whole matter is simply an educated, vol-

untary, discriminating loyalty on the part of the individual to motives and standards which he honestly and sincerely considers valid.

What this nation desperately needs today is a mental and spiritual vision properly focused. That is to say we need a culture capable of producing such a focused vision, and a method of education capable of producing such a culture.

Culture would enable individuals consistently and steadily to *see*, as by an inward light, how desirable, possible, practicable, and even *easy* it is to be loyal to those human rights which evidently transcend the rights that are merely primitive, and which, because they are primitive cannot, of themselves, meet the needs of our complex civilization.

It is relatively easy for a fireman—acting on the code and *culture* of his profession—to risk his life to the utmost in order to rescue persons from a burning building. His education has produced that culture, that inward light, which never leaves his proper course in doubt, and so makes it practicable and inevitable that he do a thing which runs counter to the raw and primitive instinct of self preservation. And yet firemen are ordinary men, with all the common frailties in those departments of conduct in which their education has been less thorough. There are many other similar instances of voluntary right conduct on the part of ordinary men and women, and all of them point to some educational process, fostered by the necessities of our civilization, as the source of it all.

Primitive, raw desire, as compared with this cultured insight, is a shabby and vulgar thing of relatively small authority. Its impulses are mechanical, extemporaneous, unreasoned, and ill considered. Of course they do serve a necessary purpose and do play a necessary part in life; and their normal processes should, therefore, be interfered with as little as possible—in spite of the teachings of many puritanical theologians to the contrary. Indeed such interference should be resorted to only when the primitive instincts clearly run counter to that cultured insight which has authority over them.

The primitive desires attain undue authority over individuals in any civilization whose methods of education fail to produce a culture capable of placing a right valuation upon such desires. I must add, though I say it with reluctance, that in view of many of the conditions that are described in this book, it does not seem to me that we can, at present, lay any large claim to such a culture. I think also that the Facts, as they pass in melancholy procession through the Juvenile Court of Denver, abundantly prove that the failure of our effort to make law and authority serve in the place of culture is, to put it mildly, rather conspicuous.

Persons who have been rightly educated regard living as something of an art, and life as a thing which may properly be loved only if one care to make it lovely. Necessarily this involves the voluntary avoidance of that which, to trained and fastidious sensibilities, seems unlovely and offensive. Simply as a matter of taste and preference, and of loyalty to the verdicts and findings of culture—and not at all as a matter of law or of authority externally imposed—such persons avoid conduct which is irrational, crude, raw, and merely "natural." They avoid vulgarity of speech and manner because there is something they like better. They avoid loose and sloppy thinking because dishonest or unskilled thought arouses their aversion and possibly their contempt; and they have a standard of life and living which demands the best, not merely in material comforts but in spiritual pleasure. When Lear said of Cordelia that "Her voice was ever soft, gentle, and low; an excellent thing in woman," he was expressing, even in a moment of terrible personal agony, an habitual and cultured preference. And Cordelia doubtless chose to speak thus for the same reason. Such things make for charm in all the affairs of life; and the human race will choose them when law and custom cease to make certain of them obnoxious. In like manner, rational conduct in matters of sex may make Sex one of the loveliest things in life. The human race will particularly choose that, when law and custom shall cease to make Sex ugly.

But by what criterion are such standards, either in art or in conduct to be arrived at? Is the independent judgment of the individual sufficient? No, I don't think it is. Any standard of voluntarily adopted conduct has to be formed as a compromise—if compromise be needful—between the sincere, independent, fearless, unfettered judgment of the individual on the one hand and his reasonable willingness to respect and candidly consider all that is universally conceded to be best and ripest and soundest in human thought and experience. This does not mean that every individual would inevitably swing around to a complete acceptance for himself of the judgments of even the best human culture in all matters, but rather that he would be powerfully influenced by them, accepting some wholly and others perhaps with modifications. Such departures as he made would thus tend to work for good rather than for harm, and make for progress and change rather than for headlong revolution, destruction, and a reckless burning of those bridges that link us with the wisdom of the past.

Such an individual would never depart wantonly and

rashly from the way of the majority, and yet he would feel at liberty to do so if the reasons for such a course seemed really right and adequate to him. With such liberty of action many would doubtless make mistakes— some of them would make fatal mistakes. Hence they would need to become accustomed to their liberty by degrees. But the final result would be to strengthen the moral fiber of the race, and to give to our social life a stability it lacks at present.

Just now we are so hedged about with laws, customs, and censorships that rob us of the power of critical choice in a thousand and one concerns of conduct that it seldom is predictable what the average American will do if his usual moral crutches be suddenly taken from him by circumstances. We theoretically recognize the unwisdom of guarding children so closely that they never learn to take care of themselves or to learn by their own blunders; but we make that very mistake with regard to our adult selves. The fact is that our inherited, puritanical fear of sending our souls irrevocably to hell if we happen to blunder into doing what we have been told is wrong causes us to protect ourselves from temptation beyond all reason. Our younger generation, I think, feels this instinctively. One fiery youngster said to me when I was urging on her the folly of something she had been doing, "It seems to me that I've got a right to make my own mistakes." And she was not altogether wrong. With a right cultural background she might have been trusted to make them wisely.

I am not saying there is no peril in freedom; I am merely insisting that in the long run freedom will be a less perilous thing to the race than the excess of law and custom by which we now make ourselves morally weak, flabby, and soft.

Nor is this to say that no restraints are necessary. At some time in the future we may reach the point where everyone will do right, and laws will be unnecessary. We might reach that goal in a few hundred thousand years, perhaps, and maybe very much sooner. But in the meantime, there is no getting around the fact that Society *has* to be intolerant, and that it has to prescribe certain kinds of conduct and to proscribe others. It will have to do this till we all learn, by right education, to control the Ape and the Tiger within us. This it would be folly to deny. Somewhere or other Society has to draw the line between conduct that can be allowed and conduct that can't be allowed.

What we have so far failed to comprehend, however, is that there should be as little of this *verboten* business as possible. Also that there should be in the public mind a clear-cut, educated conception of the value of originality, of initiative, and of the impulse which some individuals have to be different in thought, word and deed from their fellows. Progress comes through those persons who are never satisfied, and who want to think critically and to do things differently, often in violation of customs held by the majority to be sacrosanct. The liberty of these human variants to shock the conforming majority should be very large.

Our lively younger generation has *naïvely* assumed that that liberty *is* rather large, and they have rather beautifully gotten away with their assumption. The first flappers who shortened their hair and their petticoats shocked a conventional majority which, today, has so far forgotten what it once called its "morals" that it is now doing the same thing and pronouncing it entirely moral by which it means entirely customary.

CHAPTER 12

In the light of these considerations, let us now come back to this question of personal liberty in matters of Sex. When judged by what is universally conceded to be best and soundest in human thought, certain "natural" forms of sex conduct are objectionable, not because of law and custom, but simply because they are raw, crude, and often unclean and piggish—largely lacking in those cultural restraints and refinements without which the educated mind finds existence an unlovely thing.

Let me give one more example. No man with the normal code of a man will take money from a woman or live on a woman's earnings. In the underworld such men are known as pimps. Normal men look down upon the pimp and the near pimp with loathing. Normal men feel the utmost, the most intense aversion to accepting money from a woman. Even young boys feel that way about it, and the normally masculine youth who takes his girl to the soda fountain, to dinner, or a show, would scorn to let her "pay the freight."

I don't mean that there are no exceptional circumstances where individuals might not reasonably and rightly do otherwise, but simply that in general men do adhere to this code and depart from it only for the weightiest of reasons. It is a point of masculine self-respect. It holds true even of the man who would not hesitate to seduce the very girl from whom he would nct take money—all because his code permits the one thing even while it says of the other that no gentleman can do it. Why is this? The answer is that it is a positive item of culture. Men have learned from childhood to accept it, to see its value and its eminent fitness, and *therefore* genuinely to prefer it. Thus it holds good for most men; and yet it is not in any law and it is not under the jurisdiction of binding custom.—This is a form of sex conduct effectively regulated by a free culture, which would be equally potent in regulating all sex conduct if we would give it a chance.

Now let us come back to Mary. Is Mary a bad girl? In the domain of law and established morals she undoubtedly is. But in the domain of her own point of view she is not. She is crude, I admit. Crudity and rawness are indeed among the chief and most regrettable defects of the generation to which she belongs. But perhaps if she lived in a social order more considerate of her needs, with conventions less cruel and less rigid, and less blind, she would not have to assert herself in ways so objectionable to those of us who believe real marriage a beautiful and sacred thing. The path would be kindlier and smoother to her feet, and she might walk in it, instead of turning from it in flouting rebellion.

In the meantime, you may agree or disagree with her about marriage, but you cannot deny that she is following a code which commends itself to her. True, it permits sexual satisfaction out of wedlock, but it definitely excludes promiscuity, petting, booze, and the things that Maude, in her greater rawness and crudity, indulged in. In that sense it smacks more of restraint than of license. Note that the restraints are absolutely voluntary. Mary used her self-assumed liberty in a way not wholly insane. In her case at least the claims of those who insist that nothing but law and morals can prevent sex from running wild, are not borne out. Nor were they with Maude; for I easily dissuaded her by bringing to her attention considerations which she had not hitherto thought of.

Mary's voluntary code includes further the requirement that marriage, to satisfy her, must have a permanent foundation—a scruple that never bothered her divorced friends. It also demands of any man she may marry the ability to make a fair living and to support a family properly. Whatever may be said of Mary's conventional morality, her judgment seems to function pretty well; and she is on the whole taking better and more intelligent care of herself and her legitimate interest in a productive future than are many of her moral and respectable friends who are remaining strictly within the realm of law and custom, and—are keeping the divorce courts busy untangling and unscrambling the highly moral, technically legal, messes they have made of their lives.

I don't know where such drifts in modern life are leading us. I can but record them as I see them in my work; and I can but register my faith that they do *not* indicate a breakdown in our racial fiber but rather promise an improvement in it. I think the process is constructive.

The bald fact is that Mary was and is engaged in altering our present defective code for her own protection, and that she recognizes that the marriage contract, as it stands today, is a thing quite as likely to enslave and destroy a woman as to protect her. She isn't rejecting marriage, but she has a clear intention to look out for her own safety and she refuses to be anybody's property. In that she is typical of hundreds and thousands of other women.

Of course this view of Mary's conduct does not meet the further, conventional, objection that her fault lies, not in her determination not to be anybody's property, but rather in her failure to abstain from sex relationships before marriage. This raises a question that must be frankly, courageously, and candidly faced. I propose to face it here; and I want to do it in a way that will not give offense to those who, like myself, uphold and believe in the institution of marriage. And yet I want to be fair and sympathetic in my attitude toward this girl and the generation of Youth that she represents. Thus I find myself between the upper and the nether millstone; for it is exceedingly difficult so to state my view that it will not be open to grave misinterpretation.

I can only ask of my readers that they will bear with me in this, and accept here and now, as applying through every page of this book, my assurance that I believe in marriage, and that I demand of it that it shall mean the love of one man for one woman in a harmony and companionship—if I may speak personally—as perfect as that which I have always had with my own wife. When it does not mean that or something like it, then I am unable to see that it is marriage, regardless of whether there has been a marriage ceremony or not. The love of one man for one woman is marriage. Nothing else is. The marriage ceremony is simply the public avowal of a man and woman that such a relationship exists between them in all its fullness; and it is further a formal recognition on the part of Society that such a relationship exists. If it shall later cease to exist I see no clear reason why Society should keep up the fiction that it does.

But Society does keep up that fiction. It keeps it up to such an extent that it will not grant divorces merely on the ground the two parties want their freedom. Such an agreement is pronounced "collusion," and if it exists, must be kept in the background during every divorce trial. Instead it must be shown, often by deliberately manufactured testimony, that one or the other or both of the parties have been guilty of some reprehensible conduct toward each other, such as adultery, cruelty, and the like; and thus, in order to break away from each other, they must stand up in public and accuse each other of offenses that would often be impossible to either of them.

It would be monstrous to maintain that an institution safeguarded and bolstered up by such fictions as these is free from imperfections or that it needs no alterations. I am therefore obliged to go on record with the view that until Society shall consent to make the institution of marriage sufficiently flexible to conduce to the happiness and freedom of persons who enter it, it is, in my judgment, going to be regarded by an increasingly large number of men and women as an intolerable yoke, to be avoided at all costs. This would be unfortunate, to say the least. It is also unnecessary.

For instance, Mary, this girl of whom I have been telling, avoided marriage because she objected to entering on a contract so nearly irrevocable and so hard to break away from. Had it been possible for her to enter marriage with the knowledge that she could get out of it with reasonable ease, she would probably have married Bill.

What she demanded was a kind of marriage that would leave her a free agent; but she couldn't have it. Therefore she rejected the whole institution, even while admitting that, with certain amendments, she was for it, and could see many advantages in it.

It may be contended that it was Mary's duty, as a law abiding member of Society, to conform to the institution of marriage as we have it, and take her chance with it; and that if she could not bring herself to that she must remain celibate and deny her sex life the normal expression it craved.

To that Mary gives answer, rightly or wrongly, that she will not sacrifice herself to any such fetish of conformity; that she will not submit to having to make a choice between two such demands, both of which she considers monstrous and unreasonable.

Instead, she raises a flag of defiance, and says, "No, I and my generation will find a third way out. Whether you like it or not we will make among ourselves a marriage pact of our own, one that will meet our needs. We believe we have a natural right to a companionship and an intimacy which we instinctively crave; we have a knowledge of contraception which precludes the likelihood that unwanted babies will complicate the situation; we don't admit that such a course on our part imperils the safety of human society; and we believe that this effort to replace tradition with what we think is common sense will do good rather than harm."—In substance that is the way they put it.

Now what am I, a man occupying a responsible judicial position, to say to a challenge like that? On the one hand I can't commend Mary's conduct without disregarding the grave practical difficulties and social dangers which may be involved in any headlong application of her theories—the kind of application she herself is making of them, for instance. On the other hand, I cannot, with sincerity or honesty, say to Mary or anybody else that I think the institution of marriage *as we have it* capable of guaranteeing happiness to persons who enter it. I cannot escape admitting that if marriage is ever to merit the unqualified support of society it must be able to show results reasonably commensurate with its claims; and that for whatever unhappiness it produces by reason of its present rigid code it must be held answerable. Nor can I pass in silence over the fact that marriage is ordained for the welfare and happiness of mankind, and that mankind was not made for it; that marriage is not an end but a means; that when a shoe does not fit, it is the shoe rather than the foot that must be altered. As to the demand for celibacy as an alternative to a possibly disastrous marriage, why waste one's breath making demands which people would never meet and which would do violence to a necessary instinct if they did meet it?

And yet this is by no means to say that marriage is a failure and should go into the discard to make way for Free Love or any other social Ism. However imperfect the institution may be *we can't do without it*. It must be preserved by means of sane and cautious alterations in its code, to the end that it may create in people's lives the kind of happiness it should, under right conditions, be capable of creating. I believe enormously in the beneficent possibilities of marriage, but I can't ignore the fact that we are not permitting it to fulfil those possibilities. I hope I make myself clear.

I hope, too, that I make it clear why I deal tolerantly and gently with Mary and her kind; and why I admit that they have a case; and that in their effort to be honest and to face facts frankly, they "acquire merit."

But here comes in the question of their sincerity. There are many who think Mary and her kind are not sincere; that they are neither honest nor intelligent; that they are simply trying to "make the worse appear the better reason" in order that with some appearance of respectability and justification they may satisfy their "lusts."—Unquestionably this is true of some. But it has always been true of some, even in marriage as we have it. I am unable, therefore, to see that such a charge has any serious bearing on the point at issue, namely, whether responsible men and women have any moral right to experiment with the institution of marriage in an admittedly perilous effort to amend its imperfections. Such experimentation can hardly fail to be dangerous, and it can hardly fail to result in mistakes that will wreck the lives of some of the experimenters. Moreover, if it is to take place at all, it must in the nature of the case constitute a violation of established convention. The question is whether the fact of such violations puts the whole matter out of court. Some think it does, and that we must on no account go near the water till we have learned to swim. Others maintain that such social adventuring can produce no more misery than does our present marriage code, and that if we will but see it through it may reasonably be expected to result in much good. That's the issue; and to me it seems unfortunate that conventional-minded persons should refuse to face it, and that they should cover their own want of courage by attacking the moral character of those who differ with them.

In short, I deny that it is proper to question, wholesale, the sincerity and honesty of those who believe such experimentation with marriage to be moral and right. Such a method of attack is too suggestive of the proverb known to every lawyer, "When in doubt abuse the other attorney." Intolerance is the very last weapon with which to defend Marriage As Is at this juncture.

I think this is a reasonable view to take. But when all is said and done, I know what most conservatives will say about my way of dealing with Mary. They will say, "You should have stood up stoutly and unqualifiedly for Matrimony As Is, whatever your real opinion. You should have put up an uncompromising front. You should have known that Mary would take instant advantage of any tolerance on your part, and would interpret it as a tacit commendation of what she was doing. You should have used both your influence and your authority as a Judge to force her into conformity with social law and custom. You should have assured her that she was all wrong, and that the matter was not open to debate; that it was and is a closed question."

In other words, I should have protected Mary from her tendency to do rash things by playing the hypocrite with her. That's the traditional method of dealing with the young. They must not be guided, they must be commanded. Lie to them; keep up appearances for their souls' good; it is the easiest way.

But I can't do it. I can no more pretend to Mary that I think our present Marriage code a perfect one and herself without a shadow of justification in rebelling against or in trying to amend it than I can fly to the other extreme and recommend Free Love—which is a form of sex relationship that would be as impracticable to us, in our present stage of social development, as philosophical anarchy, founded on the assumption that all men would do right if there were no government whatsoever, would be in our present state of political evolution.

Why not be candid about this? Why not recognize what is a fact, that Mary and her generation are actively, and often mistakenly, seeking a solution for the marriage problem; and that if they cannot get tolerant coöperation from their elders, they will seek it alone, with a correspondingly greater risk of doing things that are unwise and dangerous, and wanting in common sense. For a lack of common sense in us begets the same in them; and there can be no common sense in our present attitude of intolerance.

To me one thing seems sure: if we of the older generation refuse to regard these departures from our conventions with kindly sympathy and tolerance and in a spirit of hope, even when we don't agree with them, our intolerance will create an added and needless danger in a situation that is already dangerous enough.

Old heads and young heads working together may solve this problem; but if they can't be persuaded to get together on it, then indeed our race may have to reach the longed-for goal at the expense of needless social disorganization, license and human misery. But that we shall finally reach it, by one path or another, I do not doubt.

I may now go forward, I hope, in the confidence that no matter what I may henceforth say about marriage, I shall not be understood as being hostile to it, or of discounting it or of wishing for it any other fate than an ample development of the great possibilities that are within it as a force making for the biological and the spiritual regeneration of our race.

CHAPTER 13

And now let me turn to another aspect of my subject. Ignorance of the facts of sex and want of suitable guidance is not the only thing lacking in our way of training the young. My experience with the senior girls of that high school in the western city confirmed another conviction which many years of work in the Juvenile Court had already created in my mind; the conviction, namely, that the home and the school had brought them up densely ignorant of the most elementary laws of health.

There are two reasons for this. One is that most parents and teachers don't know anything about the elementary laws of health themselves; and the other is that a frank dealing with the natural and essential functions of the body seems to them almost as indelicate as frank speech about the facts of Sex life. I suppose it is safe to say that the two most important facts about bodily health are adequate nutrition and adequate elimination of waste. Well, most parents and teachers know nothing whatever about adequate nutrition and therefore can't talk intelligently about that. And most of them know still less about adequate elimination of waste; and they would regard the thorough treatment of such subjects in the class room as repugnant and impossible, even if they did know.

I am, of course, aware that "hygiene" and "physiology" are taught in practically all our schools, and that most students get some instruction along those lines. But I am also aware that both subjects are taught by teachers whose knowledge is derived from the lily-white text taught in the class—which is as much as to say that it doesn't amount to a hill of beans.

I don't know what the school authorities and educational big-wigs may think about this, but when hundreds of girls coming under my care are suffering from chronic constipation, and from all kinds of complications that result from intestinal stasis; and when, on questioning, I find them completely ignorant of the whole matter, I don't need any further evidence that their expurgated physiology and their refined hygiene has been a mess of bunk.

The first thing to be understood about this matter is that normal, moral, restrained conduct cannot be had from adolescents suffering from malnutrition, acidosis, and auto-intoxication. The second thing to be understood is that a very large number of our adolescents are suffering from these things. The third is that nobody—including most of the medical profession—is doing much about it. There are, of course, notable exceptions; and I number among my friends many Denver medical men who deplore the conservatism of their profession in this respect. Physicians of this type have always been ready to volunteer their services to the Juvenile Court, and have made possible the biggest part of our work in the sex life of children.

Why the medical profession as a whole is so passive in such matters I don't know, unless it be that its interest centers chiefly on the problem of curing people after they become sick, rather than in teaching them how to keep well. At any rate the medical profession knows that a very large per cent of cases of sterility in women are the result of chronic constipation, which sets up irritations in the intestine that are communicated to the ovaries till those organs finally cease to function normally. Chronic appendicitis, another result of constipation which is very common among women, is a particularly active cause of sterility, and of many acute disorders of the reproductive organs. But I find that these girls, headed straight for such conditions as I have named, have never been told such things. Their own parents don't know the truth, and their teachers don't know it. And the medical profession with such exceptions as those mentioned, permits this condition of black ignorance to continue, and disciplines as "unethical" those of its members who make themselves conspicuous by "talking too much."

It goes without saying that even when sterility does not result from stasis, there is a probable impairment of the generative organs, and also of the general health, which is most disastrous. The same impairment is evident, though to a lesser degree, among boys. Boys are more active physically than girls, and are perhaps less delicately organized. At any rate, they apparently do not suffer so much from malnutrition and constipation till somewhat later in life, when sedentary living breaks down their natural resistance.

Although I cannot pretend to speak with scientific authority on medical matters, my own observation has satisfied me that wrong eating is the main cause of the faulty elimination. The ordinary American meal is a dietetic horror, not merely as a result of our bad cooking but also as a result of wrong food combinations, commercial refinements and adulterations, and the like.

Because meat, boiled potatoes, white bread, and white sugar are the four corners of our dietetic temple, constipation and acidosis are our two basic national diseases from which most other diseases come. We are a nation of starch drunkards; we carry an overload of refined, demineralized carbohydrates which, reckoned in calories,

ought to run a steam engine; and when we aren't stuf-
fing the fire box with "energy producing" carbohydrates,
we are filling it with an excess of meat proteins—which
is even worse. Milk we use stingily; whole-grain cereals
we use hardly at all; salads we nibble at; fruits and
natural sweets we consider a luxury more expensive than
a doctor's bill; vegetables we eat sparingly after we have
boiled the organic salts out of them and poured the
precious liquor down the drain.

I am not raising the point here because I'm a dietetic
crank, but because of the effect I see it having on Youth.
The first thing I have to look into and correct in the
case of most incorrigible children, is their health—and
nine times out of ten, wrong eating is back of their bad
health, bad teeth, bad eyesight, nervousness, colds, ade-
noids, tonsils, anemia, and every other evidence of faulty
metabolism.

I have observed another thing which connects itself
in my mind with ill health, and that is that an abnormally
early maturity, together with a perilously early arousing
of the sexual instincts, seems frequently to be associated
with malnutrition, and perhaps with other faults of bodily
function. I don't know whether clinical observation would
bear this out or not, but I should like to see the idea
tested.

Children who have been insufficiently nourished look
old. The old look on the faces of slum children, for
instance, is proverbial. Of course, with slum children
there is often an insufficiency of anything to eat at all.
But among the children of the well-to-do it is evident
that malnutrition might also result from—let us say—
a diet overburdened with proteins, and with refined and
demineralized carbohydrates, for instance white flour,
and white sugar; for there results from such a diet an

acidosis which makes proper assimilation of needed nutritive elements in the food impossible.

Red Cross workers in the famine districts like Armenia remarked on the fact that very young children who had been subject to starvation looked old, and had minds that were curiously mature and cunning. Many of them had hair growing all over their bodies, as if they had been little monkeys. These manifestations faded out with proper feeding. I leave it to some endocrinologist to speculate on the disturbances of gland function that accompanied this condition; but I think it suggestive, particularly with relation to the thymus, the "gland of childhood," whose functions normally cease with the approach of maturity; and whose atrophy would presumably give to the characteristics of maturity the right of way.

In short, it is my opinion that well-nourished children, other things being equal, are likely to mature more slowly and normally than ill-nourished children; and that since early maturity is likely to bring with it a tendency to easily aroused sexual activity, and so-called "Immorality"; the whole problem of malnutrition has a direct bearing on that of sexual continence in the young. Our young people are maturing early. In a race whose members die of degenerative disease at an average age of around forty, it is natural that they should. If you want to be old at forty you have to start your acidosis diet early.

I have in mind two children, a boy and a girl, who have been brought up on a correct diet. They will never need attention from my court. The boy is now fifteen, and the girl thirteen. Both of these children are growing like healthy young weeds; their health is apparently perfect, their bones are large and well developed, and both of them are several inches taller than children of their age with whom they associate. Both of them are still very childlike and immature, as compared with their school fellows. Sex doesn't seem to have come to the surface in their lives as yet; and the girl, unlike most of the girls she is associated with, is apparently going to come to a rather late maturity. And yet both of them, in spite of their relative immaturity, rank very high in their school work.

Of course one can't conclude anything positive from an isolated case. But I believe that those two children have at present a spontaneous, natural tendency toward sexual continence which may be traced to the slow maturing of their bodies; and that that slow maturing is in turn due to the fact that nature has been given enough building material to keep her busy with the normal process of growth for a maximum length of time. If this conclusion is correct its application to the diet of the children of this country would have a profound effect on our national morality in the space of a generation; for early maturity, coming before the mind is ready to cope with its imperious demands, is as I have already indicated, a grave problem, particularly in the conduct of girls.—To put it bluntly, I am more interested in the health of these young people than I am in their "morals." This does not mean that I am indifferent to their morals, but simply that since everyone is talking "morals" this is my way of emphasizing health and beauty as two things which make for morality. Conventional thought is too much inclined to put the cart before the horse.

It would be a mistake, however, to ascribe too much to any one cause. I have already pointed out, for instance, what an enormous stimulus toward early maturity is afforded by such instrumentalities of modern life as

the automobile, the telephone, and a thousand other con-
veniences of living and methods of speed.   There is so
much to engage the faculties, to arouse the mind, and
particularly to arouse the desires!   The bait hangs forever before our noses, and we strain to reach it, like
an ass traveling forever on a straight line because his
driver has hung a bundle of hay just ahead of him.

It does no good to find fault with all this.   The conditions are here; and the only way to deal with them
is to see them in their relation to the important and the
permanent values which impart to them whatever worth
they have.

I once had a conversation with John Grass, the successor of Sitting Bull as Chief of the Sioux Indians.   In
the course of our talk I asked him, "Do Indian boys ever
steal?"

"No," he replied.   "They never steal.'

This was an entire surprise to me.   I had had another
impression.   Moreover, I was a bit chagrined because I
knew I couldn't say the same for white boys.

"Why don't they steal?" I asked.

"Ugh! Nothing to steal!" said John Grass; and though
his face was as impassive as a block of wood when he
said it, I could have sworn he was laughing.   Indians
have a keen sense of humor which they are usually at
pains to conceal in their dealings with Americans less
aboriginal than themselves.

I thought extendedly about that conversation later.
To me it explains a great many things.   An Indian boy,
like any other primitive, has three basic desires in his
life, founded respectively on sex, egoism, and the herd
instinct.

The sex problem is easy because women are property.

He is reasonably sure to get the girl of his choice because he can buy her.

His egoism, embracing the possession of property, is not extensive or hard to gratify. It includes a bow and arrows and a pony, and maybe a rifle. And his whole paraphernalia of living is a home-made affair which his squaw looks after.

As for his herd instinct, that of course is satisfied because his life is identified with the life of the tribe, which is not so large but that every individual in it can count for something.

He has few suppressed desires; he wants little beyond what he already has; he and his fellows go through life, as it were, in Indian file, walking in each other's footsteps. It is simple.—And so he makes a wonderful citizen. There is, as John Grass said, nothing to steal. He can have his desires almost automatically without violating the rights of any one else or of the tribe. There is plenty of room, and there is enough to go 'round.

Compare the lot of this Indian boy with that of any boy or girl growing up in our present civilization, beset by growing and complicated wants in an order of things where there is a very unequal distribution of property, and where it is not easy for people to obtain a great many things it is right and proper for them to want. Life is holding up all kinds of attractive things to our young people, and holding them just out of reach. Civilization, with its glitter and its great possibilities, is simply a tantalizing bait to these fresh young palates, eager to taste and compare all strange new flavors, and almost as untaught as so many young aborigines in any principle of choice and judgment.

In other words, there is something to steal. We all feel the pull of it; and the plain truth is that while we of the older generation are sanctimoniously forbidding these youngsters and saying, "Don't," we don't hesitate ourselves to wallow in the trough up to our ears. Naturally our "Don'ts" fall on ears already filled with our grunts of satisfaction, and fail to get themselves heard. In the circumstances, it would seem that the youth of this day, instead of being immoral, are relatively far more moral than their elders, and that their power of self-straint and good judgment goes far beyond what could reasonably be expected in the face of such inducements to excess.

CHAPTER 14

A high-school girl came to me recently for advice. She came of her own accord. I had never seen her or heard of her before. She said she had a personal problem which she could not talk over with her parents because if they knew about it they would no longer be capable of acting like reasoning beings. It was one of those matters which parents are likely to consider a closed subject, not open to debate because it had only one side instead of two.

Her father, formerly wealthy, had lost his money. Now she would have to leave school and go to work. She had taken a position but had later given it up; and recently a wealthy man had asked her to become his mistress. What she wanted from me was an opinion as to the wisdom of such a course. Should she accept the offer, or look around for some other kind of a job.

All this she put to me as calmly as she would have discussed with her mother the choice of two ordinary positions, of the sort that would involve no question of conventional morality.

"You see," she explained. "I can't ask my parents for an opinion about this because they would merely rave. They would consider it immoral for me even to think about such a thing, or to debate it in my own mind. But I don't think it immoral to try to think straight, do you? Why should I take their word in such matters, as if they knew it all? I can think of lots of reasons why I might become that man's mistress and be no worse than I am now."

"You have a perfect right to reason about the matter," I told her. "And you also have a right to decide the question for yourself.—I'm not shocked at your question, and I certainly don't propose to throw a fit. Since you are a minor I could threaten you with the official power of my court, and force you into conformity with the conventions that way. But I shall not do that either. You are to decide this for yourself; and I will neither interfere with you nor violate your confidence.

"Now, as to your question: Do as you think best. Follow your own judgment. Be this man's mistress *if that's what you want to be*. But first, let's you and me consider the facts and see if that is, after all, what you want, or do you merely *think* you want it."

Then I showed her, as cogently as I could, what seemed to me the folly of what she was contemplating. In conclusion I said to her, "Don't try to decide this off-hand. Think about what I have said, and see if my reasoning does not appeal to you after you have cooled off. If it doesn't do as you think best; and if you go to this man, and he doesn't treat you right, come to me, and I'll wring his neck."

She thanked me, departed, and in due time came to reasoned decision, *not* to accept the man's offer.

I may add that today she has settled down, is happily married, and is the mother of a beautiful baby about whom she wrote me only the other day. In that letter she repeated what she had already said many times, that I had been responsible for her turning to the right in that crisis in her life, and that she would never cease to be grateful for the way in which I approached her problem that day.

What do you think would have happened to that girl

if her parents had learned what she was actually contemplating? She'd have gone to the devil, as so many of
them do in such circumstances.

Now what I want to make clear is this—the usual way
to treat young people when they try to think about such
things is to shriek at them hysterically and say you shan't,
you mustn't, this is wrong, this isn't debatable, it's a
sin, you'll get into prison, you'll go to Hell, and other
similar bunk.

"Doubtless ye are the people," said Job with fine
irony, "and wisdom shall die with you."

Why is it wrong? *Why* isn't it debatable? *Why* is it
a sin? In God's name, give them the facts, all the facts
we have, and let them decide it for themselves. Maybe
we are not so dead right as we think.

If our system of sex ethics can't survive that free
and open encounter between truth and falsehood, then
it doesn't deserve to survive; and any moral code that
has to be bolstered up by taboos and dogmatic affirmations, isn't worth preserving. If our conventions are any
good, let them come out and fight. There are places in
the Alps where, it's said, mountain travelers must not
speak above a whisper at certain seasons of the year for
fear the impact of the sound waves might start some
delicately poised avalanche on its course. There's some
sense in silence under such conditions; but if we have
to have social balances so delicate and perilous as that,
we had better seek points of safety to the best of our
ability and then fire some dynamite.

Perilous stuff, is it?—Not half so perilous, believe me,
as the other thing. Moreover, it is *not* perilous. I have
in mind scores, and hundreds of cases, wherein I have

told Youth the truth, and trusted it to find its way to right decisions in the light of such wisdom and experience as I, with my greater years, could furnish; and I have never been disappointed.

So uniform has been the success and natural compulsion of the Truth in this court that I can only record my utter conviction that Youth will in time save itself from the lunacies in our social system, and will retain what is sane and of valid worth. Also, that our efforts violently to stop or restrain this process can merely delay it somewhat, and drive many individuals to their destruction.

Finally, I maintain, if this sifting and questioning of our most revered and respectable traditions be a "sin" on the part of Youth, let's agree to call it that, and admit here and now that Youth had better "sin" its way into heaven than conform itself into hell. Better the pain and the strife than that the race should remain smugly at ease in Zion, false to itself, dishonest with its instincts, and willfully blind to the inadequacy of many customs and ideas held by our fathers to be sacrosanct.

As for those of us who cannot see this, and who insist on censoring the universe by forbidding everything in sight and out of it, and on curdling the heavens with predictions of Judgment, why—God is patient. He is letting the conservatives of the human species acquire shorter and shorter tails as the æons progress; and most of them have already reached the point where you have to use an X-ray to see what is left of it. It ill becomes any of us, therefore, to assure his brother too loudly that his tail hangs down behind.

There are still people who believe it to be contrary to the will of God that women should vote. There are even some who still object to giving women anesthetics in childbirth on the ground that God intended them to bear children in pain. We have people who, with the best of intentions, would have laws forbidding the teaching of "evolution." People of this same type of mind years ago secured the passage of laws forbidding the dissemination of information about "birth control." We still put a blight on the "illegitimate" child, though we have never defined how he differs from ordinary children. We still make outcasts of mothers who are not parties to the marriage contract, though in what respect unmarried maternity as maternity, differs from other maternity—especially as to the rights of the child, is not clear. And we cling vigorously to still other relics of the past, many of them worthy of the intelligence of an Australian bushman.

No society can live such lies as these and at the same time have machinery and science. If it does, machinery and science will destroy it; for machinery and science, without moral health, are a curse. The World War proved that. We are living in a fool's paradise if we don't see this; but maybe, if Youth proves sufficiently insistent on coming at the truth, it will save the world.

Youth is at least trying to think straight. It is trying because of the contagion of science; for science is an impersonal thing, and no respecter of traditions; and science is freeing the world. Modern youth is growing up under the wing of science; and since that is so, we shall see what we shall see. Coming? It is coming like a tidal wave.

The boy who can grind the valves or adjust the carburetor of an automobile, or who can put together a radio set with a technical understanding of its complexities, has learned a way of thought and scientific respect for facts to which his father at his age was a stranger. Likewise, the Flapper who makes her own living, votes, holds her own in competition with men, refuses to let the corset makers put stays on her, and snaps her fingers at "styles" dictated by the makers of clothes, is capable of doing things her mother couldn't come within sight of.

And remember that they will both be grown up to-morrow, and bringing up their babies after their own notions, not ours.

I do not agree with the talk which is popular just now that this present younger generation is like all others and that Youth has always been thus. It is true that Youth has always been rebellious, and that it has always succumbed finally to conservatism. They had the "new woman" in the mid-Victorian period, and old-fashioned people wondered in alarm what the world was coming to.

But Youth couldn't get away with it then. It didn't have the economic independence. Now it has it. Machinery has made that possible. Once Youth paraded and shouted with a wooden gun; but today the weapon is loaded. Make no mistake about it; this revolt of Modern Youth is different; it is the first of its kind; and it possesses means for making its will effective.

The agencies of modern life have had so direct and powerful an effect even on us of the older generation that they have in many ways demoralized us. As for the effect on Youth, that has been perfectly resistless. But there is no point in blaming the new conditions, nor in raving that they must be changed by censorship, new laws, more force, more ignorance, more silence, fear, and other nonsense. We are trying to bring up by the standards of fifty years ago a generation that has never known what it was to lack a host of things which were unknown fifty years ago. Naturally the gap between ancient precept and modern practice is making trouble; particularly when we persuade ourselves that modern practice rather than ancient precept will have to yield the right of way. Why we should want it so I can't say, unless it be that we hate the effort of breaking new trails.

I have already named in a general way what these agencies of modern life are, but let's name the most evident of them over, just to make the issue clear. Some are good and some are not so good, but they all have to be in the reckoning. Those that immediately present themselves are the automobile, (and soon the aeroplane with the kids spooning in the clouds) the telephone, the motion picture, the radio, the jazz dance, jazz music, jazz booze, jazz journalism, "crime wave," the permanent wave, the permanent passing of the chaperone, the parking of the corset, the feminine invasion of the barber shop, growing and changing standards of living, rising wages, enough to eat and enough to wear in thousands of workingmen's homes where such abundance feels like a spree,—and so on. One could continue the list indefinitely. For instance, electrical appliances that make women something more than drudges in their homes; bath rooms, steam and hot-water heat that make the whole house usable all the year 'round, electric lights that enable people to read in the evening instead of sitting around till bedtime as they did with oil lamps. The list, you see, includes among other things physical comforts and speeding-up devices of all kinds; and the effect of it all is enormously stimulating. Most of the things I have named are direct and powerful inducements to freedom, well-being, independence, leisure, and freedom of thought, speech, and action.

Of this great combination of influences, present-day Youth, with its present-day notions of conduct, is a result. What makes these agencies of modern life so often destructive and harmful is our insistence that they must blend with standards with which they have and can have nothing to do. Take the automobile, for instance, and the unchaperoned rides. You must take your choice. Either you must keep on with the chaperone—which is impossible—or you must prepare young people for the new convention by seeing to it, not only that they have a voluntary, informed, and responsible code of conduct, but also that they know all about Sex, and its place in the lives of men and women. So far we have refused to do this, on the ground that Sex is an unclean and shameful thing, rather than a sacred and lovely thing. If you, by implication, by silence, by innuendo, by concealment, by putting up veils, by talking in cryptic phrases, by winking, nodding, and looking significant, make it clear to children from their very infancy that Sex is essentially and fundamentally bad, what can you expect of them later? The most wicked thing in life, the uncleanest thing in life, turns out to be one of the most necessary and pleasant things in life. And so, convinced that they are doing wrong and yet determined to do it, they proceed to investigate Sex for themselves, with frequent disasters of a totally needless sort; and so the new freedom, instead of liberating them, destroys them.

Or perhaps you would insist on doing away with the automobiles. All right,—insist! Many silly people are doing it. It's a favorite indoor sport. Don Quixote, in his determined effort to revive the dying age of chivalry, did even better; he robustly got onto a horse, and rode into the great out-of-doors where men used to be men, and tilted at windmills. It gave him lots of exercise.

Forty years ago John Smith took Sadie Brown driving behind old Dobbin. Dobbin ambled along, and John made love within the natural limitations prescribed by Dobbin's six miles an hour, the nearness to town and neighbors, and all that. Today John makes his date with Sadie by telephone—easily, and, if he so desires, secretly. Today he sits at the wheel of a car that may be good for anything from two to eighty miles an hour. He can whisk Sadie far from all accustomed surroundings. There are roadhouses; there are long stretches of road where the solitude is complete and easy to reach; there is every inducement under the moon to irresponsible conduct.

In a word, John and Sadie have money and freedom. Since that is so, protests and scoldings can but antagonize them. To handle them, approach them with as much tact as if they were adults, not to be coerced; for coercion, never wise, is no longer even possible. You can't abolish the closed car, but you *can* abolish the closed mind and the shut mouth.

These are facts, as I see them daily revealed in the work of my court. If there are persons who still insist that this change in youth is not a change but a mere repetition of history, meaning nothing in particular, I can only repeat that they are flying in the face of the facts. The truth is that the thing is unique. It has never happened before.

It has been the fashion for some time now to hold

the motion pictures responsible for the present changes. Well, they doubtless have had a lot to do with it. They have visualized in a dramatic way most of the activities of sex for youngsters who have never been given their bearings in any other way.

Here again, you can't suppress the movies, nor can you keep them from dealing constantly with love, as the most dramatic and universal thing in human life. Not even censorship can do it, though it tries hard enough.

If people's minds and hearts were right there would be no question about whether it is right to dance, go to movies, drive automobiles, smoke if they feel like it, and live completely, fully, fearlessly, and heartily—yet moderately—with all the zest and happiness possible. The way to make such freedom possible is not to suppress these things but rather to make the heart right through understanding. All that is needed to make the whole system work for righteousness is the internal restraints and codes of conduct which derive their power from within.

"There is nothing from without the man," said Jesus, "that going into him can defile him: but the things which proceed out of the man are those that defile him. . . . For from within, out of the heart of men, evil thoughts proceed, fornications, thefts, murders, adulteries, covetings, wickednesses, deceit, lasciviousness, an evil eye, railing, pride, foolishness: all these evil things proceed from within, and defile the man."

We, however, think we know better than that. We think we know that it is the things from without that defile people. We think the path must be made smooth for the feet of Youth; and the idea of teaching Youth to walk sure-footed on paths of natural roughness occurs to nobody. On this theory we suppress books; on this theory we talk of censoring even department-store windows and expurgating them of women's lingerie.—What I should like to know is the effect of all this on the angels; does it make them laugh or does it make them weep? It is, I should say, a first-rate measure of their sense of humor.

CHAPTER 15

The damnable and destructive thing about this multitude of taboos and these varied censorships of the most minute details of conduct is that it removes from individuals all real responsibility for their own conduct. They make no choices. It also relieves the church, school, and home of responsibility simply by saying a sweeping "Don't" to every practice in life that is capable of abuse or misuse. It is like putting a man's arm in a sling and expecting it to be strong. It is like putting the whole human race on crutches.

There is no one remedy for the spiritual diseases that afflict society, and are the cause of our failure as a race to attain to the mental and physical standards of complete living. Many students of human behavior have tried to devise remedies fundamental enough to correct our want of health at a sweep, but they have uniformly failed, and I do not propose to put myself in their ranks by offering a panacea here.

And yet the situation does suggest certain measures that might cure it, and in time doubtless will. The evil in the world is a massive thing, but perhaps we might move it, if we could construct a few ingenious levers. In other words, there are a few relatively simple ideas and principles of conduct which, if they could be made general, with the help of wise legislation perhaps, would automatically tend to straighten out our human affairs. My thought is that legislation can make certain principles in education possible; and that right education can make anything possible—for this is the throttle that controls the engine of the mind.

Some of these ideas and principles are already present in the thought of many persons; and they are springing today into vigorous life among individuals of our restless younger generation. Many of them need nothing but a chance to grow. Given that, they would become beneficent principles, medicinal for all who might accept them.

But such principles find it hard to thrive in any but an atmosphere of freedom—by which I do not mean license, but simply a reasonable liberty of thought and action. And that, too, is a problem in enlightenment and education. At present the United States of America is, in this respect, one of the least free in the world. It seems absurd that in a country where freedom is talked and thought about and professed in season and out, there should be imposed upon individuals an absolutely crushing rule of standardization in thought, behavior, and speech. It is not merely that we have traditions and conventions, but that they tyrannously concern themselves with the minutest details of our lives—and woe to him who rebels against them.

The first thing we must come to, the key that would unlock many other doors, is Liberty. But it is the Truth that brings Liberty; so we are right back at the old, old question of education. And since we have, in most of our schools and colleges, a system of education carefully designed *not* to educate anybody in any essential thing and to take no chances on what people would do with the truth if they should happen to get hold of it, we find ourselves traveling in a vicious circle.—Censorship of this and that is one means of safeguarding the public from the dangerous and contaminating truth which is very much in the newspapers just now. It ranges from a censorship of school histories that tell the truth about the

American Revolution to the suppression of books that
try, in dramatic terms, to tell the truth about sex.

And yet an instant difficulty that arises, even in the
minds of reasonable and broad-minded persons, is that
some kind of restraint is necessary; and that in literature,
and on the stage, *some* kind of censorship is especially
indicated, if only as a safeguard against evident por-
nography which neither enlightens nor educates. Where,
they ask, is one to draw the line?

I admit the difficulty. A reasonable censorship of
some kind in literature and art may for the present
continue to be necessary. But in our present laws
against obscenity, when properly interpreted, we do
have such a sensible censorship applied through trial by
jury,—quite a different thing from a state censorship
whose tyrannical and arbitrary powers are not only depriving people of their constitutional rights but, because
of their tyranny, are themselves a far greater evil than
any evil they can ever prevent.

There are books written for purposes evidently corrupt. And yet, why should such despicable trash be able
to corrupt anybody?

Education of the young in the whole subject of sex
would sweep most of this evil out of existence; there
would be no need for censorship of anything because an
enlightened public opinion would be its own censor by
virtue of its genuine preferences and its educated tastes.
Instead, we try to cure one evil of ignorance and concealment with another. It can't be done.

There is also a class of books that deal with subjects
conventionally forbidden, but whose value to society is
undeniable. They are not intended for immature minds;
but there should be other methods than censorship of
protecting such minds against them. The destruction

and suppression of such sources of truth for such reasons, involves the payment by society of too high a price for any advantages that it may gain.

There is hardly an ancient classic that could have survived the present censorship laws. Shakespeare would never have been heard of after the *Rape of Lucrece* and *Venus and Adonis*.

A tree is known by its fruit. If the fruit be corrupt, the tree is corrupt. The natural way to maintain a claim that a given tree is a good tree is to demonstrate that it produces good fruit; and if this demonstration fails, then the honest thing for such a one to do is to admit that the tree is bad, and cut it down.

There are defenders of our criminal code, and of our prison system, for instance, who remain defenders though the fruit of the tree they are defending is obviously bad. Likewise, there are defenders of ignorance and repression in matters of sex who remain defenders though the fruit of the present conventions and laws in these matters is clearly bad. In like manner the foes of birth control are unable to point to anything but evil in the results of the laws that forbid the use of contraceptives, or the spread of contraceptive knowledge and advice. The foes of changes in the marriage code are in the same case. They can't escape the charge that they are upholding a condition wherein we now have almost as many divorces and separations as we do marriages. It is the marriage muddle that is responsible for the fact that there are at least fifty thousand girls in New York living with men who are not their husbands;—girls who should become mothers, and don't dare to have children because of the attitude society would take toward them. It is the marriage muddle, combined with the deliberately fostered ignorance about birth control, that is responsible for probably at least a million and a half abortions performed in this country every year—a million and a half living though unborn children deprived of the right of birth because the mothers didn't know how to prevent life from starting, and because our conventional notions about love as a thing necessarily identical with legal marriage cast a needlessly cruel stigma on motherhood out of wedlock; a stigma which strikes not only at the mother but at her innocent child.   Motherhood is so honorable a thing that nothing—no convention—can possibly make it dishonorable; and from the standpoint of the right of the child, the unborn—the unmarried mother should be granted by society the same reverence and regard as the married mother.   When a million and a half women —at least—every year deprive their own living, unborn children of life, the *fruit* of our conventional tree can hardly be called good fruit, can it?   If this object of our worship and sacrifice were a true god instead of a fetish the fruits of our worship would be different, would they not?   The claim that it all comes from the corruption of our natures is a theological superstition.   It comes from our inevitable rebellion against an inherited order that does not fit in with the plain and natural necessities of life.

I am not alarmed by what I see happening to the institution of Marriage today.   In fact, I think the sooner something happens to it the better.   I have already been at pains to explain that I regard it as a necessity and that I do not believe in its abolition, but rather in alterations that will make it work.   What those alterations will be I don't pretend to say.   They lie in the future, and the future will be responsible for them, whatever they may be.   I think, however, that among the things that will enter into the new order of things will be the economic independence of women, now developing; birth control, now developing; and divorce by mutual consent, now common enough though it has no sanction in our laws.

And then, there are still other changes which may come about in time, even though they at present run violently counter to what society at present sanctions. One of these is the right of competent, unmarried women to bear, rear, and support children out of wedlock if they wish. Another is the right of "trial marriage," which some persons today erroneously regard as the same thing as promiscuity, and therefore equivalent to Free Love, while others believe it feasible and desirable. Concerning these last two possibilities it is impossible at this time to make predictions. No man can say whether they would work or not. The whole thing is debatable. And the fault I have to find with those who believe that Trial Marriage and Unmarried Maternity are necessarily wrong and immoral and that they always will be, is that they will not admit that the question is even debatable. That is simple bigotry. There is no such thing as a non-debatable question. Any point on which people differ is a legitimate subject for discussion; and neither side has the right to assume in the premises that it is right and that that settles it. Sex ethics differ so widely in different parts of the world, and meet the needs of so many different kinds of civilization, that the assumption that our present sex traditions are final for our race for all future time is in the highest degree absurd.

I am obliged further to point out what I know to be a fact, that *all* these departures from our present day marriage code are being practiced right now by many persons whom it would be monstrous to accuse of being "immoral" in any ordinarily accepted meaning of the word. These persons, however unconventional their

lives, look upon Love as a sacred thing, order their conduct toward each other accordingly, and live in a way
which often seems to me more truly moral than the relations of persons who are legally married, who cohabit,
and yet do not love each other.

I have already said that I regard such departures from
convention as debatable and perhaps unwise. But I cannot consent to any wholesale and reckless condemnation
of such persons; since I know many of them to be both
sincere and courageous.

These then, are facts. Such things, I repeat, are being
widely practiced today by persons who confide their
stories to me in confidence, and by others I never even
hear of. Most of them are canny about it. They do
it in secret. In fact most of the people who practice
these ways of living don't even know that other people
are doing the same thing. It is like a secret society,
none of whose members know the others. It has no pass-
word and no grip. It isn't organized. But if it ever
does organize, or crystallize into a body of conscious public opinion, then something is going to happen to the
Marriage Code. I see no escape from this conclusion; nor
do I see any reason to believe, as many do, that such
a prospect sounds the doom of human society. I think
such an assumption is preposterous; and that nothing
but an overweening conceit in our own ways of doing
things could make such an attitude on our part possible.

The dangers that attend upon such changes are evident,
and I have no wish to minimize them. The Sex instinct
is the most violent instinct, possibly, that the human
race knows anything about. When misdirected it can
work more destruction in society than any other instinct.
It is very easy, therefore, to understand the alarm of
those who are afraid that any change of any sort in

the Marriage Code will open up the way for Free Love;
that is to say, undisciplined, irresponsible, and unre-
strained promiscuity. This fear is based on the belief we
are as a race so lacking in poise and intelligence that
we would convert any considerable sex liberty we might
have into license.

My reply is that the major contention of this book
is the precisely opposite claim that people are likely to
do wrong from perverse preference when they are placed
under restraints imposed from without, but that they have
a normal preference for doing right when given a reasonable liberty of choice. And I maintain that this is
as true in the relations of sex as in anything else.   In
sex relations it is certainly true of most women, whether
it be true of men or not. I shall have more to say about
that in another connection.

In the meantime let me make this point, that Free
Love and Marriage As Is have one thing in common;
namely, that each of them offers certain inducements to
irresponsibility. Everybody can see where irresponsibility may enter into Free Love with dangerous ease,
but only by looking closely does one see where it enters
into Marriage. It enters into Marriage by reason of the
finality of the thing. Husbands irresponsibly tyrannize
over wives and wives over husbands for no reason on
earth than that the law gives them a power over each
other from which they can escape only with the utmost
difficulty. Some churches and states make this condition
worse by allowing no grounds for divorce whatever; or,
in exceptional cases where they do permit divorce, they
deny to the parties involved the right to lead a normal
life thereafter. Irresponsibility begets after its kind, and
thus the rigidity of the marriage code is one of the most

common causes of Free Love that we have. It is also the cause of abortions and other frightful evils.

For instance, here is a series of cases that came before me in a single day.

The first is the case of a mother of two children. She is a Roman Catholic. She tells me she has not lived with her husband as a wife for several years. She loathes and despises him. "But," she declares, "it is against the law of our church for me to have a divorce. What I want out of him," she continues, "is $150 a month for support of myself and my children."

"But," I say to her, "you can get that in a divorce case." But to this, on religious grounds, she is obdurate.

Now this man, though he is a Roman Catholic, is, as I learned later, living with a young woman whom he loves, and whom he would marry if he had a divorce. This young woman becomes pregnant, and through the fear of unmarried motherhood sacrifices her maternal hopes to the abortionist.

Thus we have the crime of the murder of the unborn, and crippled womanhood besides—all for lack of a divorce, and in order that the too-stringent law of the church might be respected.

Another case, from my notes of the same day, and again concerning a Catholic woman.

"I have long since ceased to love my husband," she said, "and I would get a divorce but for the laws of my church. But I must continue to live with my husband, for the support of my three children."

I again explained that her husband was just as liable for the support of her children if she was divorced. But she said she felt it was her duty to live with this man she did not love. She had been advised, it appeared, to make this sacrifice for the children's sake so as to keep the father with them, since he was a good provider.

"But," she continued, "he demands the right of a hus-band; and my church forbids the use of contraceptives." Then she admitted to me that in consequence of the preg-nancies resulting from this conformity to the rule of the church, she had had three abortions performed, had wrecked her health, and had made herself unfit to care for the three beautiful children she had brought into the world, to say nothing of the three she and her hus-band had murdered—all to escape the consequences of their blind obedience to what they believed was the law of God.

Such a rigidly fixed and enslaving marriage code may produce results quite as bad, immoral, and disastrous as irresponsible Free Love, of which it is supposed to be the exact antithesis.

It thus becomes evident that this rigid marriage code, in direct proportion to its rigidity, not only has certain things in common with Free Love, but by its very in-justices and absurdities often promotes Free Love.

Marriage as we now have it is absolute; as an institu-tion it assumes a weight of authority and responsibility which the records of our divorce courts show it is not capable of carrying. Even successful marriages are more or less absolute despotisms by reason of their rigid and evident finality, and therefore contain within them the seeds of their own possible destruction.

The first notion we have to admit if we are ever to accept marriage on a workable basis is that human beings cannot live without freedom—the principle we always talk about and seldom practice. If we can't take a chance on the ability of the human race to survive under conditions of freedom, and to accept the responsibilities of living with no other restraints than these voluntary ones which come from within, as the fruit of an educated preference, then we had better shut up shop and move to another planet. If our civilization has to be bolstered up with artificially created props, if every marriage has to be set in a plaster cast, if ignorance of Birth Control must be required by law in order to insure the propagation of the race, then we'd better commit race suicide as the only thing that will put us out of our misery.

Marriage, as we have it now, is plain Hell for most persons who get into it. That's flat. I defy anybody to watch the procession of wrecked lives, unhappy men and women and miserable, homeless, neglected children who pass through my court, and come to any other conclusion. And it is Hell for the simple reason that it is despotic, that, constituted as it is at present, it readily converts itself into a denial of freedom to human beings, who can't live in bondage because the most sacred instincts in their nature forbid it.

I am perfectly willing to regard Marriage as a religious rite, just as I am ready to regard a contract to pay for a suit of clothes as a religious rite. If I am honest I will pay if I can; and if I am honorable I will be a good husband to the limit of my ability. In that sense all right conduct is religious. But the theological concept of marriage, as a thing registered in Heaven, where they don't have the institution themselves by the way, is something else again. We've got to get rid of it with all speed.

With this theological concept of marriage goes the notion that Love and legal Marriage are necessarily synonymous. It is true that they do have a very evident connection, and that they fittingly combine themselves in the lives of men and women who love each other and who intend to have children.

But Love and Marriage are nevertheless capable of being considered separately. For Marriage is a legal and social contract whose main purpose, so far as the law is concerned, is to safeguard the rights of children, who must be assured of the protection and support of their two parents, if possible, while they are growing up.

If it were not for this necessity to protect children Marriage would be needless, save as an agreement between a man and woman to live together so long that they might find the arrangement mutually desirable.

What I see constantly, both in my dealings with Youth and also with older people, is evidence that there is growing up in this country a rapidly spreading conviction that Love *without* Marriage may be a moral and chaste thing, harmful neither to society nor to the two persons concerned; beneficial rather, and making for happiness and efficiency.

I should be the last to say that there is no danger involved in this view; and I record the fact here simply as a fact, admitting that it is indeed full of dynamite. The point is that the thing is happening, quite regardless of whether it alarms and disturbs you and me or not. I don't know what will come of it, and I am watching the change with keen interest, and with the feeling that it is not in the province of any man to pass cocksure judgments on what is clearly a vast process of social alteration, determined and brought about by forces we as yet know little of.

Along with this changed attitude toward Love without Marriage I see a steadily increasing resort to the arrangement of so-called Trial Marriage, by which is meant an informal agreement on the part of a man and woman to live together till they change their minds—usually with the intention of *not* changing them. Such marriages are usually known, recognized, and in that sense witnessed, by the immediate friends of the couple. I have known many of these "Trial Marriages" to ripen into legal marriage, especially when pregnancy results. Such couples seldom refuse to carry through their responsibilities when there is a child in prospect.

One grave objection to such relations under present standards is that such persons, because of the pressure of convention, refuse to have children. They do not, themselves, however, consider their relationship immoral, and they regard it as not different, in point of actual fact, from regular marriage. To them it merely lacks the form of legal sanction.

CHAPTER 16

I have in mind the case of a brilliant girl whom I knew to be living in "Trial Marriage"—in plain English, with a lover. They regard the relationship as proper. The young man calls regularly at the girl's home, and is highly respected, and liked by her rigidly conventional parents, who, of course, do not dream of the real relationship between them. This girl told me herself that she would have a child if it were considered proper as growing out of such a relation.

I asked her why she didn't get married. She replied that all her friends were getting divorces, and she preferred this arrangement *as promising a more permanent relationship*. I am obliged to add that, so far, it apparently has; for I know one of her girl friends who has been married and divorced twice in the interim.

If the reader knew this very charming and brilliant girl of nineteen, and were in her confidence, she would, in the light of her own experience, be able to put up a very interesting argument in defense of her conduct.

One of the first points she would make would be that marriage without love is prostitution; and she would compare herself favorably with some of her girl friends whose mothers had forced them into marriages of convenience. She would differentiate between such marriages and ordinary prostitution only in the fact that prostitution is promiscuous.

"Any person who marries without love," she once said to me, "contracts a debt which he cannot pay—which is dishonorable. Persons who love without recourse to marriage, however," she continued, "are in a status which is biologically and psychologically moral even though it may be socially immoral."

From these ideas of modern youth it would therefore appear that the day may come when society will recognize that the only thing that can place a definite time clause in the marriage relationship is the coming of children—a fact which this girl apparently recognized when she told me, "You know, Judge, I would just as soon have a child by Paul if it were not for the silly attitude of society." And she added with a laugh, "There's Alice, for instance! She has a baby by her first husband, but she hasn't got her husband—they're divorced. Isn't it funny that she is perfectly respectable with her child, without her husband, while if Paul and I, who have a real enduring love, had a baby, we would be perfectly disreputable?"

If such reasoning on the part of our modern young people shall ever result in changes in our marriage standards it would seem apparent that in cases where there were young and dependent children, then the parents should be expected to see things through together at least till their joint job of rearing their children is completed. By the time they had gone through the fire together for so many years, they would probably remain married the rest of their lives. It is also evident even under such changed conditions, that young people would have to be taught that they must carry the responsibilities of parenthood even at considerable cost to themselves—a thought which fails to register, apparently, with many legally married couples who come before me with their marital difficulties.

With this duty fulfilled, and this obligation recognized,

it might be the decree of the society of some future time that such a relatively loose arrangement as that entered into, through "Trial Marriage," by this nineteen-year-old girl, terminable at will, might be returned to, after the children were reared. Would the flexible psychology of this plan work?—Does the rigid psychology of the present plan work?—These are matters to be pondered. As I have already said, I can but record the things I see and formulate the questions which they inevitably suggest to any unprejudiced observer.

Into this new order of things, if it ever comes, Birth Control may enter as a factor of safety. Birth Control, when science has finally perfected adequate, certain, and easy means of contraception, would mean that there would be no unwanted children. Thus there perhaps would be less likelihood of headlong marriages. The impulse toward love would have free and normal satisfaction in a type of marriage easily dissolved; and couples who found, in due time, that they were fitted to remain together indefinitely, and to undertake the joint responsibility of children with a fair chance of carrying that big undertaking through happily and willingly, would deliberately have children. Those who found by experience that they could not pull together that well, but who found the mere sexual bond satisfactory, would not commit the crime of bringing into the world unwanted children who would not on arrival have the benefit of a happy home and of correct rearing. More than that, *unfit* couples would not commit the even greater crime of bringing into the world children with an inferior physical or mental inheritance. Rather they would satisfy their wish for parenthood by adopting children who have first been given their physical life by fit parents. Such an order of things might make this race over within a very few generations. It might result, if linked with adequate education, in the creation of a race such as this old earth has never seen.

In such a social order, should it ever develop, the unfit of the human species would virtually cease to reproduce their kind. In fact, such reproduction would probably be stopped practically altogether. Under such conditions society might face a situation in which the state would require persons who were not legally licensed to have children, to practice Birth Control. The license to have children might, in such circumstances, be made supplementary to the marriage contract—which would be equivalent to saying that we would then have two kinds of marriage contracts, the one sanctioning the conception of children and the other merely sanctioning cohabitation. This, after all, might be regarded simply as an extension of what already exists in some states where the marriage license is based on the result of a physical examination showing fitness for parenthood. With an adequate method of Birth Control this double arrangement might be possible, because it would not be undertaking the impossible task of forbidding to people a free, normal, and decent exercise of their sexual cravings. Permitted that, they would be ready in most cases to forego children if they were plainly not fitted to produce or to rear them. Such a restraint would be a reasonable, not an intolerable one—nor would it be an infringement on personal liberty comparable to the taboos we take for granted today and violate continually because we can't endure them.

To many this might seem simply another name for Free Love. I do not believe, however, that it could be so regarded, since Free Love implies promiscuity. Indeed it might well make for a truer, more thorough-going, and more effective monogamy than we have at present. At present we cling to the name and lack the substance. It may ill become us too freely to condemn the civilization of that day before it arrives.

For the benefit of anyone who is disposed to argue against these views for the asinine reason that "it has never been done," let me here draw attention to the fact that it has. There was an ancient custom in the British Isles known as "Handfasting," which comes from the Anglo-Saxon word "handfaestnung," pledging one's hand, and was an Old English synonym for betrothal. According to the *Encylopœdia Britannica,* from which I here quote by permission, Handfasting was "later a peculiar form of temporary marriage at one time common in Scotland, the only necessary ceremony being the verbal pledge of the couple while holding hands. The pair thus handfasted were, in accordance with Scotch law, entitled to live together for a year and a day. If then they so wished, the temporary marriage could be made permanent; if not, they could go their several ways without reproach, the child, if any, being supported by the party who objected to further cohabitation."

Presumably the Scotch, who I believe have never been noted as a licentious people, found that handfasting had its advantages, or they would not have practiced it. Presumably, too, the complicating factor in this method of trial marriage was the always possible child. The child was the fly in the ointment. But with a recognized system of Birth Control, and with a development of methods of scientific contraception, sanctioned by law and public opinion, that would not have been so. It would then have been understood that handfasting was *not* a permit by society to have children; and the result would probably have been a system recognizing two kinds of marriage, much as I have described it above. It is quite possible that with a system of scientific birth control the Scotch would have continued handfasting to this day. At any rate, history establishes the fact that the custom was "repectable," and thus suggests the shocking thought that it might, under right conditions, become "respectable" again.

In the meantime, whether we like it or not we have to face the truth that people are always going to make mistakes in choosing their mates. There is no doubt, even under our present conditions, that when average people marry they really mean it to be a life contract. But in making such a contract, either in the present state of society or in that foreshadowed, perhaps, by the aspirations of modern youth, there will always be a percentage of error, a very considerable percentage; and it is simply common sense that when such mistakes are made, the parties should be permitted to release each other from what has become a loveless bond. But the percentage of error may be greatly decreased as a result of changes in the conventions and laws through which people will arrive at marriage, particularly the marriage which is intended to involve the birth of children.

The bond of a union of mere cohabitation, not involving children, will, in the event of such changes in society, probably be of the lightest. It will be easy to assume and easy to discard. It ought to involve the conception of a sincere and faithful love of one man for one woman which is true marriage; but such a union, doubtless, would have no strings tied to it, and both parties would at all times be conscious that the duration of the arrangement depended on their wish to continue together and on nothing else. Or they might deliberately choose to change their marriage contract, and so commit themselves

to having children, in which case they would owe their
children a special duty while the children were dependent
—and longer, if they found it possible, as in most of
these cases, they would.

Under such conditions, in this hypothetical future,
would love unions of the type I speak of, easily con-
summated and easily ended, lead to a riot of sexual
license? I know that there are plenty of persons who
insist that such would be the result. I am ready to admit
that in the case of some individuals that would be the
result. But I doubt that the majority of normal persons
would behave that way. I doubt it for several reasons:

In the first place, women, under such an order of things,
if we ever arrive at it, will have economic independence,
and will, as I have already indicated, determine the scale
of sexual ethics in a way that will protect them and protect their unborn children. *They would do this inevitably, for biological reasons of a most final and imperative
sort.* That fact alone disposes of the question of license.

But there is another reason, quite as powerful. Experience with human nature demonstrates abundantly that
license is almost always a rebound; it is extreme indul-
gence in a thing that has been forbidden, or unattainable.
The conduct of Americans at home, and especially abroad,
in the matter of drinking since Prohibition is a striking
example of this. Standards of moderation establish themselves in the minds of most of us when we are let alone.
I see it constantly among children. Every wise teacher
knows that the disorderliness of a school is directly proportional to the number of rules on the Don't card; and
that when the teacher has enough faith and courage to
give her pupils their head, with liberty to do what is
right, they will do it. It isn't a liberty to do what is
wrong, though that is what it looks like to cynics and

cowards. My boys always go through when I send them by themselves to reformatories, though my enemies jeer, and even some of my friends can't quite see how I "hypnotize them" into it. I don't hypnotize them. I tell them the truth; and they understand perfectly that the seeming liberty to run away is really the privilege of playing square and acting on a code of honor.

The difference between me and many persons who differ with me is simply that I really believe this; and the reason I believe it is that I find that it works. And it works in sex relationships just as it does in other relationships. It would work in the problem of marriage and divorce, if we could only bring ourselves to have faith in that magic spell of personal responsibility which Liberty throws over the human heart.

There is another angle to this, too. What *is* license? When conservative thinkers insist that the possible changes suggested and perhaps foreshadowed in the psychology of modern youth, would lead to a riot of Free Love, what do they mean? That life would become one grand petting party? That every woman would have many lovers; or that she would get married once a month; or what?

Patience is a virtue. I can only repeat. Women, for biological reasons, would *not* permit such a development. Some individual women might, but some individual women already do. We would be no worse off in that respect than we are now—probably less.

The point I wish to make—even at the risk of shocking somebody—is that we place a superstitious meaning and importance on what we call chastity, particularly in women. The idea is commonly accepted without question or debate that sex experience, if it takes place out of wedlock, changes a woman in some mysterious way; that the effect on her, for example, is quite different if she should have such an experience today while unmarried than if she should have it tomorrow after marriage.   If she should have it today, and the man should die before her marriage to him tomorrow, she would be impure and unfit for marriage with another man.   But if she should have it tomorrow, after marriage, and her husband should die the next day, she would then be a widow, and entirely eligible for marriage—a perfectly pure woman.

Of course as a matter of cold, scientific fact the only difference in the two experiences comes in the difference of the psychological reaction.   In the one case she is conscious of doing something which Society assures her will damn her right into Hell—unless the man will marry her later, in which case it will probably put her into purgatory and let it go at that.   In the other case she is conscious of the approval of Society and the assurance of the Church that the marriage ceremony completely changes the effect of this union on her—which is certainly not a fact.

It doesn't!   She is the same woman in either event, and the notion that she is not is one of the most diabolical of our tribal superstitions.   She has violated the social code, of course; but there are other ways of violating the social code which are much more anti-social, and which do not carry anything like the penalties that follow a sex offense.   Had she been guilty of some other violation—had she stolen, or slandered her neighbor, or lied, or showed an ugly temper, or scratched her rival's face, or put arsenic in the soup—she would still have been in fairly respectable standing.   At least she would not have been "impure" and "unclean" and all that nonesense.   No, that particular violation of the social code flouts and tweaks the long puritan nose of our pet racial fetish—

the fetish whose nose we all want to tweak, and in whose defense therefore we all become hypocritically violent. She may fail in her worship of our other tribal gods, but to this one she must bow in public; and if she neglects her devoirs in private, she mustn't get found out.

Many Gods? I say it deliberately. We deceive ourselves into the belief that we believe in One God, but we don't. Instead we bow down to more idols made of mud than do the "heathen"; and we violate the second commandment thereby with far worse effect on ourselves than if we kept it and broke the seventh. As a matter of fact we do a thorough job and break them both.

My own observation, in dealing with actual flesh-and-blood people is that girls who have had sex experiences are like other girls; and that they get along first rate unless Society happens to find out that they have "gone wrong."

I remember an instance of that sort. A certain high-school girl, very fine and lovely, became too intimate with a boy. Her remorse afterward was based, not on the fact that she faced pregnancy, for she did not; it was based on what she had been taught about such things. Her conscience reproached her so terribly that she felt the necessity for sympathy and support and understanding. So she went to one of her teachers, an old maid, who would have been a far better and wiser and more charitable person if during her own girlhood she had been guilty of the same misstep this child had made.

This woman immediately took the girl's story to another old maid, who spread the news. The school authorities got hold of it, called the girl up on the carpet, grilled her, smacked their lips solemnly over the details of her story, and then expelled her as a moral menace to other students.   She was bad; she was contaminated; she was impure.

Unfortunately, she believed their judgment, and the effect on her own psychology was devastating.   I had a big job on my hands later making her see that she was not ruined, that she had simply made a mistake, that she could come back, and that her judges were a gang of savages wearing too many clothes.

But she never really held up her head again.   The weight of social disapproval was too heavy for her.   She finally solved the problem by getting out of Denver.

And yet she was a very fine girl, with a moral sense about her that placed her infinitely above the two she-cats who dragged her down, and above the purblind pedagogues who finding her on the edge of the cliff kicked her over into the abyss.   Those two women are active workers in one of our large Denver churches.   They go to service every Sunday, and are socially well known. They deserve to be in the penitentiary.

Other girls I have known have gone down utterly under such persecution.   What amazes me is that apparently reasonable persons, who admit, theoretically, the injustice and the savagery of such things, usually join in the hue and cry when a concrete case of "immorality" crosses their paths.

> "By the Hoof of the Wild Goat up-tossed
> From the cliff where She lay in the Sun,
>   Fell the Stone
> To the Tarn where the daylight is lost;
> So She fell from the light of the Sun,
>   And alone!
>
> Oh, Thou Who has builded the world!
> Oh, Thou Who has lighted the Sun!

Oh, Thou Who hast darkened the Tarn!
Judge Thou
The sin of the Stone that was hurled
By the goat from the light of the Sun,
As she sinks in the mire of the Tarn,
Even now—even now—even now!"

CHAPTER 17

In a recent issue of the *Atlantic Monthly* I find a letter printed in the Contributors' Column which throws a sidelight on this question of marriage and morality. The letter relates how a bride and her husband, known by the writer of the letter, went to South America, and there devoted much of their time to betterment of conditions among the peons. One of the first things they undertook was to urge the men and women living together on the plantation to get married. They found the men willing enough, but to their astonishment, encountered opposition from the women.

"Finally," said the bride later to the writer of the letter, "an old woman of more than ordinary education and intelligence—really 'une grande dame' in her class, solved the mystery for me. She walked ten miles over mountainous country roads from her village to beg me to confine my missionary activities to securing better teachers for the children and vocational schools for the older girls. These she heartily approved.

" 'But, Señora, do not make my people think it is wrong to live together without the ceremony of a marriage. So long as a woman *consents* to live with a man, he treats her with respect and is faithful to her, and is considerate of the children. When she *has* to live with him, he abuses her, takes the money she earns, and is not afraid to go openly to another woman. And if the children belong to him he hires them out and pockets the wages or even sells them. Oh, don't you see, Señora, we women have more freedom and happiness and our men are better when we are not bound to them—when we can pick up and leave them if they don't behave?'

" 'And,' added my friend, 'all the old Dona said is true of these people. And,' she laughed, 'I sometimes encounter an attitude toward one's responsibilities among my own friends which almost makes me wonder—Oh no!' she interrupted herself, putting up her hand to shield her from my horrified expression, I suppose, 'I still believe in the institution of marriage!' "

That letter seems to me one of the most illuminating comments on the marriage as we have it that I have ever read; and it bears out exactly my own extended observation of the way marriage, *as we have it,* works. What the old Dona said was not merely true of those people, it was true of all people and of all human nature; and that is why the generations foreshadowed by the perplexities and yearnings of modern youth may find it absolutely necessary to make our marriage code as flexible as the welfare of children will permit; and perfectly flexible in all unions where there are no children.

The conclusion of the letter is illuminating, also. There you have the usual insanity—the one woman instinctively horrified at even a hint of an assault upon the divine Institute, and the other, in spite of the damning evidence, apparently still clinging to the Institute As Is, and implying that something different might work better—*for peons.* Something different might work better for all of us. Not an abolition of marriage, but a change in the code.

Once again let me refer to my statement that women —those peon women, for instance—are under a biological necessity to make marriage a stable thing, whether it involve a marriage ceremony or not. I have a letter in my files from an eighteen-year-old girl whom I once pulled out of a difficulty, and who still makes me her confidant; and I take from it this passage:

"I am going steadily with one boy now. He is a ———— and is 28, and is the straightest, decentest boy I've ever met. I may marry him. We have been going together for two months now, seeing each other every night and all day Sundays. I know you would approve of him for he is everything that is good and true and fine. He insists on keeping our relations honorable. To tell you the truth I don't want him to. I'm crazy about him, and I am so afraid he will go with other women so that he can continue to be good with me. I would so much rather give myself than to have him go with other women. He has promised me he won't, but it worries me."

There are two ways of looking at that passage. One is to say that the girl is immoral and is flouting the Institute. The other is to say that she may have in view a conception of marriage far more normal, healthful, vital, and *honest* than anything the Institute provides for —a view far too honest and moral, indeed, for Society, with its rigid conventions, to approve of it. But at least it is an answer to those who insist that "laxness" in these matters would lead human society into an orgy of promiscuity. The very heart and soul of that girl's letter is its recognition of love as between one man and one woman.

This girl is monogamous by instinct, just as all normal women are monogamous by instinct. By this I mean, not that she would be incapable of enjoying sex relations with more than one man, but that her maternal instinct, with an eye to the interests of herself and her potential children, is a check. Men, because their biological relations with their offspring are less close, do not experience this check in the same degree; a fundamental fact which largely accounts for the eternal conflicts of sex, the "un-faithfulness" of man and the jealous passion for exclusive possession of a mate which tends to make many women tyrannous in marriage.

This girl therefore proposes to be monogamous and likewise to exact monogamy of her lover, the possible father of her children. But she is an exception among women in that she sees his point of view as well as her own. She understands men well enough to take him as he is. She recognizes that he is human, and like all men instinctively polygamous; and, facing facts as they are, she is frankly concerned that he be not tempted beyond his strength. She also knows that he might look toward other women; and she doesn't count his natural mascu-linity against him. She has breadth of view, charity, and a fearless understanding of human nature—for she has been educated by her own mistakes and troubles. If more women had a similar understanding and charity toward men it would be well for the world, and men would go straighter through the mere fact of being sym-pathetically understood.

There is an old joke to the effect that the average man always tells "the other woman" that his wife does not understand him. There is more than a little truth in that, and more than a little misery and secret adultery comes from it. Her distrust and fear become translated, in him into a suppressed and destructive desire.

For instance I recall a case of one of the happiest and most successful marriages I know, where the wife told her husband that she placed no restrictions upon his relationships with other women, but added the suggestion that in the event he cared to make use of such freedom it would be with the understanding that it applied equally to her, if she should care to use it: They made a pact to that effect—with the result that neither has ever acted on it. The resulting sense of freedom has made inconstancy or unfaithfulness a logical impossibility simply because the terms of their pact said "We agree not to attach the name of 'inconstancy' to anything we may do." The spirit of jealous possession has never marred the happiness and harmony of this couple. This freedom has created within them those internal, voluntarily *preferred* restraints which the arbitrary conventions of marriage are notoriously failing to create.

But to return to that girl's attitude of mind, particularly her willingness to live with her lover without being married to him. I don't know what others may call it; but from her viewpoint I am sure she thinks it is moral, even though it violates the social code. This does not mean that I would have either approved of such a course of conduct or advised her to follow it. I know its dangers in a social order to whose habits of thought it is so offensive and so alien. But I hope I also appreciate its sincerity and the fundamental ethical values that derive from that sincerity. Surely, too, the honesty and frankness of this girl's revelation of what she really thinks is a thing beyond price. What a different world it would be if between all parents and their children there were a similar frankness, able without fear of hostile criticism and misunderstanding, so freely to express itself.

Our racial habits of thought keep us from recognizing what is here made obvious, that personal morality and social morality are not always identical. For here is a clear case of a self-sufficient personal morality which runs counter to the social code, while outwardly and cannily conforming to it. Socially, this girl is "immoral." Personally she is not. Thus we have a conflict which Society has not yet learned to resolve.

In another paragraph the letter throws some light on this point of conformity to tradition. This girl as I have said, outwardly conforms, like many of us, to traditions to which her judgment does not consent. For instance she says:

"What do I think of the modern girl? The same thing that I think of the average man. There is no such animal. You can't put your finger on the 'modern girl' because every girl is different and every girl is modern in her own way. Take, for instance, Madeline. She is very modern but at the same time she is very conventional. So one cannot say that all modern girls are unconventional. Take me. I am modern and conventional on the outside, at least I try to be, but inwardly I am not. I don't see why I can't smoke going down the street just as well as I can smoke in a public restaurant or on top of a bus or in the lobby of a theater. I don't see why I can't pet a man in public as well as I can in my room at home. And a number of other things I wonder. There is no solution. I just can't. Yet I'm modern, even if I am conventional."

Still one more passage from this interesting letter, written with a frankness proportional to the fact that I never say "You shall" and "You shan't" to young people who confide in me:

"I think that flappers and others who are not in that category but just on the outside, not daring to creep over the line so that they could be honestly classified with their more honest sisters, are a hoax. Their carryings on are just a pose. Everything they do is for effect, and not for personal satisfaction. Did you ever see a flapper flap when she was by herself or without an audience? I never did. They all flap for the attention of the public and the more they can hold the glances of other people the more they are going to pull their stuff. The thing nowadays is to be bizarre, and so we attempt it, the bizarrer the better. But not because we like it. But because we attract the attention of the boy at the next table and because we thrill under the disparaging glances of the middle-aged couple a few chairs away. The more comment we cause the more successful we think we are."

Of course my correspondent has not here accounted for the desire to attract all this attention, and to win disparaging glances from middle-aged people. What have these youngsters got against the middle-aged that they should want their disparagement,—unless they conceive that the old order is so completely wrong that anything it disparages must be right. It is not a constructive frame of mind—it is the headlong, iconoclastic extremism of Youth—and yet, consciously or unconsciously, it does aim at a constructive end, a reconcilement of the absurdities, a resolving of the contradictions, so badly needed in our confused social code today. It is not a final solution, but it is another step.

What I have had to say regarding the possibility that society may develop two frankly recognized types of marriage which already exist without such recognition, namely one for cohabitation and the other for the rearing of children, has doubtless shocked many readers. Doubtless too there is an added shock in the further suggestion that the perfecting of simple and adequate contraceptive methods would make the marriage of cohabitation easily practicable and possible.

For many readers are not prepared to admit that the marriage muddle requires extreme remedies if it is ever to get itself lined up in conformity with the biological and psychological requirements of the human race. Most persons are prepared to admit that Marriage, as we have it, is an imperfect institution, but they always hedge by saying it's the best arrangement the wisdom of the human race operating through the ages has been able to devise. We must get along with it as best we can and train people to the powers of self-control necessary under such a system. I can sympathize with this point of view even though I don't agree with it. The obvious answer is that the failure of human ingenuity down through the ages to solve a problem isn't a proof that it can't be solved. Human ingenuity failed till quite recently to produce so obvious and simple a mechanical device as a steam engine, or a dynamo, or an airplane. Our past stupidities are no warrant or excuse for their own continuance. Bold thought and speech, and on occasion, bold action, may carry us far. That's one reason I like this younger generation. It's bold. It has in large measure that flow of faith and courage, that swelling tide of unquestioning belief, on which the human race has always floated forward to fresh goals and new achievements.

It is when you see people struggling in concrete situations that you become convinced that here is a muddle which might be corrected by methods thus and so. Let me tell another story.

I once knew a girl whom I shall call Imogen. There had been a robbery in a garage, and Imogen, then a child of twelve years, was one of the witnesses. Imogen came to court with her mother, and gave her testimony; one look at her face caused me to request her mother to see me after the session of the court was over.

"Do you know," I asked, "that your little girl is oversexed? Do you know whether she has ever had intimate relations with boys?"—Of course I didn't put it quite as bluntly as that, but that was the substance of it; and in spite of all the tact I could use, the mother was furious. Finally I convinced her; and then she was disturbed and frightened.

She went to the principal of the school the child attended and asked if he had ever observed anything out of the way in her conduct. "No," he said; "such a charge is absolutely unwarranted; but that's the way with Judge Lindsey." Whereupon the principal came to me in high dudgeon. "That child," he said, "has been in my charge since she was in kindergarten. I know her innocent mind like a book. What do you mean by such charge?"

"I make no charge," I said. "I merely know that if she has not yet gotten into trouble, she is in danger of doing so."

Finally the mother brought Imogen to me, and I sent her out of the room while I talked with the child. Within fifteen minutes I learned from her that she had been "bad" with boys.

She was frantic, then, with the fear that I would betray her; but I told her I would tell nobody without her consent. Finally I prevailed on her that I should tell her mother—but not her father, of whom she had a great fear.

Then I called in the mother, talked with her alone, told her stories of my many experiences with cases like this, and so prepared her for what I had to say that she supported the shock very well.

When I asked her, however, if she did not want me to see Imogen from time to time she said No, that she would take charge of her daughter herself.

And she did.—

Five years later an attractive girl of 17 walked in on me. She introduced herself. It was Imogen. She said,

"Judge, I kept the promise I made you about boys till last month. Then I broke it. I've come to tell you."

Then she told her story. She was attending an exclusive school for girls. She and another girl whose picture I had seen in the papers a week before as one of our prettiest débutantes, had gone to a dancing party with two boys. After the party, on the way back to the school, they had permitted these boys to fondle them. "It wasn't the boys' fault," she said. "We were as much to blame as they were."

The result of this petting excited and frightened her. She was afraid of what might happen. I counseled her as best I could and represented to her in the strongest terms I could command, the folly and danger of such courses; but in spite of it all she went to another party with the same boy; and this time "it happened."

"I don't want to do such things," she said to me later. "I'll try again not to. But it is terribly hard for me to keep boys from going too far. Why can't I be like Dorothy?"—naming a close friend of hers. "She never has any trouble like this."

"It is too bad," I told her. "But it's the way you are. Your sexual nature has waked up early; and you ought to be married. But your parents don't understand. Make me another promise and this time try hard to keep it. Come here often."

She did so, and for a time things went well. Then one day she came to me utterly happy. She was in love with a young man of 22 who loved her and had asked her to marry him.

But on her next visit she was in the depths of despair. Her parents had forbidden the engagement. They had told her that she must go East to school, and must not think of marriage till she was twenty-five, another eight years.

"I can't stand it," she said. "Please marry us without my parents' knowledge. Then I'll go to school and see him only in vacations; and if there's a baby then I'll tell them we are married."

"I can't do it," I said. "You are under age, and I can't marry you without your parents' consent."

"But you do marry minors often, when their parents refuse consent," she retorted. "You know yourself that when illicit union makes probable the birth of a child, then the rights of the unborn child transcend the grand-parents' rights, and the Juvenile Court has the right to marry the parents of the unborn child, even though the grandparents refuse consent. You married Sadie Brown under just such conditions; and she told me just what you said to her parents."

I had to admit that such was the case; but I warned her against any such conduct.—She left, looking thoughtful. A few weeks later she came back. "Now you can marry us," she said. "I didn't tell him that it was so we could be married; but I 'went wrong' with him."

To say that I was disturbed would be putting it much too mildly.

"Don't you know," I asked, "that in that case he is likely to stop wanting to marry you."

"No, I don't," she answered. "He loves me."

"He can't support you yet," I said. "And if you marry him it means a break with your parents. You must wait."

"I want you to tell my mother," she said, "exactly what I have done and what my condition is; and make it clear to her that we ought to be married."

So I sent for the mother, and told her the situation.

She said hopelessly, "Yes, but her father wants her to go to school till she is 25."

"He is bent on her destruction," I said. "Such a delay would be a crime. She is a good girl, but she is as she is. Give her a chance."

"If I told him what she has done," said the mother, "he would kill her."

"Tell him," I said, "that you are convinced that she will elope as soon as she is 18, and that if he wants to prevent that scandal he had better let her marry now."

She did so; and the result was that the father compromised. She was to go to school a year, and then marry if she wished.—She wished. They had a big church wedding, and today she is a happy wife and mother, and one of the leaders of Denver society, a young matron above reproach.

The reason I have told this story here is to show one of the many, many situations in human life that have in them the makings of terrible tragedies because of the tricks and devices people are put to oftentimes when their natural cravings run up against the present regulations—particularly the marriage regulations—of society. In this instance I was able to straighten out the tangle; but nine times out of ten disaster would have resulted.

Speaking from a biological standpoint, marriage ought to be easy, spontaneous, and natural. It should be a normal fulfillment of our normal instincts. It should not have to be deferred year after year for economic reasons. Earlier marriages should be made possible by removing the possibility of children being brought into the world before the young couple are in an economic position to support a family. Barring the youth, and consequent economic incapacity of the young man, there was no reasonable reason why this girl and her sweetheart should not have gotten married. And the reason his economic incapacity counted as a prohibiting factor was the possibility that there would be children. And yet, grotesquely enough, the threatened advent of a child was the only condition that could make their marriage possible! What utter insanity—You must not get married for fear you'll have babies;—and yet you *must* get married for the same reason!

CHAPTER 18

Place the conception of children absolutely within the control of the people who are to have them, and the economic difficulty which makes marriage such a tragedy today in so many lives would be largely cleared up. Many a young couple could live together happily on a little money if they had no babies; and later, as their income increased, and as their certainty of each other crystallized into a permanent partnership, they could have the babies, *and would*. As it is they marry on a little; have babies when they can't afford them; and are dragged down and worn out by a burden too heavy for their shoulders. For these reasons, thousands of them are coming into the domestic relations and divorce courts. The woman becomes a neurotic drudge, and the husband finds life converted into a treadmill. Their dreams have fled, and thereafter they worry along as best they can— or if they can't, get a divorce.

Under the one system, they might have had a full and happy life, she retaining her beauty and poise, and he his youthful hope and energy. Under the other they have violated every essential law of life, and must pay the tragic penalty,—a penalty which society shares because it decreases their ability to lead full and productive lives. Marriage would seldom be a failure under right biological and economic conditions; and, by the same token, it can hardly escape failure when it is under the conspicuously wrong biological and economic conditions in which it struggles along at present.

The wonder is that our divorce courts are not twice as

busy as they are. Why anybody should be struck with
wonder, horror, or amazement at our divorce statistics
I can't understand. What we had far better marvel at
is the number of human beings who see the arrangement
through under such unspeakably idiotic conditions.

Marriage is a feasible enough arrangement if we would
but give it a chance. But Ignorance, Poverty, poor health,
and unwanted children, often physically and mentally
subnormal, combine to jam the whole works. It is a crime
that children should be conceived under such conditions.
It is a crime that we should permit ourselves to spawn
as if we were a race of frogs.

Ignorance means more than the inability to think
straight which is so diligently fostered under our present
ways of education. It means also a want of knowledge
of the basic facts which people need to think with.

In Marriage it means, among other things, a want of
knowledge of sex facts. Men and women have as a rule
only the haziest notion of the part which sex plays in
their lives. Most of them think their sex relations will
take care of themselves. And so they neglect the whole
matter, and shirk the disciplines it imposes, till their
lives are like unweeded gardens, and sex itself becomes
a byword instead of a sacred responsibility.

No art *ever* takes care of itself; and love-making is
the most vital and important of all the arts because it
is the psychological and biological root of all of them.

In this connection Andre Tridon says in his excellent
book "Psychoanalysis and Love," "Considering the artificial character of the marriage union, and at the same
time the psychological importance of its durability as far
as the mental health of the off-spring is concerned, one
of the most pressing duties of the community (and one
which it never performs), should be to devise all the

possible ways and means whereby the sex cravings of both mates could be helped to retain their freshness and strength as long as possible."

This writer then goes on to say that personal attractiveness and beauty in men and women are assets of the utmost importance, and that these should be retained and fostered, by artificial means if necessary, to prevent the dying out of erotism as a result of the humdrum and habit of daily life. In this erotic sense, if in no other, beauty and health are a duty to the race.

Poverty does much to make the retention of beauty and health in marriage impossible. The tension of fear which goes with poverty also makes love-making in marriage often impossible—for relaxation, security, and ease are necessary to courtship.

Another factor which makes trouble in marriage is partly the fruit of ignorance and partly the fruit of fear and poverty. I refer to the way in which married persons insist on modifying and changing each other's personalities. In courtship before marriage there is a scrupulous respect shown by the two parties for each other's ego. But after marriage this passes—and love is likely to pass with it.

The usual theory is that in marriage the couple should become slavishly adapted to each other. I deny it. Nobody should in this sense adapt himself or herself to anybody. When people adapt themselves they simply cork themselves up. That kind of "adaptation" is an ignoble form of domestic pacifism, wherein peace-at-any-price weaklings of both sexes sell their souls for a mess of pottage. They want comfort, and they get it—for a time. But it's simply a case where one lie and polite concealment leads to another, and where the tyranny of the one with the stronger personality slowly but surely and

crushingly asserts itself. For such suppressions of themselves thousands of married persons are paying the penalty of untoward neurotic disturbances. Often the weaker
mate in such marriages becomes sexually disabled, the
only form of revenge the harried subconscious can resort
to; and the consequent cases of chronic illness, the nervous prostrations, and the like that fill the offices of
physicians, neurologists and psychologists are legion.

What married people need is not adaptability but rather
a sturdy egotism combined with mutual respect and tolerance—and with complete intolerance both of female
nagging and of male bullying, an intolerance as complete
as it ever is in courtship. Submission to such tyranny is
fatal. But so is the heat of anger and resentment. Candid reasoning is the only thing that ever can define the
issue in such cases.

Integrity of the personality, which is possible only
through independence of thought and action, and through
freedom from fear, is of double importance in marriage
because it is the only thing that can make a man and a
woman permanently attractive to each other in a sexual
way.

There are persons who maintain that the permanence
of this attraction in marriage is not important, and that
it dies out anyway into a platonic relationship in the course
of a few humdrum years. Very true. It usually does.
And thereby hangs the tale of most divorces.

Under favorable conditions a husband and wife should
remain sexually attractive to each other during the whole
period of their physical potency; and the rich symbolism
of their sex life together should by then be so rooted
and permanent that their relationship as sweethearts will
remain vigorous and sweet, till their life's end. But the
conditions of marriage usually tend to make such a rela-

tionship impossible. And this is one of the greatest tragedies of our civilization.

The part which vigor and fearlessness of personality can play in the sex relationship is sufficiently well shown in the charming coquetry and high and mighty independence which young girls show toward youths who seek their favor. It is also well shown in the liking which women have for the so called masterful type of man, and for the overworked "cave-man stuff."

If the conditions of marriage were such that they would make possible a continuance of the independence and the freedom from fear which marks courtship, then marital love would have something to build on which it lacks at present. Such independence and freedom from fear would, so to speak, enlarge the personalities of the wife and the husband in each other's eyes, just as it does in courtship. They would thus become worthwhile to each other, and remain so; and their union would be free from that mutual indifference—the fruit of humdrum contacts —which is more truly an infidelity than adultery itself, —and is, indeed, the chief cause of adultery. Such indifference is an infidelity because it makes impossible those complex psychological conditions which lead to sex satisfaction. It thus strikes at the very root of the union.

Independence and freedom from fear are difficult to attain in any relationship where one of the parties is in the position of a dependent, living on such bounty as the whim of the other cares to extend, and perhaps extends grudgingly at that. While such a condition of things exists equality in the partnership is not possible. In fact it isn't a partnership; it is merely an arrangement by which the economically dependent party is kept by the other party for reasons which soon begin to dwindle in importance. Some persons have so little self-respect that they don't mind this; and there are men who marry women of fortune, frankly content to subsist on their bounty, just as there are women who marry men merely to exploit them. This is married prostitution.

The economic independence of women in marriage would go far to solve this problem. But it is difficult to conceive of any plan whereby such independence of married women would be practicable or possible under our present social order. Economic independence before marriage is now common enough, and grows more so; and it is true that when a woman has once proved to her own satisfaction her ability to earn a living for herself she will always have a sense of independence that will profoundly affect her relationship to her husband. She can always leave him; and she does not have to accept bed and board as if she were a mistress selling her body for these commodities.

And yet, when all is said and done, the wage earner in the marriage combination has the advantage if he chooses to take it, and if he chooses to violate the self-evident proposition that when a man marries a woman he does not employ a mistress but enters into a partnership of absolute equality, wherein the woman is quite likely to contribute more than he.

The unfortunate thing about this is that in society as it is now, the bearing and rearing of children places the woman at the husband's mercy. In consenting to have children she gives hostages to fortune. When Bacon said that the man who marries gives hostages to fortune, he might have added that this was doubly true of the man's wife. It is one reason why so many married women dread —what they naturally most desire—motherhood.

For this there is no specific, made-to-order remedy—

for obviously it is a matter of personal conduct based
on internal, rather than external, restraints. A trained
ethical sense is the natural remedy, and the only remedy.

Legislation of the right sort, it is true, may enable the
State to extend alleviation in extreme cases, such as those
which show up in my court all the time; but that does
not meet the needs of those persons unwilling to resort
to law and who prefer to bear their trials in silence.

Some have proposed that the State assure the support
of mothers and their children by a system of pensions.
But this mother has one standard of living, and that one
has another; this one lives in two rooms, and that in
twelve. What would be aid to the one would not be
a drop in the bucket to the other. However, properly
understood, there should be no such thing as pensions
for mothers. It should be rather, *aid for children*—as
it is in Colorado. The State is as vitally interested in
the child as the parent, and should therefore aid the
child for its own sake, making of the parents simply
trustees of the funds provided.

I continually find it necessary to force husbands to
support their families, and to require them, on pain of
imprisonment, to contribute certain percentages of their
incomes. But if the worst comes to the worst, and the
husband disobeys, and I send him to prison, that leaves
his family with nothing at all. If the man could earn
something substantial in prison that would help; but there
is as yet no such adequate provision in any State. A
commendable effort of this kind has recently been undertaken in California; and within another year a similar
step is expected to be taken in Colorado.

Legislation of the right sort would improve these conditions; but the only legislation I can conceive of that
would really get permanent results would be the sort pro-

viding for the adequate education of everybody, parents
as well as children; and that, needless to say, is a long
way ahead.   I have several times in recent years presented to our Colorado legislature bills providing for the
compulsory education of parents, especially in matters
pertaining to sex hygiene, and the proper rearing of children.   Since the State refuses to educate children for
parenthood my idea was that we might at least do something by educating the parents.

To those of us who believe we have a clear vision of
how things ought to be, these changes seem to come with
desperate slowness.   Sometimes it is very discouraging.
But from another point of view they are not coming
slowly.   They are coming with almost dizzy speed.   It
is astounding to consider that most of the changes which
I am discussing in this book are a product of the last
ten years, though thoughtful persons perceived long
before that something of the kind was on the way.
For instance an increasing number of married persons
are acquiring notions of justice and fair dealing, financial and economic, in the marriage relationship which
they never learned in school, and which are an outcrop-
ping of the spirit of the times.   The old idea that what
a husband earns belongs to him, and that whatever he
gives his wife and family is a gratuity provided by his
lordly bounty and generosity is no longer fashionable.
Women no longer tamely accept that view.   Women are
carrying over into marriage those practical principles
of equity and common sense which they learn in business
before they get married.   An increasing participation in
business, and in the world of affairs, has done it; and
to the shame of our schools and churches it must be
said that they have contributed little to this change.
Once women were ignorant of these matters, and the

man determined the economic basis of the marriage. Now the woman is more sophisticated, and insists *from the start* on terms similar to those of any real partnership. From the start it is made clear that her contribution in marriage is quite as valuable as money. Joint bank accounts are more common than they used to be, and the man who keeps his wife helpless simply by keeping her poor is slowly becoming a back number.

I need not add that men who, after marriage, deliberately make dependents of their wives deprive themselves of the very thing they sought in the days of their courtship, rapport with another free personality. It is also evident that such wives will nag, be jealous, and do all they can in the way of pettiness to compensate for their own sense of helplessness.

I think it is possible that a considerable portion of the race will soon become educated to this ideal of marriage as a partnership composed of two independent personalities, who must first of all respect each other. I think the revolt in which our younger generation is now engaged clearly tends in that direction. A significant thing I should record here is that in many cases of cohabitation without marriage that have come under my observation, the arrangement has apparently created this condition of mutual independence and respect between persons who might not have maintained it in marriage.

CHAPTER 19

I said a while back that conventional Marriage, like any other tree, must be judged by its fruits; and that if the fruit be bad, then the burden of proof is on those who still insist that the tree is good as it stands, unpruned, unsprayed, and neglected by human art.

Consider some of the facts about the harvest today yielded by this ancient and neglected tree, which, as we have it, is little better than a jungle product. For every marriage in Denver during the year 1922 there was a separation. For every two marriage licenses issued there was a divorce suit filed. These figures are not limited to Denver alone. They are approximately correct for many cities of the United States. I cite my own city because it is necessarily the laboratory in which I work. What happens in one city is substantially happening in all cities. I am not discussing a city but a social problem. I need not add that Denver is no worse than any other city.—Indeed I think it is much better than most.

In the last four or five years the marriage and divorce ratio, which in the cities was formerly in the ratio of about one divorce to four marriages, is now more nearly one divorce to two marriages.

The last time I looked up the matter in detail I found that in the year 1922, up to December 16, there had been 1492 divorce cases filed in Denver as against 2908 marriage licenses issued. The divorces were 49.5 per cent of the marriages. At the same time my own court figures recorded 1500 cases of non-support and desertion, though many were dealt with without the formality of filing a case. This makes the total of divorces and separations 2992. At the time I allowed an estimate of fifty more divorce cases for the rest of the year, bringing up the total to 1542; and I allowed 100 more marriages, giving a total of 3008. The corresponding figures for 1921 were 1497 divorces and 3626 marriages. Which means that in 1922 the increase in divorces was 45, and the *decrease* in marriages was 618. In other words they are getting gun shy. "Surely in vain the net is spread in the sight of any bird."

The number of marriage licenses issued in Denver in 1920 was 4002. Compare that with 3008 in 1922.

In Chicago it is reported that there were 39,000 marriage licenses issued in 1922 as compared with 13,000 divorce decrees actually signed. If 13,000 divorce decrees were actually signed, how many couples do you suppose there were who *wished* they could get somebody to sign a divorce decree for them, but who never acted on their wish? For divorce is a troublesome, expensive, embarrassing business, and persons who wish for it resort to the courts only when at the extreme limit of their endurance. If there were 39,000 marriages in Chicago in the year of grace 1922, it is absurdly conservative to say that fully 26,000 would have gotten divorces if they could, in addition to the 13,000 who did. I base this belief on the proportion of married couples who come under my own observation, coming as they do confidentially for advice and consolation, and who never go after the divorce they wish for. I believe their number is many, many times larger than the number of those who go to court with their troubles.

Recently I picked up a United Press article concerning the Marriage and Divorce statistics of the year 1924. Some of them run as follows:

Atlanta, Ga.	Marriages	3,350
	Divorces	1,845
Los Angeles	Marriages	16,605
	Divorces	7,882
Kansas City	Marriages	4,821
	Divorces	2,400
State of Ohio	Marriages	53,300
	Divorces	11,885
Denver	Marriages (approx.)	3,000
	Divorces filed	1,500
Cleveland	Marriages	10,132
	Divorces	5,256

Other cities mentioned in the report with a similar showing were Portland, Seattle, Memphis, Omaha, and many more.

According to this news article there were a little more than four times as many marriages as divorces in twenty of our principal cities and states. No doubt these were cities and states where divorce laws were liberal. In others where divorce laws are not liberal the evidence bobs up in the form of an astounding increase in the amounts of money being collected from husbands in non-support and failure to provide cases, in separations— which are simply a form of divorce by mutual consent— and in other cases where legal separation could not be had—a type of case, by the way, which leads to a great deal of adultery.

While average ratio of divorce to marriage in the cities and states mentioned in the report just cited was about one to four, it is to be noted that in the selected list given above, it is about one to two. There is no escaping the conclusion, if such facts be compared with the statistics of former years, that divorces and separations are

steadily increasing, and that if this continues, as it probably will for some time to come, there will be as many
divorce cases filed in some parts of the county as there
are marriage licenses granted.

This is practically the situation already. The reason
most persons don't realize it is that the statistics don't
cover the domestic relations situation in America. There
are thousands of divorces by mutual consent (separations) which never get into the statistics; there are thousands more entered into by informal arrangement out of
court. There are tens of thousands of cases where the
flat failure of the individual marriage is recorded in our
courts, not as "divorce" or "legal separation" but as
failure to provide, non-support, desertion, and the like.
*Materially and psychologically there is no reason why
these should not be classed as divorces—for they would
be just that if the parties to such marriages could have
their way,* and were not held together by circumstance,
children, and their legal obligations. The general name
which would cover all such cases, including divorces, separations, and all others are Marriages That Have Failed.
Under that title it would be conservative to say that there
are as many "divorces" annually as there are marriage
licenses granted.

So far as Denver is concerned I am sure, from a fairly
reliable survey, and from information constantly coming
to the officers of the Juvenile Court concerning social
conditions in Denver, that the number of separations,
including divorces, is now annually equal to the number
of marriage licenses granted. And what is true of Denver
is, as I have already said, just as true of other cities.

One thing that keeps a large number of unhappy marriages from ever getting to the divorce court is the unwillingness of both parties to break up a home in which

there are children. Legal obligations under the club of
the State add tremendously to this "unwillingness."   Another deterrent is the inertia of daily habit.   Couples
learn to endure each other though they never inwardly
consent to each other.   Still another deterrent from divorce is the economic dependence of the woman.   Most
divorce suits are brought by women; and if there is one
thing more certain than another about this whole business it is that in proportion as more and more women
find economic independence under the new order of things
now rising up around us, more and more women are
going to cut loose from mates they do not love, in spite
of all our creeds and conventions.   In other words, the
growing economic independence of women is one of the
biggest present causes of the increase in separations and
divorce, as well as the increase of unmarried unions and
"trial marriages"; and the figures are going to keep right
on growing for a time, by leaps and bounds, till some
sort of equilibrium is attained.

By the same token, however, the growing economic
independence of women will in time *decrease* the number
of divorces.   I have already dwelt on that point.   It
will cause women to be more particular and slower in
making a choice of a mate; it may also lead for a while
to a further increase in the number of unmarried unions;
and it will give women a position of independence in
marriage itself that will greatly reduce the friction and
the tension that now come from abject dependence.

In former days this friction and tension were both
present, but there was nothing that a woman could do
but submit to it, or else, by nagging, get the upper hand
of the man on whom she depended for her daily bread.
Most of our satire and humor about marriage is based
on this tyranny of weakness, by which women have from

time immemorial concealed from themselves and their mates their deadly sense of helpless dependence and half-conscious fear. Most women formerly took their dependence for granted. They had been trained from babyhood to take it for granted, as a natural and divinely established fact about a divinely ordered institution— God save the mark!

The friction and tension are still present, with the difference that they are beginning to find an outlet in action. The change is here, and those of us who are not ostriches will welcome it and hasten it. It may be that the faster the divorce figures increase from now on till we get rid of the old order, and the old maladjustments, the better. One qualification I must make to that statement is that divorce in families where there are children should be avoided if possible. But even so, there are homes where the tension between the parents is a ruinous thing for the children. It is often the lesser of two evils when such a home is broken up.

The effect of all this on the younger generation I have already indicated. Youth sees that Marriage, as is, or as convention would have it, is a failure; and youth is not in the same old hurry to try it on the same old basis,— though most couples, let us hope, will continue to live together with marriage though thousands are undeniably living together without it.

If failure comes to these unconventional unions, simple separation suffices, and they avoid thereby the complications of divorce. The big outside world knows little about this; the parties to such arrangements don't consult society. But the small groups in which these couples move and live know about such liaisons and accept them as a matter of course. In their own little worlds they are living "on the square"; and the very fact that society frowns on their way of life is an added bond between them. One live question now is, Will the time ever come when these numerous little groups will merge and form a big group, capable perhaps of imposing its will because *it* will be society?

I am conscious that in making these statements I may seem to lay myself open to the charge of advocating the changes and new practices I describe. I don't want to be misunderstood on that point because I have no wish either to be shocking or to put myself needlessly at outs with the conventions of society. This I have already tried to make clear, but it will do no harm to emphasize it here.

Let me say, in the first place, then, I am an observer with rather unusual opportunities to see things that most persons never come in contact with. As such, I record what I see. I record these changes because they are before my eyes; and I regard them tolerantly because they are a process of racial adjustment and social growth which is beyond any man's control. I believe in these processes of growth even though they may seem to my limited powers of judgment to be fraught with desperate peril for many individuals. I have faith that the process is, at bottom, a good one; and I think it should be the function of thinking people today not to try to check or thwart it—which would be silly, wrong, and impossible,—but rather to guide it, so that the percentage of individual mistakes and tragedies that may grow out of it will be reduced to a minimum. We need not let the wave submerge and capsize us; we can, by using good judgment, ride it and let it carry us forward. But to try to *stop* it by laws and denunciations is perfectly futile.

In the second place I am perfectly satisfied that some kind of a change is not only inevitable but needed; also that an attitude of mere dissent and hostility toward these new conditions conspicuously lacks common sense and real courage. True, many individuals who get involved in these new ways make mistakes; often they run amuck and require discipline and restraint. Often they do things of which I, for one, heartily disapprove. But they are at least *doing* something, however clumsily; and their chief offense is their lack of intelligent moderation rather than the wickedness and corruption of which they are accused. I therefore look with a charitable eye on errors of individual conduct that are an inevitable part of this social change. I have faith in their outcome, and in the inherent goodness of people, and in the essential divinity of the creative evolution back of it all. As for those of our younger generation who lose their heads in the meantime, they are often led astray by an excess of energy, high spirits, and bravery; together with a want of experience, knowledge, and understanding easily to be accounted for by the inadequacy of the education given them.

CHAPTER 20

My position about Marriage and my belief in its great possibilities I have already tried to make clear. But I don't doubt that many a reader of these pages will still find himself unable to reconcile support of Marriage with tolerance toward those who violate the conventional part of its code. Perhaps such persons will see less inconsistency in my view if I add that *one fundamental reason why I demand the respect of Society for men and women who live loyally together even though they may be unmarried is that the rights and happiness of unborn children are involved.* If the parents insist on doing things that way, it is clearly wrong for Society to visit on them a punishment that makes them regard it as necessary that they have no children. Very often they are precisely the kind of persons who ought to have children because they have desirable physical and mental qualities to transmit. Why force them, not merely to avoid the parenthood they often desire, but also, when accidental pregnancy takes place, to resort to the abortionist?

One thing that gives me a vivid sense of the irrationality and wickedness of this attitude is that I constantly see with my own eyes that in fully half of our conventional marriages men and women do not live loyally together, as that institution *assumes* they should and hypocritically *pretends* they do. I am soul-sick of these superstitions, hypocrisies and lies. Particularly sickening is it that the churches stubbornly maintain, in the teeth of the facts, that the trouble is caused by the corruption of our natures and the sinfulness of men and women, and not by the imperfection of the code under which they are expected to fulfill their sex needs and to produce children.

I demand, therefore, in the interests of unborn children, threatened with murder before their birth and with disgrace after it, that the social stigma now placed on unconventional unions be removed, to the end that such persons, be their way of living right or wrong, wise or unwise, may, if they wish, bring children into the world without fear that our conventional savagery will point at them the finger of scorn and shriek to the stars, "Unclean! Unclean! Y-a-a-ah! Unclean! Unclean!"—I demand further that such persons as they be dealt with by Society ahead of time through *education,* and not through persecution after the mischief is done, the persecution that drives them to despair, subterfuge, and even murder.

I am for children first, because I am for Society first; and the children of today are the Society of tomorrow. I insist, therefore, on the right of the child to be born, and that there be no "illegitimate" children. I demand for the unmarried mother, as a sacred channel of life, the same reverence and respect as for the married mother; for Maternity is a cosmic thing, and once it has come to pass our conventions must not be permitted to blaspheme it.

Always when I think of these things there passes before the eye of mind a pageant of the "wayward" girls I have dealt with in these many years. At this moment I am thinking of a girl who had had an abortion because of her fear of social disgrace.

She said to me, with a sadness I shall never forget, "I have done many things Society would consider sinful; but for all these I can forgive myself and forget them—

save one: that I didn't have my baby. Oh, why should people condemn a girl like me for doing a good and noble thing by bringing a child into the world, but let her go scot free if she does not bear it?"

I may add that her statement of the choice that lay before her is accurate. I have known many girls whose relations with men have been condoned by the segment of society they moved in, provided they didn't have a baby, and provided they put an end to life already quick within them.

Persons who, ignoring the rights of the unborn, talk glibly, with parrot squawks, about such recognition of unmarried unions being a "sanctioning of immorality" choose their words badly. If that be a sanctioning of immorality, what words can be found to characterize the murder of at least a million and a half unborn babies in this country yearly, and the murder of thousands upon thousands of newborn, natural, but "illegitimate" babies besides? These abortions and murders are the direct result of the refusal of society to sanction unmarried unions and to stop its persecution of unmarried mothers. If it be a choice between "sanctioning morality" and virtually compelling terrified girls to practice abortion and infanticide, by all means let us sanction immorality, or at least admit that it is the lesser of two evils. Mrs. Grundy won't like it, but I am confident God will—and millions of His murdered children will.

Does it seem unreal and incredible when I say that such things go on all the time in every walk of life? I suppose it does. But I, who am daily dealing with young people, frantic with fear, and ready to do *anything, anything* to escape the threatened ruin of their lives,— where can I find the words that will convince others that these things are so? My resources are limited as compared with what they should be; and yet the powers given by the State of Colorado to the Juvenile Court do enable me to bring through unscathed most of the girls who appeal to me. In one way or another I protect them from unmerited and unreasonable disgrace, provide for their confinements, and arrange for the care of their babies. Sometimes I provide a home for the child till the girl, later on, and without arousing suspicion, can adopt it.

Sometimes I permit childless people to adopt it. At such times some of the tragedies that result are almost beyond belief, for of all things I find it hard to do, I think separating an agonized mother from her newborn child is the hardest. Sometimes they don't seem to feel it at the time; but later—months and years later—they come back to me and plead with me to give them back their babies. And I can't. All I can do is reason with them, allay the pain as best I may, and send them away. Later they marry and have babies they can keep; but they never forget the one they could not keep, who is out somewhere in the world, they don't know where.

Here is a letter that came from one unmarried girl— who had given birth to a child, and who was therefore "immoral." The letter was written to the matron of the home that had arranged for the adoption of the baby after its birth. Read it carefully, and if you find the immorality in it, let me know; it has escaped my notice:

"It has seemed to me an endless eternity since I gave you my baby Sunday afternoon and I felt that I must write and ask you if the woman of whom you told me took my baby? And is the little darling all right without my nursing her? I have worried unceasingly about her taking the bottle.

"O I can't tell you how I loved her. God alone knows that my heart is breaking—but what can I do? My arms ache for her—and she is mine, mine, mine. I don't know how I did it but I know it is best for her. Sometimes I wish I might have died first. If only they had given me time to think about it—but Dad knew a quick decision was best I suppose.

"Won't you give the enclosed letter to my baby's new mother? I am leaving it unsealed in order that you may read it and see for yourself that I did not reveal my identity.

"O, won't you pray for her and for me? It is hard—God knows how I want her, and I beg that you write and tell me how she is and whether her new mother is good to her."

Here is her letter to the foster mother of her child:

"Dear Unknown Friend:

"That I should have given my baby into other arms, and other care, does not mean that I did not love her, and I wanted to tell you that it was only a deeper love than I can express that induced me to make such a sacrifice.

"And too, my darling came into the world through the strength of my love for her father because my feeling for him was not a weakness . . .

"But most of all I pray that God will watch over my baby, and build a shrine for her in your heart, and the heart of her new father, that shall be everlasting and beautiful. God surely ordained that I give her into your keeping, and I trust you to watch tenderly and carefully over her.

"Every night as the weary, heart hungry days pass,

I shall look out into the night, and know that my baby is warm and happy, and has all the lovely material possessions for which she could scarcely help inheriting a desire. I wanted lovely things and of necessity went without, and I beg of you that my baby should have them.

"Somewhere, sometime, someone may bring comfort to the longing in my heart, and in the meantime I trust you and God to bring sunshine and love into my baby's life.—"

I am happy to be able to say that in this case through our good offices, the girl finally recovered her baby. The woman who had adopted it was so affected by her grief that she consented to give the child up, though she herself had come to love it as her own; and she did this at the cost of pain and sacrifice from the agony of which she has not yet recovered.

The girl's father, however, was so angered by the step she made in taking back her child, that he informed his friends of the "disgrace" that had happened in his family; and today the girl is bravely bringing up her own child in the teeth of the united disapproval of the social set in which she moves. She is a university girl of fine church and home training. The baby's father is married to another woman, has children of his own, and earns a small salary. Therefore he can do little to help.

The trouble started when the girl and the boy were students at one of our Universities. She went to several college-set drinking parties where there were occasional sex experiences, and finally met a boy with whom she fell genuinely in love, and by whom she became a mother. I am unable to see that the complications, brought about by her ignorance and her consequent misconduct, were in any way helped by the social pressure which forced her to do an unnatural thing, in giving up her child, and which is now penalizing her because she has had the strength of character and the courage to do the natural and the right thing. Ordinarily of course it would have been impossible for her ever to see her baby again after another woman had legal possession of it; a rare turn of fortune favored her in that.

As for her mistakes, they are in the past and not in the present. She is through with them just as if, having had the measles, she had gotten over them. Because she was sick then, how silly to say she is sick now. Because she was "immoral" then it is equally silly to insist she is "immoral" now; yet into such inconsistencies and cruelties have we been led by conventional superstition, hypocrisies and lies. She is accepting her responsibility as a mother, though under needlessly difficult conditions; and I can see no difference, therefore, between her and any other mother, except that hers is the greater sacrifice. It is a perfect example of the witch-hunting frame of mind which we fondly imagine we have outgrown. In such matters we are simply savages without the savage virtues.

The courses into which society and its conventions drive these girls sometimes result in complications so strange that only a book of fact would dare to print them. They would never be accepted in fiction. They lack probability. For instance:

A few years ago a girl of eighteen entered my chambers and wished to talk with me alone. She opened her purse and showed me that it contained a large sum of money. The money had been given her so that she might with it pay an abortionist for his services.

Her name, let us say, was Mary Jessup. She was one of the type that matures early, and was beautiful and attractive. Recently she had gotten into an intrigue with a wealthy Denver business man who was married and had children. To prevent scandal and the ruin to himself and the girl which would ensue, he had supplied her with money for an abortion. She, however, decided to talk with me first; and I persuaded her, after much argument, that it would be better for her to bear her child.

When I had won her over to that I had next to persuade her to let me confide the facts to her mother. From this she shrank hysterically; but I told her that parents seldom act with as much severity as their children fear, and at last she consented. The mother, who was a woman of intelligence, and who was wealthy besides, did just as I had expected. When the first shock was over, she rose to the occasion and stood by her daughter. After several conferences with me she gave out to her friends that her daughter was making a trip abroad. Instead the girl went to a private maternity home.

A few months before Mary Jessup came to me I had had a visit from another woman. She was a society star, the wife of a young and successful business man. The name was Richardson. She had no children, and she and her husband were thinking of adopting one. But they were unwilling that the child should ever learn that it was not really theirs; and she therefore wanted to know if she could not adopt a very young baby under circumstances that would make her whole circle of friends believe it was really her own. I had met situations like this many times.

I told Mrs. Richardson that it could be done, and that

when a newborn baby was available for adoption I would send her word as to what she was to do.

Now I sent for her, told her that I had in mind a child that would be born several months later, and agreed with her that she was to inform her friends that she was pregnant. She was to engage a physician who was in my confidence, and this doctor was to take care of her during her pretended pregnancy and confinement.

When the time came, she had her fictitious confinement, and the newborn child was secretly delivered to her from the hospital where it had been born. Neither she nor the doctor knew where it had come from, and the real mother of the child did not know where it had gone.

I was the only person who knew all the particulars; and now I put only one obligation on the foster parents, that they were at once to make a will leaving a portion of their property to the child, and that they promise never to disinherit it.

Two months passed, then one day in walked Mary Jessup. With her was another girl, a close friend, to whom she had confided the fact that she had had a baby.

Simply as a matter of routine precaution I now asked her friend to step outside. As soon as we were alone Mary burst into tears. Her chum's married sister, she said, had recently had a baby whose age was about the same as that of her own child. She had gone with her chum to congratulate the mother; she had seen the baby and held it in her arms; and since then she had gone to see it many times; and the sight of it had awakened in her an overwhelming longing for her own child.

"It's the dearest baby in the world," she said. "She lets me take it up and love it; and I love it as if it were my own. The more I look at it the more I want my baby. I want my baby back; I'm crazy for it; I'll die if I can't get it; I can't sleep; I can't think. I feel like a criminal that I gave my baby up; you must get it back for me. When I see how happy Mrs. Richardson is with her baby I know what I have given up."

I looked at her in a daze. Used as I am to strange situations, the room seemed to reel around me. She had, unknowingly, fondled her own baby; and I had not even known that the two women knew each other.

I controlled myself as best I could. Then I tried to explain to her that what she asked couldn't be done; that I had warned her in the first place that she might have this desire come upon her; and that the woman who now had her baby had learned to love it, and would certainly insist on keeping it.

She called her chum into the room, and they tearfully pleaded together. "Can't you persuade the woman to give it back," asked the chum. "We would pay her whatever she asked; and my sister, Mrs. Richardson, would lend us the money."

"I'll see what can be done," I said. "But I can't give you much hope."

The girls came to me, day after day. Finally Mary's mother came. "I ought never to have persuaded her to let the child go," she said, "and I want to right this wrong I have done. I have come to tell you that I am going to employ a lawyer to trace the child and take legal steps to set aside the adoption."

Of course that thoroughly alarmed me. I made her promise that she would do nothing till I had had an opportunity to talk with the child's foster mother. She agreed to this.

When I saw Mrs. Richardson I laid the case before

her, without naming any names, of course. I told her what the child's mother had said; how she had pleaded; how she longed for her baby, how she could not sleep. But at the thought of giving up the baby Mrs. Richardson grew hysterical.

"Don't you see how impossible it is?" she cried. "It is like my own child. I love it. And besides all my friends think it is my own. What would people say? What would my sister think? What would my family say—to my giving up my own baby?"

"Yes," I said. "It is impossible."

So, with a heavy heart, I sent the next day for Mary Jessup. "I hope," I said, "that you have faith in me. You did not want to have your baby in the first place; and you did it because I persuaded you that it was right. If it had not been for me there would have been no baby. In that event you would have been spared this grief, but the woman who has the baby would not have had the joy it is bringing into her life. The legal rights are hers; and I am sure that no matter what you do you cannot get the baby back. She will not give it up. I want you not to attempt to get it back. There are things about this case that I cannot explain to you; but I can assure you that any attempt on your part to get your baby back would cause for you, and for people you would love if you knew them, a tragedy so awful that this trial you are now going through would be a pin prick beside it. Some day you will marry and have babies you can keep. Meantime, be assured that your baby has a mother as sweet and beautiful as you are yourself, and who loves it as dearly as you do. You will know, better than you think, how happy is the lot in life that has come to your child, and to another woman into whose sad life you have brought the greatest happiness that ever came to her."

Many other talks I had with her. But at last one day she came, and looking me in the eye, she said with quivering lips, "I have decided you are right. Tell her she can have my baby." But all unknown to her or the foster mother she went right on loving it during her frequent visits to the home of the Richardsons.

Many persons wonder at the way I sometimes flout the conventions of society, and the lightness with which I sometimes hold them in my judicial work. Perhaps the story I have just told may help to explain my attitude. I deal with the realities of life; and no man can do that for twenty-five years and have much respect for its unrealities, its shams and its hypocrisies. For these he can feel only a consuming hatred. Make no mistake about it. The wrong attitude of society toward the unmarried mother and the illegitimate child was the direct and needless cause of the tragedy I have just recounted. The girl was not the agent but the victim. Such tragedies pass through my court, and my heart, not once in a while, but daily; not often but always. The girl who wants her baby back haunts these court rooms like a specter. She is always with us.

CHAPTER 21

Babies weave a strange pattern in the lives of people; and the pattern becomes the stranger because there are some who want babies desperately and can't have children of their own, while others who can have children all too easily fear to have them. Generally the complications, whenever they arise, are based absolutely on society's unwillingness to permit people to work out their own problems in their own way, and on the consequent necessity for those who take their own path to keep the secret hid. Some of the most dramatic literature in the world, as I have said, is built on this fact, but comparatively little of it questions the rightness, necessity, or wisdom of these taboos.

A woman came to me who several years previously had married a foreigner. He was a younger son and had come to America to "win to hearth and saddle of his own," as Kipling puts it. A few years after this marriage several deaths in his family brought him much nearer than he had been to inheritance of a title that was in his family. He went to Europe in consequence, to take action in several matters that related to this prospect.

In the meantime his wife was uneasy. She knew the importance a man of his ideas, bred in an old-world tradition, would attach to having an heir to his title. And though he loved her, she saw evidences of discontent which convinced her that he might, if necessary, divorce her in order to marry someone who could give him children.

She therefore decided to take action. As soon as he was in Europe she wrote him that to her own great surprise she had discovered that she was far advanced in a pregnancy she had not suspected, and that in all probability there would be a baby born to them before his return from Europe.

She waited long enough to receive his enthusiastic reply by cable; then went to a distant city, sought a foundling home, and chose a very young baby, which she adopted. Later she returned home and told her friends that her baby had been born during her absence in the East. The husband returned home, and was delighted with his new son.

A year later the superintendent of the foundling home died, and as he was the only person in her confidence, the secret was now apparently her own.

For seven years she lived in greatest happiness. The husband worshiped the boy he thought was his son, and there was no cloud on the horizon.

Then, one day as he was leaving the house to go to his office, the mailman handed him some letters. She, standing beside him, saw on one envelope the return address of the foundling home from which she had obtained her child. A shock of fear went through her, but she reached out quickly and took the letter from his hand, saying carelessly, "Oh, there is the letter the club has been expecting. What other letters are there? Anything more for me?"

He gave her one other, kissed her and his son good-by, and went off. "I felt," she said in telling me the story later, "like a thief, an awful woman; and I knew, then, too, what the boy had come to mean to us."

The letter proved to be merely a formal note of inquiry. The home was compiling some statistics, and the present superintendent was delighted to know that one of their children had been taken by so prominent a woman. Would she write him an account of the child for inclusion in their records.

The other letter her husband had left with her was from her mother, and seems an odd confirmation of the belief that adopted children often come to resemble their foster parents as a result, possibly, of a similar attitude of mind built up by a similar mode of life. "We have so enjoyed John's visit," said the letter. "He grows more like his father every day. Even the little things they do are strangely similar."

In great distress and fear she came to me with the two letters. She had not dared to reply to the one from the foundling home. "If my husband ever finds this out," she said to me, "it will be my ruin."

I told her I would reply to the letter, and that I would look into the matter on my next trip through the city where the home was. A few weeks later I started on a lecture tour which brought me there; and looking up the superintendent I found him a young, sympathetic and intelligent man. I asked him, "How did you get this name and address? You are not supposed to have it."

He brought out his record book. Opposite the name of the girl who had borne the child was the name of the woman who had adopted it, written in lightly in lead-pencil. Undoubtedly it was put there as a temporary memorandum by the former superintendent, with the intention of erasing it later.

I said to the young superintendent, "There are certain things about this case I can't explain to you, but I want you to forget that name, and erase it from the records."

He instantly picked up an eraser, and he did a thorough job with it. Then he dug up the carbon copy of the letter he had written her, and together we watched it reduced to ashes. "I think I understand," he said. "Tell the lady not to worry. Her secret is safe with me."

Later, I said to the woman, "Have your husband make a will. If you should die before he does and this should afterward become known, the child would inherit nothing. You thought this knowledge died with the first superintendent, but it didn't. We hope it will die with the present superintendent, but it may not in spite of all our precautions." She acted on my advice, and so the matter stands. Thus far, all is well; but coincidence can play strange tricks. The young man is a member of the younger set in a distant city to which his people recently moved.

Perhaps some of my readers may feel that it was not proper for me to aid this woman in safeguarding the deceit she was practicing on her husband, since a great wrong had been done him. But the wrong had already been done, it was accomplished years before; and I had nothing whatever to do with that part of it. It was now a choice between letting things remain as they were and wrecking three lives, including the life of an innocent child who was in no way responsible for what had happened, by a violation of this woman's confidence, or at least a refusal to heed her call for help. In my judgment such a course would have been neither moral nor humane; it would have been unspeakably savage. I therefore offer no apology for helping the woman to maintain a condition which, in practice, was making for the happiness of all concerned. I could not betray her or refuse to help her under such conditions however strongly I might disapprove of the thing she had done;

nor could I impose my standards on her to her certain destruction and the destruction of her home. Rather, I am satisfied, it was far better to let matters remain as they were, and thus make the situation as safe for all concerned as possible.

I recall an interesting story of a wife who was barren. She loved her husband and he her; but they had been childless through many years of marriage.

She came to me for advice. She said that she had an unmarried girl friend visiting her; and that this friend was willing, because she loved her, to become the mother of the child she, the wife, could not herself conceive. She wanted to know from me what was the legal bearing of the matter. Would it be possible for them to sign papers in which her friend would relinquish all claim to the prospective child?

I told her such an agreement probably would not be legal, and that if presented in court it would doubtless be annulled as contrary to public policy.

She wanted to know if I thought she could rely on her friend's promise not to claim the child. I told her I thought it very unlikely, because the mother urge, once aroused, is likely to be stronger than any promise. No one, I said, could predict what her friend might do.

She heard me in silence. At last she rose. "Still," she said, "I think I shall trust her. When she gets married she can have babies of her own. And I know she loves me."

I am sorry I can't conclude the story; for the woman never came back. I should be interested to know the result of that strange bargain.

But I knew of another bargain equally strange, the termination of which I can here record. Nora was what

I may call a raving beauty. She combined the finest qualities, mental and physical, of her Irish father and her Scandinavian mother. Her hair was a raven black, and her eyes were blue, and she had the most beautiful mouth and perfect teeth I have ever seen in a human being.

When she called at the court she explained to my wife, as many of these girls do, that she would see no one but me. And this, briefly, was the story she confided to me:

She was the unmarried mother of a baby, about whose beauty and sweetness she paused for fifteen minutes in her tale to tell me. But this darling child was about to be taken from her through the circumstances of the very intrigue that had resulted in its birth.

Her affair had been with the husband of a friend of hers. When her pregnancy became evident she and the man decided to confess the whole affair to his wife. The wife proved to be tolerant, and herself proposed a way out of the difficulty. The three of them were to take an apartment in a part of the city where they were not known. At the time of confinement Nora was to be passed off as the wife, and the wife was to play the part of a midwife nurse.

This program they carried out to the letter, and the child's birth was officially registered at the City Hall in Denver as the child of the real husband and wife. The fact that Nora's mother was in the East on a long visit made this arrangement the easier to carry out. But a continuance of the deception was, of course, necessary, and it was therefore agreed that the man and his wife should continue to pass the child off as their own.

This worked very well till Nora suddenly realized that the other woman was taking toward the baby an attitude of possession that to Nora's maternal instinct became offensive.

This led to quarrels between the two women, with the result that Nora one day kidnaped her own child, and now, at the time of her coming to me, had it under cover.

She had now come to me because the other woman was threatening to sue her in the Juvenile Court for the possession of the child. She said the only proof she would be able to offer of the truth of her story was the physician who had attended her in her confinement.

Talk about the judgment of Solomon!—Well, I saw that I was in for it; and after further consultation with Nora, I sent for the other woman, whom I will call Mrs. Hall. Mrs. Hall assured me that Nora was not playing fair, and that she had promised her the possession of the child when it should be born. This was to be her reward for her charitable attitude.

"I have always been eager to have a girl baby," said Mrs. Hall, "because I already have two boys; and I would rather have one conceived by my husband, even though I was not the one to bring it into the world."

Nora denied that she had made any such agreement. In my judgment she did probably make such a promise under the stress of her first fears, and then later regretted it; but who can blame her?

I pointed this out to Mrs. Hall, urged upon her that Nora's maternal instinct for her own child must have the right of way, and finally got her to consent that Nora should have her child.

I may add that the fact that the Halls were still living in a strange neighborhood, and more or less under cover, without their friends knowing that they had a baby, did away with the embarrassment that would ordinarily have resulted for the Halls, and thus aided in the settlement. Had the birth of the child become known I hate to think of the snarl I would then have had on my hands.

My next task was to take Nora's mother in hand, break the news of Nora's escapade to her, and reconcile her to her daughter. In this I succeeded. The mother and daughter then took the baby, and passed it off as the child of a relative of theirs who had died.

Since they belonged to Denver's "finest" and were people of wealth, it was easy for Nora and her mother a little later to make a trip to Europe, accompanied by the baby. In England she met a young man who was the younger son of an English nobleman and fell in love with him. To him she confessed the whole story as I have told it, with the added fact that long before this affair she had been married and divorced.

What happened then seems to me extremely interesting and significant. The young man didn't take the old traditional masculine attitude that he must marry a "Pure Woman"; and that the fact of her having had intimate relations with another living man "spoiled" her for him. Instead he said in effect, "It makes no difference to me whether you had this child by your former husband or by one who was not your husband. I love you and I love this baby."

And so they were married. But the old dowager who was the mid-Victorian mother of the young man was suspicious. She wanted to know more about that divorce; and when it was granted, and all that. So they showed her the decree. And I never thought it advisable to ask Nora what they did to the date it bore. But from Nora's occasional letters to my wife and me telling of her happiness and the growing beauty of her lovely child

I am sure that what the dear old dowager does not know will not hurt her.

I particularly want to call attention here to the attitude of this young English nobleman. It is not the first instance that has come to my attention where men have married girls who have had children by other men. The fact is worth pondering, for this attitude on the part of men was an extremely rare occurrence even twenty years ago. The notion was once held universally that such a girl as Nora was defiled and unclean. What has become of that once universal male conviction? I can answer the question very shortly. We are learning to think differently. What the man recognized was the simple, bare, stark fact that motherhood is motherhood, and that Nora's motherhood was a sacred and normal thing regardless of any human code whatever. I have had in my experience an astonishing number of cases where an unmarried girl, pregnant by one man, was loved *and married* by another, with full knowledge of the truth. Such marriages, within my experience, have turned out with perhaps larger proportion of successes than ordinary marriages. I once discussed this with a youth who had married such a girl. In explaining his attitude he said to me, "Why, if Sarah had her child by a husband now dead or divorced from her, I'd love her just the same, wouldn't I; and I'd marry her, wouldn't I? What's the difference? She's the same now as she would be then." This attitude of mind among modern youth is far more common than is ordinarily known.

Only a few years ago there was a Denver girl who became pregnant, and the story became public property, and got into the newspapers. And what was the result? Simply that the girl received by mail 150 offers of marriage from men in Denver and in other parts of the country; and that she accepted one of those offers. Her husband is a millionaire, and the marriage is apparently a very happy one.

These are facts. Similar facts come to light in my court daily. What are we going to do about it? How are we going to interpret them? Are we going to interpret them constructively, and see a positive and good meaning in them, or are we to rage against them with futile bigotry?

There was a girl, the daughter of a minister in the East, who came to Denver to be cured of tuberculosis. The family physician had diagnosed it as tuberculosis to her parents; and he thus concealed from them the fact that she was pregnant, though unmarried. As her father was a man of extremely rigid ideas, of the type called "moral," it was out of the question for his daughter to confide in him.

A wealthy Denver woman, the wife of a banker, called to see me about this case, she being in the girl's confidence. She told me that she had a friend who was wealthy, and unmarried, who would be glad to adopt the child; and wanted to know if it could be arranged. I told her it could, but that I must satisfy myself first about her friend. So the two women came to see me, and finally we drew up the necessary papers.

Months later the woman who had adopted the baby came to me and said, "Judge, I love that baby; I shall always love and care for it. But having it has aroused in me a desire to have a baby of my own. You understand; I don't want to marry; I don't need a husband or want to live with one. I enjoy my independence. But I ask you, would it be wrong for me to have a baby of my own to love—any more wrong than to take someone else's illegitimate baby and care for it?"

"I can't answer that for you," I said. "As a judge I can't give you advice that is contrary to the standards of society. It is unfortunate that you don't want to be married; but the only place where you can find an answer to your question is in your own heart. Do what you honestly think is right."

In a year she came back. "Judge," she said, "the matter I spoke to you about need no longer disturb your judicial morals. I have carried out the plan I had in mind. I am going to have a baby. I selected the father of my child carefully. He is a young man who is studying for the ministry. I told him I was not enamored of him or any other man and never would be. I said I was a woman, and was entitled to have a child if I wanted one. I told him I had decided that I wished him to be the father of my child, if he considered such a course right for himself. We talked it over, honestly, and he decided that it would be right.

"The father of my baby understands that he has now gone out of my life completely; that he has no claim on me, or I on him. What I want of you now is to arrange so that I can have my baby without scandal or loss of self-respect. I understand that you have helped many women in embarrassing difficulties; and there is no reason why you should not do it for me. That is true, is it not?"

"Since you have gotten yourself into this situation," I said, "I don't see how I can do otherwise than help you; but please understand that I am doing this for the sake of your unborn child.

"Tell your friends that you are going on a trip. Go away somewhere where you are unknown and have your baby. Put it in good hands to be taken care of, and return to Denver. Then announce that you have decided to adopt another child. Have the baby brought here. A woman will bring it to my court saying that it has been abandoned by its mother. I will say that you have asked me to find you another foster child, and will send you word that I have one here for you to look at. You and your friends can then come and examine the baby, and I will have the adoption papers made out."

She carried out this plan to the letter; she and her friends in due time exclaimed with delight over the baby —which was a very fine one, as might be expected in such a case; they congratulated her on my having made such a find for her; and she adopted her own flesh and blood. She and the two children are today living in greatest happiness in a city in the Far West to which they later moved.

With regard to this case, as to others I have told of, every individual is entitled to his own opinion. My object in recording the facts is to show what is happening under the surfaces of human life; and to point out that when facts collide with theories and theologies, it is likely to go hard with the theories and theologies; and that it is more profitable to accept facts and use them constructively than it is to scold about them. You may be right and I may be wrong about theories, but the facts are not arguable. They are simply there. I've got them; and because of our confidential personal contacts I don't believe there is another place in the world where there are so many of them lying around loose, visible to the eye and audible to the ear, as there are in the Juvenile Court of Denver. Personally, I've made up my mind to accept them as they are and make the best of them; and it is my hope that the presentation of a few of them here may lead others to do likewise. For only by accepting facts as facts can any of us know the truth about society as it really is, and not as the smug complacency of ignorance and wilful blindness thinks it is.

CHAPTER 22

The question is often asked, "Would not the sanctioning by Society of unmarried unions simply put an end to Marriage as we now understand it? Wouldn't it throw Marriage into the discard?"

The obvious answer to this is that under such a condition the thing we now call unmarried unions would be unmarried unions no longer. There would be simply a changed and more flexible form of Marriage. There would still be conventional and legal restraints in marriage, but they would be of a different kind.

Whether such a change in our marriage code would be safe and desirable is the very point at issue.

Only a few years back a divorced woman was hardly more respectable than if she had been some man's mistress. Today that stigma has virtually disappeared. And this change has come about silently, in the face of every sort of opposition. Will a similar change come about in our attitude toward unmarried unions?

"Preposterous!" say some. "Why, what would become of the children of these unmarried unions? It would rob children of all protection." A distinctly humorous argument, that, from a Society that puts the brand of illegitimacy and disgrace on those very children.

The obvious retort is, What becomes of the children of conventional and legal marriages? Who looks after *them?* What guarantee have *they* of "protection"? In a recent survey of one American city it was found that 32 per cent of the children in a certain school, all of them "legitimate," had no father at home. I am running up against this situation all the time. The assumption that our present form of legal marriage automatically "protects" the future of children would be funny if it were not tragic.

Marriage, as at present ordered, does not guarantee to any child the benefit of its parents. There is no such magic of any kind of contract or ceremony. There is such magic, however, in an open and unforbidden *love* between parents, physically and mentally fit, whether they are legally married, as they preferably should be, or not. That is the only thing that can sanctify the home and protect the children; and without it there can be no such thing as real marriage. It is the very essence of marriage.

If this be true, it may surely be held that if there be any law or custom in Society that except when clearly necessary, interferes with, forbids, or destroys the relationship of open love between the parents of children, that law or custom should be looked to.

The same may be said of those of our laws which, by forbidding "Birth Control" force the inauspicious and inexpedient conception of children by men and women who don't want them or can't take care of and protect them.

These laws virtually insist on abstinence as the only legal contraceptive. Why not be honest and admit that men and women will not practice abstinence, will not confine the sex relationship to mere procreation, and will violate that law so long as it stands in the statute books?

It is a fact of course that, with or without marriage, there are and always will be some persons who will shirk the responsibilities of parenthood. This is true because such persons are biologically inadequate and maladjusted, and therefore shirk the normal responsibilities of living. There will always be weaklings who find the right way too hard for them, where a normally constituted, energetic human being would find it practicable enough.

Birth Control would cut down the number of these people to a minimum by enabling the incompetents of the race to satisfy their sex needs without danger of producing children whom they would not be competent to care for, and to whom they would have no worthwhile physical or mental qualities to transmit. Birth Control would cut down the number of these degenerates by causing their degeneracy to stop with them.

Under present conditions the world is like an unweeded garden. No sane gardener would sow tares with his wheat. But our insane gardener, Tradition, demands that we sow 90 per cent tares and 10 per cent wheat. And so our garden of Civilization is a wilderness.

But in the meantime we have to reckon with the federal law, formulated by Anthony Comstock, and supported today by thousands of good and conscientious persons who would be horrified if they had the slightest conception of what lay back of the Comstock psychology. This law forbids our race to pick and choose the conditions under which it shall bring its own posterity into the world; and it identifies contraception with obscenity. It is too high a price to pay for a fake morality, an ethical goldbrick, foisted on us by an unclean fanaticism and the infamous logic that we can have a better world through ignorance, darkness, and superstition, rather than through knowledge, liberty, light, and love.

The stock argument against Birth Control, as a safeguard against the conception of unwanted children, is that married people would have too few children, thinking of their own ease, while the unmarried would be free to indulge themselves without fear of consequences.

The notion that most people don't want children simply isn't true. My list of applications for children to adopt is always much larger than I can meet. On the other hand the notion that they don't want too many is quite true. But who is to decide that for them? Is this a free country or isn't it? As for the unmarried ones, it would seem evident from our illegitimacy and abortion figures that they keep right on indulging themselves regardless of whether they fear the consequences or not. The fear of pregnancy is clearly not an effective deterrent. Why, then, should we add to the unhappiness in the world by forcing on these people helpless children who, though innocent, will have to suffer for the dereliction of their parents?

A very nice but very foolish woman told me once that she objected to Birth Control because it would enable people to indulge in the sex relation for merely "sensual" reasons; as if they had ever, since the dawn of time indulged in it for any other reason. "Sensuality" is a big word. It does not lack a spiritual connotation when it includes love. What an art we make of hypocrisy! What a mess we make of Life!

Here is what one girl said to me about that; and I advise some of our moralists, and advocates of the double standard, and spouters about the chastity of women, who wink at the licentiousness of men, to put it in their collective pipe and smoke it:

"There can never be an equality between girls and boys," said this girl, "until girls can, through knowledge of contraceptive methods, place themselves on a par with boys; *so that if the girl makes the same mistake that a boy does she runs no more risk of ruin than a boy does.*"

I would not expect any hypocritical moralist to feel the very sharp cutting edge of that, for such people are devoid of conscience; but any man of intelligence ought to find it sharp enough to shave with. It's as good as a bill of rights. She might have added that under such a program the women of this world would establish a *single* standard of sex morality that would have few points of similarity to the standard which is now preempted by the males of the species. That new single standard would have two notable characteristics: It would be candid and it would be sane; and most of the present slough of secrecy, crime, and perversion in which we now live would thus be drained to the point of becoming decent, under the action of air and sunlight.

The risk of pregnancy indeed!—By what law of right do we, under an "obscenity" law forbidding contraception, place it *all* on the woman!—Hypocrisy? Satan himself must visit us for lessons!

If I have not by this time succeeded in making it clear that this new freedom in the relations of the sexes would not mean Free Love; and that it would be predicated, *not on the destruction of the institution of Marriage, but rather on an extension and alteration of its prerogatives within lines that would permit a hitherto unknown measure of human freedom and happiness,* then I have written to little purpose.

I am concerned, however, lest in attacking the rigid traditions we at present hold, I seem to be advocating a reckless sweeping away of all restraint. In pleading for any special cause one always runs that risk. I am aware that radical changes have their dangers, and I urge nothing sudden or extreme. Indeed, I ask for nothing of any sort, save a perceptible degree of tolerance and vision on the part of thinking people who might other-

wise try vainly to resist what they cannot stop, and so
cause added unhappiness both to themselves and those
dear to them. The change is coming. I can but predict
it in the light of my facts, and so help to clear a path
for it by making a few more minds receptive and hospitable to it.

Love is a sacred thing; and like every other vital principle of life, it is a paradox. Freedom is the only chain
that can bind it in captivity. That it be untethered and
free to depart when it will is the one guarantee that the
desire to flee will not become an obsession fed by its
own impotence. Always it must be able to say, "I
could if I would. Nothing holds me but my own wish.
I love because I want to—not because I have to seem to."

Such is the freedom I bespeak for all marriages and
such the freedom I predict.

Inconstancy—Yes, we shall always have inconstancy,
—though I object to calling it that. I think "mistakes"
would be the better word. Men and women will always
make *mistakes* in their choices of each other. It happens
in the best-regulated families. How could it be otherwise
when they have to stake their whole lives on the outcome
of a single throw, and under conditions that make their
knowledge of each other's traits the wildest sort of guess
work? If they guess right, well and good. If wrong,
they are out of luck.

The more reason for some form of marriage dissolvable
without inconvenience or discredit. At its very worst I
cannot conceive of the evils of such a system—and I
suppose it would not be perfect—amounting to more than
a pin-prick as compared with the monstrous and tragic
drama of Sex in Chains, which is being enacted by human
society today, with the world for a stage, men and women
for players, and weeping cohorts of angels, perhaps, for

witnesses. One act of that drama is the Butchery of Babies, or the Out-Heroding of Herod. You can guess the others. One you might call the Vice of Commercialized Virtue, which would show how organized puritanism lives on the sins of people, and holds them in line with the Whip of Superstition.

The trouble with most of us is that we won't take a chance with Human Nature. Perhaps that's why I'm rather an exception. I'm a born gambler when it comes to betting on these Humans; and I always win. The secret of loading the dice in this game is simple: You remember always that the loneliest thing in the world is the Human Soul; that it hates to travel in the dark; and that if you reach out a hand to it in the dim regions where it lives, it will seize it and hold on.

Just what happens when Society and the Church interfere in the relations of men and women with uniform rules to which all lives are supposed to conform themselves, is well illustrated in the story of a woman whom I shall call Mrs. Herring. It runs strikingly parallel to another story I have already related, but I give it here. It illustrates the point I am trying to make.

Mrs. Herring before her marriage was a stenographer, pretty, wholesome, and "innocent"—that is to say grossly ignorant of the most elementary facts about sex. She told me in court that before her marriage the Roman Catholic priest who performed the ceremony told her the truth in private. The information shocked her, and gave her a feeling of repulsion toward the whole matter from which she never recovered. However, she was married, and submitted with what grace she could to what, rightly under the circumstances, she regarded as a repulsive ordeal.

One warning the priest strongly emphasized in his

instructions was that she must never "interfere with nature." Birth Control, he assured her, was contrary to the will of God.

Well, as a result of that warning, which she swallowed whole, she bore three children, close together. As her husband's income was very small, three was a whole lot too many. When the fourth baby was evidently on the way, therefore, there was trouble. Mr. Herring burst into a fury of wrath at the news that his wife was pregnant. He threatened to leave her and the whole family forthwith unless she would go to an abortionist. She did this—three times in the next three years. Abortions became a custom in the Herring family. It must not practice birth control, since that was a sin, and an interference with nature and with God's purposes—rather remarkable that human beings could interfere with the plans of the Maker of the Universe, is it not?—but abortion would do very well as a substitute for it. So, in three successive pregnancies, she had her living but unborn children killed before their birth.

"Don't you think it would be better," I asked "not to permit life to start than to take life after it starts?"

"Yes," she said, "I do. But he demanded his marital rights in spite of my protests; and the priest says it is sinful to interfere with the beginning of life, and also that I must obey my husband. So I submitted. But later, how could I bear to lose my husband's love, and his support for our three living children?"

In other words, she yielded to fear, and to the economic pressure that threatened her living children, and largely for their sakes she killed three that were unborn, I don't think the question as to whether this was a case of superstitious terror or of religion needs extended comment here.

Another woman with whom I talked said to me, "*I* practice birth control, whether it's forbidden or not, and nobody is going to scare me out of it. Believe me, those who do the forbidding don't bear the kids. We women do!"

All of which would seem to indicate that our mechanical and "materialistic" age is at least doing something for people's minds.

The story of the Smith family attracted a good deal of attention in Denver not long ago. The father of the Smith family was a man with a highly developed conscience and no ballast in the way of ability to think straight. He had been told by his religious mentor that birth control was a sin, and that *abstinence* was the only remedy for him if he didn't want more children than he could support. Since one had arrived nearly every year of his married life more children would have been a calamity in that family, and since abstinence didn't seem practicable, and wasn't, Smith came to our court for information about contraception. Such information could not legally be imparted here, and I sent him to a medical clinic, where, owing to their fear of the law, they played safe, and refused the information. Smith settled his problem by killing himself.

Then friends raised a fund for temporary alleviation of the Smith family's material wants—since they were deprived of their natural supporter.

Thus between the Church and the Law, the Smith family was crushed to something like a pulp.

A degenerate family by the name of Clark was another. The Clark family grew steadily, at the rate of one about every year. They didn't want to. They couldn't afford it. It wasn't fair to the other Clarks when a new one arrived; but since it was a choice between that and going to hell if you practiced contraception, or undertaking an impossible asceticism if you abstained, the Clarks multiplied and replenished the earth.

Today one of the Clark boys is in prison for a degrading sex crime against a child. He is a degenerate. The sum of sin and misery produced in that family by the lie they had to live has laid a burden on society beyond calculation; for the whole run of them are potential criminals who ought never to have been born, and who never would have been born if the poverty-stricken parents, with their own evil inheritance, had had full and effective knowledge of contraceptive methods, and had been trained and taught to use them. They had no real wish to continue their line and to have children they couldn't support. They were forced to.

The only possible excuse or justification for the marriage of this degenerate couple in the first place would have been that they should be able to establish a relationship between them that would be sexually satisfying and natural, and yet safe against the possibility of offspring. But our laws, and for the most part our churches, insist on the other arrangement—a thing so loathsome, so immoral, and so completely unclean and repulsive that one can only wonder at the thinness of our veneer of culture and the magnificence of our bluff that we are thinking beings.

If the Clark family (I have of course disguised the names in all these stories) were the only case, or if such cases were merely occasional, I would not be so emphatic about it. But how can I convey to any reader who has not seen conditions with his own eyes, a picture of the procession of unfortunates who pass through my chambers in the course of a year, subject to the jurisdiction of this court because the incapacity of so many of them to live right affects the rights of the children they should never have conceived? A large number of the people with whom I deal are, as I have already related, normal. But there is an astoundingly large percentage who are not.

Society *permits* these people to marry, and then virtually *requires* them by *law* to abstain from the use of contraceptives, thus virtually forcing them to reproduce their kind, and thus adding to our already enormous army of criminals and degenerates. Not only do the children of such people come into the world with an inadequate biological inheritance, but they suffer from malnutrition in childhood and are subjected to a kind of rearing at home which often cripples them, physically and spiritually, for life. Such people are mostly chronically poor, and socially impotent for anything but evil, by reason of their own inherited lack of energy or intelligence. The only way to save society from the blight of their presence is to find a way for them to die off without offspring, or with very few offspring. And in this they themselves would usually be more than willing—the women among them in particular.

Merely to impart to these people what is already known about methods of contraception would not be sufficient. We must go further. There must be a change in our federal and state laws that not only make legal the imparting of contraceptive information, but will make it possible for science to investigate and experiment in this field so the proper combination of simplicity and effectiveness may be found. The present methods are better than none at all, but they are clumsy, uncertain, and imperfect.

The argument that such measures would result in race suicide is nonsense. The notion that people would not have children if their ignorance of contraception did not force them to it is an old chestnut. The thing for us to do is to follow the dictates of an enlightened common sense and let such results follow as they will. Our present notion is that by permitting and even forcing what is clearly wrong and unscientific we can put legal props under our civilization that will hold it up. We think that the circulation of *many* human dollars of debased coinage will save the world. We won't adopt the gold standard in society though we were quick enough to see the utility of it in finance.

This isn't an advocacy of small families. I think people should have as many children as they can rear successfully. Boys and girls should be taught this; it is a part of any right education; and they should be taught what a lovely and regenerating influence children are in any household they bless with their presence—provided the material equipment there is adequate to their maintenance, and provided they are wanted. But we are as a race very far from that thought. We've run amuck. And what a price we are paying!

CHAPTER 23

The plain fact is that we are stupidly permitting the conception of illegitimate babies in wedlock by thousands. We've got the notion that an illegitimate baby is one that is conceived *out* of wedlock. We are mistaken. *An illegitimate baby is one conceived by parents who are biologically unfit.* Such a baby is illegitimate regardless of whether the parents are married or not. Or perhaps it would be truer to turn it around and say that it is the parents who are illegitimate. What illegitimizes parenthood is unfitness for it. Some of the saddest little "illegitimates," some of the saddest little "orphans" I know have both parents living in "legitimate" conventional wedlock.

Let us not deceive ourselves as to the true status of our present notion of "illegitimacy." Let us not blink at what goes on under the surfaces of our minds. Society does not want "illegitimate" babies lying around, not because it is concerned about the "morality" of conditions under which they were conceived, *but because it is afraid it will have to take care of them.* To escape such a threatened burden it imposes a heavy penalty, a penalty which defeats its own purpose by making it impossible for the parents of such children to undertake openly and without reproach the responsibility for their act. The whole business is grotesque as well as heartless. The hypocrisy and the pretense of morality that accompany it make it the more repulsive. There is no truth or health in it. It is of the devil.

Hundreds of "illegitimate" babies have passed through my hands. Of many of them I have pictures, wonderful little beings born often of wonderful parents. I have gone to certain hospitals or homes merely that I may feed my heart by looking at their loveliness, like the loveliness of flowers. I have seen for myself the joy and happiness they have brought into the lives of their foster parents, and the great promise many of them hold out to the world. At such times I can only wonder at the blindness and the unintelligent cruelty of our "moral" civilization.

I find in my files a copy of a note which I once sent, with a gift of flowers, to a young girl from one of Denver's best homes. Because of my urging she had consented to have her baby, at whatever cost to herself, and had just given birth to it.

Here is the note:

"To a brave, pure, sweet little girl whose suffering and nobility in doing what God and Nature would have her do rather than the cowardly thing thousands not half so good have done, more than atone for any mistake of conduct she has ever made, and now entitle her to all the love and respect that any girl in the world was ever entitled to; and which endear her, besides, to one who is very proud of her and her folks—for a brave, plucky fight.

"From her friend,
            "BEN B. LINDSEY."

With the secret kept that girl afterwards with great credit completed her course in school and is now happily married with another bouncing baby of her own. The other had to be sacrificed to her "self-respect," which meant its adoption into a home where it actually saved a couple from divorce and unhappiness. That baby worked a miracle in their jaded lives and rekindled a love that had dwindled to the breaking point. Now, I know of no happier family blessed with any lovelier child. Recently, when our paths crossed in a distant city where they now live, they told me they loved "their" child as much, if not more, than they could conceive of loving the natural child that had been denied them; that it had been the welding force that seemed to have united them forever; that they lived for their darling.

We do a lot of sentimentalizing about such cases in song and story. Audiences laugh and weep over plays like "Way Down East," and other stock melodrama, with the stern father, and the girl sent out with the child into the storm. We've always stood for that kind of thing in the realm of the imagination, and have sympathized with all the people concerned, and doused them with quantities of mush and slush to show it. And then, as in the case of certain recently censored books, we turn on any person who pictures such things as going on in our own lives, or as being otherwise than remote from us. By the same token we destroy anybody who does such things and gets found out. Thank God even for the follies by which this Younger Generation, in its revolt against tradition, is forcing that old notion to the wall.

Not long ago I had in my court the case of a girl who was unable to care for her child because it was illegitimate, and concealment was thought to be necessary for the maintaining of her reputation among her friends. Because the circumstances of the separation did not permit her to nurse her baby, the child died, as many babies do when fed with a bottle.

Since it was necessary for the girl to make a living somehow, a position was found for her. She became wet nurse to two weakling children whose own mothers could not nurse them, and who were likely to die in consequence. As it was the babies thrived. Never shall I forget the tragic despair in that girl's face as she told me her story. "It seems hard," she said, "that my own child should have died for want of what I was permitted to give to someone else's babies."

Do I hear some puritan say that that was a just punishment for her offense? All right—let's say for the sake of the argument that there is truth in that statement. *What about the child that died,* and who had nothing to do with the failure of its parents to get married? Did it not have as much right to the nourishment of its own mother, "moral" or "immoral"? As much right to life as those others to save whom it was permitted to die? What would the dead baby say about such "morality," such "justice"? Have we sunk so far that we imperil the lives of children by harrying and persecuting their unmarried mothers, robbing these baby innocents even of their natural food in infancy as well as pointing a finger of scorn at them later, if they survive the first murderous assault?—Have we sunk so low as that? We have.

One of our most treasured social traditions is to the effect that whenever any upstanding he-man discovers that some other man has established an undue intimacy with any of "his women," be the lady a wife or a daughter, there is just one thing for him to do—get a gun and use it. Stripped of verbiage and hot air, the meaning of this tradition is that a man *owns* his women, and that a seducer is not so much a seducer as a thief, in a somewhat lower category than a horse thief. The woman thus becomes a passive bone of contention between males, and the question of what part her will and personality have played in the situation is immaterial. At any rate, there must be a shooting; and this is fairly safe, because there are few American juries that will convict for a killing under such circumstances.

Once I had one of these stalwart males to deal with. John Chalmers was a middle aged man with a punch, considerable fighting spirit, and a daughter. He was rich and a broker. He had gotten rich by strangling weaker men than himself in the way of business. Inasmuch as he was among the bitterest enemies I had in Denver, owing in part to a decision I once made against a franchise grab he helped to engineer, I was greatly surprised when he one day presented himself at my chambers and asked for a confidential interview.

When we were alone he told me that he was in family trouble of a kind he had least expected. His son and daughter, he said, had been reared with all the care and skill that money could provide; outwardly they had always been well behaved and their moral conduct apparently above reproach. Now, however, he found that his daughter was going to have a baby, as the result of a liaison with a young man.

"I made her tell me the name of this scoundrel," he said. "And he would be dead by now for having brought this shame upon my family—for I had made all my preparations to shoot him; but I have changed my mind. On consultation with my attorney I find that since my daughter is under 18 the fellow has committed a penitentiary offense in seducing her; and that a life sentence is possible. If I can put him in prison for life, that will be a better revenge than killing him.

"Now that," concluded Mr. Chalmers, striking his great fist on the table and frowning down at my five feet something from his six feet something, like the formidable captain of industry and all around go-getter he was, "is why I've come here.—I know you. It is your habit to go easy with these fellows. But I don't want any miscarriage of justice in this case. I want that fellow to get the limit; and I'm going to find the best lawyers in this country to give him hell. I want your promise that you'll hand out a life sentence if I don't shoot him."

I could hardly refrain from laughing, though doubtless I should have upheld the dignity of the august bench I occupy by getting angry at his high-handed talk. But why be angry at people merely because they are foolish and misguided. "You understand, of course, that I can't condemn offenders in advance of their trial," I said. "Also that——"

"The damn scoundrel," he roared. "What I ought to do is gather a mob and lynch him."

"Only the other day," I observed, "I read an interview in the papers quoting you as saying that respect for the law was the cornerstone of liberty, and criticizing some strikers for not respecting it very much. Now you don't want your example to belie those words. Why not let the matter rest till four o'clock this afternoon when my day's work is over. Then we'll get together and talk some more."

But he was very much dissatisfied as he went off rumbling and grumbling like a restive earthquake, but unlikely, I thought, to do any shooting.

A few hours after Mr. Chalmers left a plainly dressed woman with a sad and worn face called at my court. Her name was Mrs. Dreer. She was accompanied by her daughter Gladys. Gladys, she said in a story told through tears, had "gone wrong." She had questioned the girl, but could not persuade her to "name the man," as the phrase goes in melodrama. She had now brought her to me in the hope that I could extract the information; a statement at which Gladys, who was a very pretty, spirited-looking Miss, shook her head and pursed her lips stubbornly,—an old story with me.

"If we are to get the truth I must talk with Gladys alone," I told Mrs. Dreer. And she left the room, withdrawing to the limbo in which I always keep the party of one part while I talk to the party of the other part. For more than twenty years I have "tried" such cases that way.

When I had Gladys by herself the usual thing happened. All I had to do was convince her that I was not particularly horror-stricken about her mistake. As usual I told Gladys I would not betray her secret without her permission, no, not even to her mother, and that I, in short, as my friends and enemies would put it, was "an encourager of immorality." She told me the whole story. She would have told it to her mother just as readily if her mother had understood her as I did. But her mother was one of these people to whom conduct, especially in matters of sex, is either black or white, according to the presence or the lack of a ring.

When she readily gave me the name of the boy in the case, however, I got one of the shocks of my life—not a moral shock, but a shock of coincidence. You've guessed it, Reader. His name was Chalmers, Clifford Chalmers, son of John Chalmers, my capitalistic friend. She had thought she loved Clifford and she was sure he had really loved her, she explained, but things had changed and she was not sure she'd care to marry him.

I let the matter rest there for the present, and sent the mother and daughter home with the promise of another conference which I hoped might straighten the tangle. At once I called the office of one of our leading banking houses and asked for young Chalmers. He agreed, by telephone, to reach my chambers early that afternoon. He turned up very soon after my return from lunch. As readily as in the case of the girl he admitted what he had done, and said he had considered marrying Gladys, but had not been sure it was the best thing to do. He was sure his father would object—and it was evident that he feared rather than respected his father. He was very straightforward about it. I was favorably impressed with him.

Because I had several pressing appointments, I finally asked the lad to sit down in one corner of the room till I could talk with him further.

At three o'clock, with the boy still there, the door of my room burst open, and in rushed John Chalmers, white hot with rage once more. He had worked himself nearly into a fit by continuous brooding over the outrage that had been done to his daughter.

"You were not due here till four o'clock, Mr. Chalmers," I said rather sharply; for a meeting of the father and son was the last thing I had contemplated at that time.

"I thought you said three," he answered. "Anyway, here I am; and I want to know what you are going to do with that young scoundrel. These damned seducers ought to be burned alive. And he's going to get what's coming to him if I have to fix him with—"

Just then I saw the boy get up, white and trembling. "Father," he cried. "You don't understand."

Chalmers whirled and faced his son in astonishment. "What are *you* doing here?"

"I came about the case."

"The case!" snapped the father. "I'll take care of the case. You leave that to me." Then he looked at his son sharply. "But what do you know about it?"

"You're being too hard on me, Father," said the boy.

John Chalmers turned to me in bewilderment. "What's he driving at?" he asked.

I motioned toward the door with my head, and the boy, thankfully enough, I guess, slipped out of the room.

Then I turned on John Chalmers and let him have the truth, for once in his life, without gloves. "Now," I concluded, "you left here this morning more than half determined on a killing if I didn't lend myself to the revenge you sought. On your return you found your son, who has done the very thing for which you want to shoot another man's son, and a boy no worse than he is. I didn't arrange this meeting between you and your son. It happened because you came early.—Now figure it out for yourself. If you are right, and if *killing* is the remedy for these two situations, begin with your own son, whom you have brought up with such care, and who, judged by your standards, is a villainous seducer, but by mine is a mighty fine lad who is the victim of your methods of child training, and who now stands ready to shoulder the responsibility for his mistake—and yours. Or perhaps you prefer that I should send both of these boys to the penitentiary for life. But I don't think that is the remedy."

I stepped to the door and recalled the boy, and explained to him how the meeting had happened—while his father stood and glared. It's a long story, but it concluded there in the privacy of my chambers as the boy half hysterically blurted out: "What shall I do? I'm ready to do whatever you think I ought to."

"Marry her! You've got to now!" shouted his father. And then burst into a flood of invective which showed that the poetic justice of the situation had taught him little.

"I'll marry her," said the boy.

As he left John Chalmers turned to me, with a gesture of despair. "I give up," he said. "I thought I knew my own children; but I don't.—You'd better take charge."

"Send your daughter to me," I said. "Let's clear that up first."

When he left it seemed to me that his bulk didn't loom quite so large as it had. "I'll send her," he said, thoughtfully, almost tearfully.

She came the next day. Like the son, she was a splendid example of modern youth—and very much a credit both to her burly father and to the stirring age that had produced her. "What my father probably didn't tell you," she said, "was that we are Roman Catholics, and that he can't tolerate the notion of my marrying a Protestant. I love the father of this child I am going to have, and I wanted to marry him. But father forbade it, and said I was under age—and that was why we took matters into our own hands."

When I next saw John Chalmers I said, "There is no need of my making a decision in this case. You decided it yourself yesterday when you said to your son that he should marry his sweetheart. It works both ways."

He shook his head subbornly, like an angry bull. "This is different," he snorted.

"Suppose we submit the question to your religious adviser," I suggested. To this he consented, grudgingly.

When the priest heard the story he considered a moment in silence. At last he looked at John Chalmers.

"They should be married," he said, "by a civil ceremony."

With that Mr. Chalmers gave in, and I married them.

What was supposed to be a wedding trip was spent by the bride in a maternity hospital in a distant city. It was the intention that later the couple should go through the form of adopting the baby; but it died.

Clifford Chalmers proposed marriage to Miss Dreer,

but she refused him. I sent her to a maternity hospital, and later arranged for the adoption of her child by a couple that wanted a baby and could not have one of their own.   Later she married another man, and now bids fair to live happily ever after unless some old harridan of her acquaintance finds out by accident about her "past."

Her refusal to marry the father of her child seems to me highly significant of the change which is coming in these matters. It was a typical thing for a member of the younger generation to do. In former days the girl always accepted marriage in such situations thankfully. Any other course, in conditions under which women were helpless dependents, meant destruction. But times have changed. This girl delighted me by sweeping aside the usual hypocrisies and pretenses with fine courage, when she said:

"It was all a mistake, but as much my fault as Clifford's, just fifty-fifty you see, when it happened. He really loved me, I am sure; and I thought I loved him. Now I know I don't; no, I don't love him any more and I won't marry him." In other words she objected to making a married prostitute of herself.

CHAPTER 24

I need offer no apology, I hope, for stringing together these stories as they occur to me. A story is its own good excuse; and these experiences from real life convey in the form of action the human side of the ideas I have been setting down. It is impossible to have contact day after day with people whose lives are a snarl and a tangle without finding out what it is that makes the snarl and the tangle. What I have discovered is that many of our social traditions are simply a concealed trap into which people walk before they know the thing is there. To put it differently, the evil is a double one. It consists first in the ignorance and bad education which keeps people from thinking straight; and secondly in certain unreasonable, inherited social restraints which are enough to drive even informed and educated people into a state of mind where straight thinking is next to impossible, even for them. The effect of all this on the unthinking and untrained minds possessed by 95 per cent of the race may be conjectured.

Keep this in mind while I tell another story, the story of the Koudenhoffen baby.

A little white girl, five years old, golden-haired, blue-eyed, was playing in one of the outlying streets of Denver; a street of tumble-down, ramshackle, unpainted houses occupied by negroes.

A white woman passed that way. She was gray-haired, well to do, and had been active in social work. She was much interested in negroes. The sight of this apparently white child playing in the heart of a negro quarter, therefore, arrested her attention at once.

She stopped and smiled down at the child. "Whose little girl are you?" she asked.

"Ah'm Mammy Fink's little girl," said the child; and her words, her accents and all were a precise duplication of those of the pickaninnies that swarmed in that street.

Just then a portly negro woman, with broad, black heavy features, appeared at the doorway of the nearest house. Apparently she had overheard the question and was enraged by it. "She's my chile, she is," she said coming menacingly forward. "An' I don't stand for no white folks comin' here to mess up in my affairs. Flossie," taking the little girl's hand with a gentleness quite at variance with her manner toward the unwelcome visitor, "you come inside."

Whereupon, with a final glare she withdrew, slamming the door with decision.

The social worker came to me. "It is no place for that child to be," she said. "She is beautiful, and evidently white. There is something wrong somewhere. The place where these people live is a shanty town, close to the railroad tracks and the freight yards. This child should not be left there. I hope you will have the case investigated."

I sent an officer to make inquiries. From the negro woman he encountered angry defiance. The child, she insisted, was hers; and when the question of color came up, she pointed triumphantly to her husband, who was a light-haired, fair-skinned white man, driver of a moving van.

The neighbors testified that the child had been with Mammy Fink since her birth; and that she had been

kept secluded in or close to the house till recently, when
her demand for playmates had resulted in her being
permitted to go out onto the street.

The further the inquiry went the more questionable
Mammy Fink's story looked. At last, on the strength
of a petition of dependency I summoned the child and
her reputed mother to court. When the two of them
walked in, with a cloud of their dark-colored friends, it
was a scene dramatic enough for a Eugene O'Neill
play.

The negro woman was a typical southern Mammy,
corpulent, big-bosomed, round faced, a dark mulatto. I
knew the type from memories of my own childhood, and
my heart went right out to her when she marched in
there like an army with banners, ready, obviously, to
defend her own with her very life—but beset, withal, by
a deadly fear of the Law, as represented in my—as I
hope—not too forbidding presence. She was leading by
the hand a tiny, fair-skinned, flaxen-haired sprite, beautiful and dainty as a Dresden doll.

Instantly the woman burst into a violent, bitter, and
excited telling of her story. Negroes often have a natural
dramatic gift; and as that woman stood there, her rich
voice booming through the room, I thought I would have
liked to see her on the stage.

The gist of it was that the child was hers, and that
white folks had no right to take it from her. I questioned her gently and at length. The fact that both
Mammy Fink and I had come originally from Tennessee
helped greatly in winning her confidence; and though it
cost me a great deal of tactful effort, expanded in several
more interviews, I finally got a real story—the truth this
time—out of Mammy Fink.

Mammy Fink had had a lively past. She was a ver-

satile and energetic personality. One of the things she
had long tried her hand at was midwifery. In that capacity she had made the acquaintance of certain nurses
of the sort whose business hovers on the line between the
legal and the illegal. Sometimes, where concealment was
desirable, little lifeless bodies that had come into the
world were brought by such "nurses" to Mammy Fink
to dispose of; and she burned them in her stove.—Mark
the fruits of fear.

One night, long after midnight, a knock sounded at the
door. Mammy Fink, always on the alert for such knocks,
opened the door and admitted a nurse who carried still
another of those tiny bundles in her arms. The bundle
was wrapped in gunnysacking. "This child is dead,"
said the nurse. "Get rid of it."

She left, and Mammy Fink prepared to throw the
bundle into the fire. Suddenly she heard a faint sound,
the cry of a newborn child. She took off the wrapping.

"Dat wan't no dead chile," she told me. "It was a live
chile; but the life in it was jus' a spa'k, a dying spa'k.
Dat baby was blue and stiff, like a dead rat. I couldn't
lay it down for it to die; I couldn't leave it there that 'er
way. I tuk it up; I put it on my bosom; I warmed it
back to life; an' it lived. 'Cept for me there wouldn't
been no chile. I put de bref of life into it. I guv it
life like I had borned it. It's mine like I had borned it;
and white folk ain't got no claim on it." Her voice rose
to a passionate shriek as she went on with her plea. "Dey
said it was dead fur dey done brought it ter me same as er
dead rat; I got to thinkin' that night that I'd keep that
chile. So I did. I kep' it, I raised it. I didn't let no
one see it more'n I could help. I didn't know where it
come from, but I knowed white folks didn't want it,

and that I did. Now no pryin' white folks is goin' to
get that chile 'cept over my dead body. I'se goin' to
keep her, and she's goin' to grow up with me to be a
gran' white lady. I'se raisin' her to be that."

I let her get it all off her ample chest. She told me
her story many times over; and while she told it I thought
hard. It was plain that the child was of more importance to her than if it had been her own. If cruelty could
be avoided in this difficult situation I wanted to avoid
it; and my hope was that it wasn't simply one of those
Gordian knots that have to be cut.

"Mammy Fink," I said at last, "you don't want your
love for this little girl to work an injury to her. If she
is going to be a grand white lady as you hope, she ought
to be brought up among people of her own race. Now
suppose I could find a white family that would adopt her
—if we can't find her real mother. Perhaps—"

But a flood of tears, mixed with wails and groans interrupted me.

"Listen, Mammy Fink," I went on. "We could pick
someone who would let you visit her. Perhaps we could
even find someone who would let you take care of her.
I'll let you help out in making a choice, and we can surely
find someone who would suit you."

At last, in spite of the obvious agony in her own heart,
she acknowledged that the thing I proposed would be
best for the child. Having brought her to that I asked
her if there was any way of tracing the child's mother.
She didn't want the child's mother traced, and was jealous
at this suggestion in an instant. But finally she gave me
the name of the nurse who had brought her the baby;
and I sent for the nurse.

The nurse proved to be one of those fox-faced, quiet
women who say little, and seldom offer you the truth

gratuitously,—the kind that are a link between the upper and the under world. They are silent partners to the shady segment of the medical profession who perform abortions, take "confidential cases," and blanket a multitude of iniquities by means of medical certificates obtained the devil knows where.

This nurse had in her house, which was near the home of Mammy Fink, two rooms in which she took confinement cases that wanted, for one reason or another, to avoid the light.

One day, five years before, a girl of twenty had come to her to arrange to be taken into one of those two rooms. The girl evidently had money. She wore expensive gowns, and she was beautiful. She gave the name of Adams, and a telephone number which proved to be that of one of our leading hotels.

Within a few days she was settled in the nurse's home. She was not happy. She appeared to be going through a great mental struggle, and wept a great deal. She expressed the hope many times that both she and her baby would die.

When the girl's time came, the nurse called in a physician with whom she drove a pretty constant trade. ·After the child was born its mother begged the doctor to tell her that her child could not live. As the child was very, very weak he did better than that: Considering it as good as dead, he told the mother that it was dead.

"Did you tell Mammy Fink the child was dead?" I asked the nurse.

"I may have done so," she said. "I thought it was."

From the nurse I got the name of the physician, and summoned him. He was a very seedy, shabby, gray-haired sort of person with "failure" written all over him; —about what I had expected.

Yes, he remembered the case. He had been certain the child could not live, and had told the nurse so. He had taken it for granted that if it did live, the nurse would take care of it, and had not concerned himself about it further. Later the nurse had told him the child was dead. The woman he saw only a few times. She had paid her bill in cash, and as no birth certificate had had to be filed, he did not even know her name.

On the register of the hotel we found the name of Mrs. Adams, but that led to nothing. The nurse, however, began to remember things. She recalled finding in the baggage of "Mrs. Adams" a small apron with a name on it. She thought the name was Koudenhoven or perhaps Koudenhoffen.

By this time the mystery of Mammy Fink's baby had begun to interest the newspapers, which spread the story far and wide, with a picture of the child. One paper mentioned that the name might be Koudenhoven, or possibly Koudenhoffen.

In the meantime several first-rate families in Denver had offered to adopt the child. From among these, after punctilious consultation with Mammy Fink, I selected the minister of one of our churches, whom I had found to be particularly kind in his attitude toward Mammy Fink. He told her that she could see the little girl when she liked, and could come and work in his home if she wished. Indeed he would adopt Mammy as well as the baby. She assented to this; the papers were made out, and all parties concerned had gathered to go through the legal formalities of adoption. I had indeed picked up my pen to sign the papers when suddenly the doors of my chambers burst violently open, and there stood a woman, pale, hysterical, agitated. "It's mine, it's mine, it has come back from the grave," she cried. "It has come back from the grave."

She dropped a little suit case she was carrying and ran forward to me. "You have my child," she said. "My child—my child, I know it." In her hand she clutched a fragment of newspaper that sufficiently explained where she had gotten her information.

It was several minutes before she became quiet enough to talk connectedly. Finally, however, she told her story.

"I was always good," she said. "I was a good girl. I don't know how it happened. He had promised to marry me, but it was not till three months before it was time for my baby to be born that he kept his promise. I was his wife, but I knew that would not save me from becoming the talk of our neighborhood. My family are deeply religious; and my mother had often told me that any girl who went wrong had committed a mortal sin. I was afraid it would kill her if she ever found out about me. And so I decided to come away, and I told my mother that I had gone to visit a school chum.

"Before my baby was born I prayed that it would die. I thought that would be the best thing for it, since it had been conceived in sin. When the doctor said it was dead I was thankful.

"I went back to my husband, and no one knew what had happened. But one night I had a dream. In it my baby came to me and said, 'I am not dead; some day you will be sorry.' I told this dream to my husband, but he laughed at it and called it a fancy. We never had another child, though we wanted children.——

"Two years later I dreamed again about my baby. She was growing up now, and was beautiful. After that I dreamed of her continually. She grew up in my dreams, and I cried with longing for her.   And always I wondered if she was really dead.

"One day there came a letter to my husband.   It was postmarked Denver.   I never open his mail, but I did open that letter—I don't know why.   Inside of it was this newspaper clipping, with the picture of my child, and I screamed, 'It lives; it lives!'

"With it was a letter—this letter."

Here she placed the letter in my hand.   It was a business letter from a traveling man; and it bore a postscript:

"Old man, there is a funny case in this town about a very beautiful child.   Of course, ugly old mug, it don't look anything like you, but the name looks funny.   I never knew but one Koudenhoffen, and you're it.   Say, is this one on you?"

The woman went on with her story.   "I hurried to my husband's office.   'You see,' I said, 'I was right.   It is our child.'

" 'You must tell your mother what has happened,' he said, 'and then take the first train for Denver.'

"I told my mother, I took the train, and I am here. I want my child."

While Mrs. Koudenhoffen was talking I had forgotten in my astonishment to send out word that the little girl was to be kept out of the room; and at this moment, as luck would have it, Mammy Fink and her little charge appeared at the door.   Instantly the woman rushed toward the little girl, crying out "I am your mother!   I am your mother!"

Whereupon the child uttered a piercing scream, clung to Mammy Fink, and burst into tears, crying, "You can't have me.   You're not my Mamma.   This is my Mamma! Mamma, Mamma, don't let her take me!"

Mammy Fink said nothing, but what she did was an eyeful. She thrust the child behind her, and stood, big arms akimbo, looking at the strange woman as if she would eat her.

"You nasty, low-down white gal," she said, suddenly finding her tongue, "runnin' about and doin' as you please; you wanted this chile to be dead, an' she's dead to you. I'd give her to anybody before I'd give her to you. The Judge won't let you have *my chile*." And Mammy went on with such fury of denunciation as I have seldom heard.

The mother fell on her knees before the angry negress screaming, "I was afraid! I'm not bad! Please let me tell you! They said it was dead!"

In the meantime people were rushing in, alarmed by the screaming; and the child was clinging to Mammy Fink and adding to the uproar. It took me some time to quiet them down; and when I had them so that they would listen, I said that nothing could be done one way or the other till the mother's story had been investigated. After that we would see. Of course that didn't satisfy anybody, but they couldn't object to it, and it gave me a much needed spell for getting my breath.

Investigation established later that the mother's story was true and that she could give her child a good home. Then I began to work on Mammy Fink. I conferred with the two women together, as they faced each other across my desk, sometimes glaring at each other, sometimes weeping in sympathy with each other. It was a stormy business. But gradually Mammy yielded.

At first Mammy Fink refused bitterly to accept the $2,000 settlement that was offered her. "You can't buy my chile," she said. But at last she accepted on the understanding that she was to be allowed to visit the little girl.

Then came the task of reconciling the child to her mother, who had so unfortunately frightened her. That took days. But finally the idea "took"; and one day she slipped from my knee and ran to her mother. And that was that.

Today the child is a schoolgirl in a mid-western city. Her connection with Mammy Fink is not wholly severed, because Mammy still frequently visits her "chile." Some day Flossie will marry and have babies; and I like to think of Mammy Fink as their nurse.

As to the moral of this tale, I have already stated it. Fear of a social disgrace she did not merit drove Mrs. Koudenhoffen, in self defense, to expedients which finally resulted in an incredible mess of coincidence and confusion. Thousands of Mrs. Koudenhoffens do the same kind of thing from the same kind of motives. Most of these never get found out; they take the chance and pull through. The small number who do get found out usually face ruin and social disgrace, and take refuge from that in measures that range from suicide to a stoical acceptance of the monstrous penalty imposed by "good" people on such offenses against the social code. Only by a miracle did Mrs. Koudenhoffen's tangled affairs get straightened out, and only such a social instrument as the Juvenile Court of Denver could have helped her. Ordinary court methods in disposing of such cases would have destroyed the happiness of everybody concerned.— I repeat, therefore, that our sex taboos, saturated as they are with superstitions, are a trap that destroys human happiness. They are no more rational than were the Salem witch-hangings, and they work out to a perfectly logical conclusion in the occasional tar-and-feathering practices of the Ku Klux Klan when it deals with persons of whose morals it does not approve. Society applies some kind of tar and feathers to all women who violate its sex code. It is time we re-appraised that code and found a more rational way to treat those whose natural impulses lead them to violate it. Mrs. Koudenhoffen would not have made her first mistake had she been differently educated; and she would not have made matters worse by her desperate concealment of the truth had she not been driven mad by Fear. Fear of what? Fear of a social superstition, a Fear exactly parallel to the Fear which must have possessed those poor women convicted of witchcraft in Salem. They knew they were not witches; but how could they prove it to that beastly monster that held them in its grip, mad with an ignoble belief which blasphemously claimed sanction and approval from God Himself. Religion—the theological kind of religion—did that, in a Christian community, among people who knew by rote, though not by heart every word that Jesus ever uttered. Mrs. Koudenhoffen knew she wasn't bad; but the same monster that used to hunt witches would have hunted her had it found her out, and would have been as deaf to the voice of reason in dealing with her. The only difference would have been that it would not have destroyed her body. It would merely have applied a hot iron to her soul.

I cannot see that the one kind of superstition is any less loathsome and ignoble and unworthy of reasoning beings than the other. I cannot see by what right we plume ourselves with the belief that we have ceased from our witch-hunting. But I think we might cease from it. Indeed, I think we will. Modern Youth may bring about the change; Modern Youth which laughs so shocking loud when its elders talk of Witches! And yet Youth alone is not enough. The wisdom, the experience, the caution of Age are also needed. But there is no room for its conservative stupidities. If those stupidities persist, Age can contribute nothing but fresh trouble, and Youth will have no choice but to go forward alone and take its chance over this admittedly perilous path without a guide. That, indeed, is what it is already doing.

CHAPTER 25

One of my reasons for writing this book is that I think the way to come at the truth of these matters is through a free discussion of them. It isn't necessary that everybody should be right, but it is necessary that everybody should talk, and talk freely, if we are ever to develop a sane public opinion about anything. At present we do not discuss sex morality—at any rate we don't discuss it with candor, and we question the morals and the intent of those who do. It is a mean way of thought. Look at it hard, Reader, and you will perceive that you are face to face with the meanest, vilest, most cowardly thing on earth, Superstition!

The first thing to admit and recognize is that there is *nothing in the world* that is not a legitimate subject for honest discussion—yes, even for dishonest discusson. I wouldn't shackle any kind of discussion whatever. I'd leave the truth to survive by its own strength, as it infallibly will.

At present our notion of preserving what we think to be the truth is to gag all who don't think it's the truth. We win our arguments by forbidding argument. We combat anarchism, socialism, bolshevism, birth control and the like by forbidding people to discuss them on street corners or in cellars and attics. The churches used to win their arguments against atheism, agnosticism, and other burning issues by burning the ism-ists, which is fine proof that there is a devil but hardly evidence that there is a God.

What an amazing state of mind! Suppose the churches,

for instance, instead of trying their dissenters for heresy would, as some of them have already done, open their pulpits to honest thought, and give it a chance beside the often dishonest thought to which some of them now give the right of way. Suppose they opened their doors as freely to such thinkers as they now open them to men who are sworn, like a "fixed" jury, to uphold given sets of theological propositions, set forth in *ex parte* state- ments and disingenuous half truths,—what interesting places our churches would be. How much religion they would have and how little theology. How much light they might produce for the guidance of the world. What a moral force they would become!

If such were the case there would be less hostility against Birth Control and other enlightened movements. The opponents of Birth Control certainly have a perfect right to their views. Those who oppose it on the ground that it is forbidden in revealed religion, have a right to do so. But they are not content to let their presentation of what they consider the truth survive by its own ex- cellence—if it can. They want to ram it with the help of the law down the throats of other persons who refuse voluntarily to accept it. This is all very enterprising and energetic, of course—but it is hardly an ethical way to spread the Truth, particularly in the name of the Man of Nazareth, who would never countenance such methods.

Let me pause at this point to make myself very clear on one matter. The theological opposition—I do not call it religious opposition—to Birth Control has come from Protestant churches as well as from the Roman Catholic Church. The reason I emphasize this here is that I don't want the references I have made to certain Roman Catholic women to be interpreted as a shaft aimed in that direction. Those of my readers who are familiar with my recent collision with the Ku Klux Klan in Denver will already know that I consider the "200 per cent Americanism" attitude toward Roman Catholics—not to mention Jews, negroes and aliens—to be a yellow streak in our national life, a streak so yellow that a sane yellow dog would be ashamed to own it.

And yet, perhaps I put it too strongly. Perhaps in putting it that way I am permitting myself a spasm of the very spirit of intolerance I denounce. One must be moderate, even toward the Klan. Many well-intentioned and misled people belong to it because they don't see the underlying meaning of it. When I stop to think, I know that impatience, anger, and judgment are wrong; I would fain discipline myself even to a point where I might be truly tolerant toward the mistaken spirit of organized intolerance itself.

I have an added reason for harboring the kindest thoughts towards the Roman Catholic Church, even when I find myself obliged to take issue with certain of its teachings—particularly on the subject of Birth Control, with regard to which its clergy put up a united opposition. That reason is that the Church of Rome associates itself in my mind with many warm and treasured memories.

Some of my most valued friends are Roman Catholics. My mother, a convert, was buried in that faith. I once studied at Notre Dame University; years afterwards Cardinal Gibbons there conferred an honorary degree upon me; and they have such affection and regard for me there that my picture hangs, rightly or wrongly, among the pictures of their worthies.

My father was at first a member of the Protestant Episcopal Church. One of my earliest recollections of him is in a surplice, acting as lay reader. But he was a "high churchman," and the Oxford movement, led by Newman and others, carried him over into the Church of Rome. After that I was brought up in his faith, and remained there till he died.

When I was fourteen I left Notre Dame and attended the Baptist College at Jackson, Tennessee, where I was born. Here and during earlier periods of my childhood I came under the influence of my Welsh grandmother, who had been brought up in the faith of John Wesley. She was an intense Methodist of the old South. Then too, came the influence of the blood of my Scotch Covenanter ancestors on the side of my North-of-Ireland Scotch-Irish Presbyterian grandfather, with whom much of my boyhood was spent. That must have spoken within me also. At any rate, I suppose it was only natural that I should return to the Protestant faith of my forebears, as I did in my early young manhood by uniting with the Methodist Church.

But to come back to the point at issue, Birth Control. One of the clearest and most decisive utterances I have seen against artificial contraception and in support of the view taken by many fundamentalists, Catholic and Protestant, comes from Cardinal Hayes. Here it is:

"Children troop down from Heaven because God wills it. . . . He blesses at will some homes with many, others with few or none at all. They come in the one way ordained by His wisdom. Woe to those who degrade, pervert, or do violence to the law of nature as fixed by the eternal decree of God Himself! Even though some little angels in the flesh, through the moral, mental, or physical deformity of the parents, may appear to the eye hideous, misshaped, a blot on civilized society, we must not lose sight of this Christian thought, that under and within such visible malformation there lives an immortal soul to be saved and glorified for all eternity among the blessed in Heaven."

That, I think, is a fine and clear statement of the point of view of those who believe artificial contraception to be a sinful frustration of God's purposes. But to me it does not seem logical. To me it seems that those who are guilty of bringing deformed or perverted children into the world have, to paraphrase the words of Cardinal Hayes, degraded, perverted, and done violence to the law of nature as fixed by the eternal decree of God Himself. It seems to me also that many such persons have permitted their theological beliefs to do away with their common sense.

The logic of the view so admirably expressed by Cardinal Hayes is that abstinence from intercourse, which is the one contraceptive countenanced by those who oppose artificial contraception on theological grounds, blocks and prevents the entrance of children into the world much more effectively than the use of artificial contraceptive devices, and must, therefore, also constitute a frustration of the purposes of God.

But according to that way of reasoning every trick and device by which man makes, for his own advantage, alterations in the course and common effect of natural law, is a "frustration" of God's purposes. It isn't "natural." The steam engine, by which we attain speeds which God clearly didn't intend us to make, since He didn't give us wings, is an example of this. It isn't natural. Neither is a surgical operation. There are plenty of religious people today who think the probings of science into the secrets of nature are a sin against God for the reason that if He had intended us to know these things, He would have revealed them—in the Bible, perhaps.

This whole way of looking at the matter seems to me

impossible. Cardinal Hayes himself would not hold it with regard to most of the inventions by which man improves his lot. By what logic then does he, and those who are of his way of thinking, draw an arbitrary line in these matters, and authoritatively say of this, "God intended men to work out these new inventions and discoveries; and they are not a frustration of His purposes but clearly a fulfillment of them"—while they say of another thing, for which their minds are less prepared, and which infringes on the jealously guarded domain of Sex, "God never intended men to regulate the propagation of His own species by any method save abstinence. He chooses the number and kind of children we men are to have; He's got it all planned and determined; and He certainly will be displeased *if we step in and upset all His carefully formed calculations.*"—To me such reasoning seems presumptuous. I can't see how a finite being can in the least degree upset the plans and wishes of the Infinite Being that made him. I can't see why God should have intended us to use our brains and our common sense in one department of life, and not to use it in another. Finally I cannot admit that any man born of woman has either the knowledge or the authority to tell other men, as a statement of ascertained fact, what God's purposes are in this or any other matter. I refuse to give to any man or body of men the right to form my opinions for me, to think for me in the slightest degree. But the churches, both Catholic and Protestant, have long claimed that right, that authority, that knowledge. By the morning paper, for instance, I see that the Board of Review of the Protestant Episcopal Church has pronounced Bishop William Montgomery Brown a "heretic." Theoretically, at least, that sends the good bishop to Hell.

It is time that we had done with our superstitions and puerilities of thought and turned ourselves to the task ahead—the great scientific task of regenerating this race along the broad lines of reason and common sense prescribed by Christ as the Way of Life.

It is also time that the American people clearly understood that just as there has never been a discovery of first-rate and revolutionary importance in medicine and law that did not have to establish itself in the teeth of practically united opposition from the medical profession or the legal profession, which should have been the first to accept new truths, so there has never been a discovery of revolutionary importance in science or sociology that has not had to encounter the opposition of established theology.   Birth Control is a capital example of this.

So we come back to the question of the Truth, and of daring to search for the Truth, whatever betide, until we find it. *Many of the established forces in this country are bending their energies to the suppression of some sort of Truth.* Isn't that startling?   Most of our established forces have one thing in common: they try to uphold one set of ideas by suppressing, hiding, or minimizing all ideas that run counter to them.   I encounter this all the time in Denver; and anyone who tries to tell the truth anywhere will encounter it.   This has been true all through history.   Perhaps it always will be true; for most of the human race, in the present stage of its evolution at least, thinks in a rut and lacks imagination. And the lack of imagination is just another name for conservatism.

The organized forces of society are static.   That is what they are organized for.   That is their function. The maintenance of a static order, a stable order, is their reason for being; and if the static and stable order hap-

pens to be a lie that makes no difference. It is sufficient that it be static.

The Truth? What could an established, static order
of things care for a thing so fluid, so protean, so elu-
sive, so difficult to come at as the Truth—save to kill
it if possible?

The Truth is destructive to things established; everything we call fixed, settled, and stationary it sweeps along
before it like so many chips on the surface of a torrent
that rushes through the Universe—and *is* the Universe!—
"The *truth* itself is motion," says Ouspensky in his *Ter-
tium Organum,* "and can never lead to arrestment, to
the cessation of search. All that arrests the motion of
thought is false. Therefore the true and real progress
of thought is only in the broadest striving toward knowledge that does not recognize the possibility of arrestment
in any *found* forms of knowledge at all. The meaning
of life is in eternal search. *And only in that search* can
we find anything truly new."

"*Panta rei!*" cried Heraclitus the Greek, looking out
upon that infinite flood; "All things flow!" And thereby,
if you will, by a divine relativity, he posited his own Soul,
as it looked out there from the sure-standing watch tower
of its Being, telling what of the Night.

Most of us are afraid of roaring torrents. We want
to be comfortable. "What will become of civilization?"
we cry. And then we set to work, with dams of sand,
to stop the flood.

But I would not stop it if the mere crooking of my
finger would turn the trick. I would not stop it, not
though I knew it would drown me—which it won't. If
Truth would drown the world, I say, let it. It isn't
much of a world if such living waters as these won't buoy
it up.

But what is Truth? I don't know; But I do know that such glints as we get of that majestic Face, such sounds of the Voice as reach us through the whirlwind, are the result of not being afraid, and of talking, thinking, and acting as honestly and straightforwardly as we can. And I don't think that our established hypocrisies or unyielding dogmas can have any part in such a program.

That the Youth of today makes mistakes disturbs me somewhat but not excessively. That it is honest heartens and delights me much. Here it comes, with its automobiles, its telephones, its folly and its fun, and its open and unashamed refusal to bow down to a lot of idols made of mud; and it makes me hope.

This revolt of Youth, with a scientific and mechanically grounded civilization back of it, offers the world more hope than anything that has happened in centuries. About once in so often, the human race rediscovers Fire. This younger generation, Prometheus-like, is doing it now.

A friend of mine once visited the home of George Bernard Shaw in London. Over the arch of the fireplace in Mr. Shaw's library, he saw a quaintly phrased line which seemed to him so characteristic of Shaw's own angle on life that he asked the happy owner of the line if he would not give him the American rights to it.

"It isn't mine," said Shaw. "I stole it from an ancient Frenchman. Help yourself."

My friend did so. Later he told me the story; and when not long afterward Mrs. Lindsey and myself went to England I made up my mind to see the arch of the Shavian fireplace for myself, and, with the owner's permission, appropriate the now twice-stolen treasure.

But as luck and circumstance would have it, though

we had a delightful visit with Mr. Shaw, it did not take place at his home. That, however, did not prevent me from summarily shipping the coveted thought across the Atlantic, smuggling it past the customs—to which it is most contrary—and putting it safely over the arch of my own fireplace. There, of an evening, when I sit before my hearth, I read and ponder:

"THEY SAY—WHAT DO THEY SAY?—LET THEM SAY IT!"

I have a belief which is part of my religion that any man who puts that over his fireplace will never lack for a flame wherewith to warm his spirit.

CHAPTER 26

Having gone thus far with my subject I am still conscious of having left much unsaid, either for want of space or because it would carry me far afield from the relatively narrow subject I have chosen, the Revolt of Modern Youth.

And yet Life is a thing so homogeneous that it is not possible completely to isolate such a theme from the bigger chain of cause and effect of which it is a part. The Revolt of Youth needs at least some interpretation in the light of matters with which, superficially considered, it may seem to have little to do.

For the Youth of Today is the State of Tomorrow. What Youth is, and what Youth thinks, that State will be. By the same token, it is not possible for the Adult of Today to determine in his own person what the State of Tomorrow will be; and yet he can influence its destinies in a measure, for Tomorrow we are gathered to our fathers, to add our mite of strength to that dead and mighty hand of the Past whose tyranny has, in so many sinister ways, made us what we are, and reaches out forever to clutch the very unborn future itself and strangle its will.

But is it necessary that we adults of today so wholly identify ourselves with that old and tradition-ridden Past? Can we not start, as it were, a New Past which will disown and repudiate the shackles and chains of the Old while clinging to those things it offers that are good?

We can indeed! We can let the numbing poison of irrational tradition stop with *us*—the poison that has warped and cramped *our* past in the racial life. Oh that our race might seize upon that truth, and then damn this Tribal Incubus into the limbo of Forgotten Things,— setting Youth free forthwith,—putting into its strong and eager hands the keys of Life and Death,—saying, "We from whose loins you have sprung trust you! Make of yourself a force that shall work for righteousness, to the creation of a new heaven and a new earth. Do it in your own way, and by whatever means may commend themselves to you as just, right, and able to stand the test of use."

This is the heart of the matter. It is not necessary that we should predict and prescribe what the specific plan of action is to be.—If we could only see this! It is *not* necessary, I say, that we should dictate that plan in any respect, nor that we should lay upon it the dead hand and the lifeless arm of the Past, as we are trying constantly to do.

We are not called upon, for example, to say specifically what shall be the future status of marriage; nor the standing of "Birth Control"; not what is "loose conduct"; not what is the proper length for a skirt; nor whether a woman's hair is her glory; nor whether "damn" is a swear word; nor whether abstention from Sunday golf constitutes keeping the Sabbath holy; nor what is the line between moral dancing and immoral dancing; nor in just what respects individuals are morally bound to go the easy downward path spontaneously and mechanically followed by unled and unintelligent majorities; nor any similar thing.

All that is needful is that by means of a right system of education, we lay upon the hearts of our young people the conviction that they have a solemn duty to be good and productive citizens of the world: that we plant in their minds the suggestion, the faith; that it is their normal desire to be such; that we make it possible for the Good Will and the spontaneous Idealism, which are Youth's natural gift from God, to grow unhampered, as grow the flowers of the field; that we protect them from Fear and from the acceptance of second-hand, standardized, cut-to-pattern thought as from a plague; that we give them a background of essential knowledge which withholds no Fact on the ground that there are things which must not be known or discussed; and, finally, that we teach them the Art of Living, and permit them a philosophy of effort which will carry them through, and keep them headed wondering, yet fearless, toward the far horizons to which they naturally aspire.

If we can consciously and deliberately bequeath them, to the limit of our ability, an unstinted, ungrudged heritage of Health, Beauty, Honesty, Fearlessness, and the Knowledge that casts out Fear, we shall have done *our* duty by the future and handsomely disowned every part of the Past that cannot prove its own fitness to survive without artificial rejuvenation at the hands of worried conservatives. Thus we shall have made of our own warped minds and crippled bodies a bridge over which our children may cross to better things. More, we shall have laid upon the State a benison that will protect it from all harm, because we shall have placed it, unfearing, in the hands of God.

These things are possible, and I think inevitable. But the trouble at present is that we are afraid. We can't believe that excellent things survive by their own excellence, that necessary things are stronger than our worst follies, and that any rigid custom or tradition which cannot stand this test does not deserve to persist unchanged. We lack the faith for believing this. That is

why we refuse to encourage in our young people sound
fundamental motives of action which they must be free
to use according to their judgment, even at the cost of
blunders and mistakes.   Rather we insist on saying precisely how they shall use them.   I repeat that our fundamental sin is our lack of faith.   We are idiotically
convinced that any departure from *our* program, which
we took second-hand from *our* fathers, will destroy the
world.   We don't realize how habitually we insist on
this, even in prescribing our own conduct.   I have often
wondered that our national sense of humor should have
been so dormant that it kept right on sleeping while
Henry Cabot Lodge and his cohorts were presenting,
as one argument against our participation in the League
of Nations, the fact that *Washington* had warned us
against entangling alliances.   And yet Henry Cabot Lodge
was, in what seemed to me an evil way, intelligent.   Perhaps that was why he used such an argument.

In my mind at this moment there hover two pictures,
two memories, that seem to me admirably to set forth
how society, in the interest of many of its conventions,
confuses dross and gold.

Sonia is a Russian girl, gifted with a magnificent energy, both of mind·and body.   She is the kind who ought
to give the world many splendid babies; and the world
should be humbly thankful for the gift.

Sonia, because she had a fine mind, graduated from
high school when she was barely sixteen, and then entered a university in another state.   Soon after her
matriculation a strange ailment came upon her.   She went
to several physicians, but none of them could name the
cause of the trouble; and the real cause, which was pregnancy, never occurred to them.   For Sonia is not a "wild"
type.   At last one of them guessed it, and told her;

and then Sonia, crazy with fear, took the first train for Denver and came to me. When I suggested taking her father into our confidence she nearly fainted. "He is an orthodox Jew," she cried. "He would disown me and cast me out; he would spit when my name was mentioned; he would forbid my little brothers and sisters and my mother even to remember me! It is impossible!"

"Very well, Sonia," I said. "Yours will be one of the first cases under the new Maternity Law of Colorado, a law which empowers this court to provide money for the support of your child—both before its birth and after."

I provided, therefore, for her to have her confinement under conditions that would not betray her to her father. It was difficult, but I managed it. The next step was to get the money. It was to come from a fund that had, nominally, always been in charge of a certain social worker. This woman, for the purpose of getting the upper hand of me, had had put into the statute books of Colorado certain provisions to the effect that financial aid could not be extended to mothers unless it could be shown that their character was thus and so, that they had been in residence so long, etc. She had thought thereby to put a spike in my guns; and she now flared up in a way which is common among a certain type of social worker when the question of illegitimacy is on deck, and said, with an air of unconcealed triumph, "I will *not* give over the required amount until I have investigated the girl for myself. What is her name?"

"Impossible," I said to her. "You can't have her name. To tell it would be to expose her."

"Such girls," she snapped, putting an indescribable venom in her voice, "*deserve* to be exposed." That, mind you, from a social worker, whose professed purpose is to help people.

"You will turn over to me that money I require, Miss Thorpe," I said. "For it happens that you have overlooked the fact that the new Maternity Bill says this money is provided by the State *for the child, not for the mother*. This girl's character, place of residence, and so on, does not enter into the question because the money is not for her."

On that ground I was able to force her to obey the court; and a limited sum became available for Sonia to administer in trust toward the support of her baby.

Never have I seen a human being endure more wretchedness and woe than did that girl in the months that followed. Sonia had her baby, which we had to take from her to prevent discovery. Very soon after she had recovered from her confinement, she became seriously ill, and had to undergo a major operation, which was performed by a physician in my confidence. "That girl," he said to me, afterward, "has been through enough, in the way of physical and nervous strain, *to wreck her for life*. But she's exceptionally strong, and I think she'll pull through." And then he added with sudden fervor, "Damn society! Why can't they let her alone!"

Pretty soon I discovered that since the amount provided by the State for her assistance was not enough to enable her to support her baby, she had in her desperation figured out a way to plug the cash register in her father's place of business, and to take money from it without being discovered. Her fear of society and of her "respectable" and "moral" father had driven her to that. The result was that later I increased the amount contributed by the State to make such thefts unnecessary.

That's where the case of Sonia, hounded by society and religion, and frantically trying to protect her baby and herself, stands now, at the time of this writing. What

will happen later I cannot predict. I can only say that
I propose to stand back of Sonia against these damnable
persecutions to the last ditch, and that any aid and comfort I can possibly give her she shall have. Only yesterday she appeared timidly at the court, and asked to
see me alone.

"Yes, child," I said. "What is it?"

"I was blue," she said, her eyes filling with tears. "I
just wanted to hear you say it again—that I'm not bad,
and that things will turn out all right."

So, while I kept a dependency case waiting—the case
of a married man who didn't love his wife and baby
and didn't care a whoop what became of them, I talked
to Sonia, comforted her as best I could, and sent her
away only when I saw that the corners of her mouth
were turning up instead of down.—In a few weeks,
back she will come for more comfort. What can one
say of her Pecksniff of a father, typical in his "morality,"
staunch upholder of the conventions? Is there *any* light
that could penetrate that darkened mind, or any impulse
of simple humanity that could enter that barnacle-en-
crusted heart? Would the fact that his own daughter
has stolen from his own cash register to support her
baby be anything to him but fresh cause for offense?
Have we no sense for the spiritual splendors of motherhood—no notion of the wonder and the weight of Life—
that we should behave toward each other as though we
really were, as Dean Swift cynically thought us, a race
of vermin?

Oh the pity of it!—I told one woman this story.
When I had finished her eyes narrowed like the eyes
of a cat. "Are you sure," she asked slowly, "that that
was the *first* time; I don't believe it was."

"What if it wasn't?" I demanded hotly, hardly able to

conceal the rage that rose within me. What I wanted to add and didn't, was, "I have seen Sonia's baby; and I tell you she has done the world a bigger service than dried up old cats like you do in a lifetime."—But of course I didn't. I shut up.

At the time these things were happening to Sonia there took place in Denver a splendid wedding. Money flowed like water. The presents to the bride would have filled a store. Thousands of dollars were spent for flowers alone; and amid that floral profusion the purity of the lily was conspicuous. The wedding took place at the church, the bride having said that she would not "feel really married" if it didn't; and all the wealth of Denver turned out to see it. The organ played the well-known wedding march. The newspapers played the story to the limit under banner heads. It was as overflowing with respectability as Sonia's poor little affair with a young man of twenty, married himself and supporting two children, was wanting in that readily purchased commodity.

Such was the way this society wedding looked *on the surface* to all who saw it, and to all who read the account of the papers of the next morning.

But what *I* knew, by reason of things that had come to light in my court, was that the ushers at that wedding had, on occasions known to me not long ago, had intimate relations with certain girls who were present at the wedding, and who were shown to their seats by their former paramours. Also that at least one of those ushers was suffering from venereal disease at the time of the wedding. I was the only person in Denver, I suppose, outside the parties involved, that knew these facts or even dreamed them.

But it was "respectable!" The bride won't have to

have her baby in secret, if she takes to babies instead of lap-dogs; and she won't be driven by her respectable relatives to theft from her father's cash register, in order to support her child after it is born. No father will spit when her name is mentioned. She's respectable! It was a respectable wedding!

CHAPTER 27

Keep those two stories in mind while I quote, on the subject of "respectable marriage," the Reverend R. P. Schuler, pastor of Trinity Methodist Church, Los Angeles. Mr. Schuler, according to an Associated Press report, has recently given the California State Board of Education something extra to think about by writing it a letter in which he denounced, says the dispatch, "certain illustrated text books on mythology as having a demoralizing influence on boys and girls."

Mr. Schuler attacked me in print not long ago for certain of my views about marriage and the rights of unborn children to be born instead of being murdered, and to be "legitimate" after birth, regardless of every parental Who, What, Why, Where, When, and How. Mr. Schuler denounced my views, and accused me of favoring Free Love,—whereupon I protested. He replied with the following letter:

"My dear Judge Lindsey:

"I thank you for your very kind letter of May 17, and in reply will say that my editorial was based upon newspaper clippings which I have in my possession, and which undoubtedly placed you in the position of declaring that society would be forced to take a different attitude toward children born out of wedlock and therefore toward the necessity of the marriage relation as a prerequisite to respectable birth, etc. I read the first article that I saw concerning the matter very carefully, and also an editorial discussion of it by some editor,

whose name I do not now recall. It seemed to me perfectly clear that you were taking the position that society would be forced to modify its attitude toward the
marriage relation or rather the necessity of the marriage
relation.

*"I confess that I am so tremendously concerned about
this wave of looseness that has hit our country* that I
possibly was a little strong in the editorial which I wrote,
and if you feel that I have wronged you in the matter,
I will be mighty glad to do anything that is at all right
in order to put you in the right light before my readers.
If you will give me a very brief statement of your exact
position, I will be delighted to publish it.

"Yours ever,
"(Signed) R. P. SCHULER."

The italics are mine.—It is needless for me to comment on the evident courtesy and fair intent of the man
who wrote that letter. But what a pity that people with
such big hearts and minds can't go the whole distance, and
cease trying to impose their standards on a future which
has a right to make its own.

Here is my reply to Mr. Schuler's letter:

"My dear Mr. Schuler:

"I thank for your letter of May 21st and wish to say
that jury work has delayed my answering sooner.

"I am a member of the Trinity Methodist Church
here in Denver and I have no disposition to promote
looseness in the marriage relation as I understand that
relation and believe it ought to be. . . .

"I am sure that anyone in the position that I am in
is much more likely to know society as it is than the
average minister in most any church. Therefore, no one

could see more of the looseness you refer to, or, I believe, be any more concerned about it than I am. It is the rights of the child that are involved in that looseness which also concerns me. I have not any doubt at all that there are two million illegal operations in this country every year. I feel that I know positively from my experience here that there are a thousand in Denver—perhaps more. I do not propose to see the butchering of these unborn children go on in the way it is going if I can help it. It is the attitude of society that is largely responsible for the murders and slaughters of innocents today. There is a reason for it—at least I think there is, and I am going to help to point it out regardless of the misunderstandings of people who misjudge me—some of them unintentionally and some intentionally. The rights of these children are just as much involved as the concerns of morality.

"I believe we should do to the unborn as we would have the unborn do to us. If it is necessary, to prevent this slaughter of millions of children, that society should modify its attitude toward the marriage relation in order to prevent the worst kind of sin, I am in favor of that; and I do believe that society will be forced to modify that relation to what I consider real marriage in order to prevent this appalling slaughter. But whatever may come in that regard, these murdered innocents are not responsible for the stupidities and crimes of our present social conditions, and I do not propose, so far as I have anything to do with helping to change conditions, that any one of these little ones shall be made to suffer because of the sin, ignorance, or poverty of the parents.

"I have often said to my wife, because of the many misunderstandings which seem to follow any public statement I make in this regard, that my only hope to be really understood is to write a book on the subject. That I hope some day to do; but in the meantime I have expressed myself in general terms about as well as the situation permits.

"I may say in conclusion that I have been rather appalled at how little the average minister knows about what is frequently going on under his nose. I am not saying this applies in your own case because I assume that you do know; but if you do you certainly know that there must be a great many changes in society before we can have the fine morality that all of us would like to have. For no one appreciates the sanctity and the importance of a home, and the real marriage relations that ought to be, more than I do.

"Again thanking you for your kind letter, I am
"Yours very sincerely,
"(Signed)   BEN B. LINDSEY."

That letter, although it was hastily dictated amid the harassments of a crowded docket, seems to me to define the issue; and I don't see how Mr. Schuler or anybody else can walk around that issue. If those who cling to the old order insist on having their way, they have to have it by consenting to an evil which is terrible, cruel, and murderous beyond words. I hope I shall not be understood as favoring any orgy of sexual license if I say that if it came to a choice as between seeing every man and woman in this country practicing "Free Love," and the saving of possibly two million unborn babies a year by removing the social pressure of Fear which leads to most abortions, I would choose the former of these abominations, particularly if the "Free Love" were linked to effective "Birth Control." And if it be a choice between two million abortions and a

perfectly possible and sensible modification in our marriage code, not even remotely akin to "Free Love," then
the matter does not seem to me debatable; and those
who cling to the old order appear to me to be forcing
on the world the continuance of a hideous evil *which
will continue so long as the present arbitrary, Fear-
ridden standards of sex morality remain unmodified.*
One or the other of these things we must choose. There
is no escape; there is no third way. Mr. Schuler and
those who think with him are on the horns of a dilemma.
To me it seems amazing that presumably sane people
can fiercely denounce irregular and unconventional sex
conduct, expending their energy on that, and yet remain
perfectly oblivious of the murder of children deprived
of their right to be born because the parents, for good
and sufficient reasons, are afraid to bring them into the
world.

As I stated in my letter, I am just as much concerned
about the "wave of looseness" Mr. Schuler speaks of
as he is. But I am concerned for a different reason.
I am concerned with its causes and their removal. *Those
causes inhere mostly in the rooted conviction of the older
generation that certain of its customs and received traditions are not conventions, merely, but ultimate verities.* What is making the trouble is the effort made by
the adult world to impose this point of view on a Younger
Generation which questions it, rebels against it, and wants
to do its own thinking.

This unwarranted attempt to place Youth under the
authority of the Past is causing thousands of our young
people to overshoot the mark of wisdom and moderation
in their blind plunge away from arbitrary restraints and
penalties. Remove the restraints and the penalties, on
the other hand, and permit our boys and girls to make

their own under wise counsel, with no savor of arbitrary restraint about it; and they will be moderate; they will test every new idea and new custom with due caution and responsibility. If our conservatives say that the young are incapable of using such freedom aright, and that their search for new things is immoral, dangerous, and destructive, *per se*, then I for one ferociously deny it; I deny it on the authority of a personal experience with young people which I venture to say has not been duplicated by any man in the world. I am no arm-chair theorist. The affirmations of my opponents, particularly as regards Marriage, emphatically do not stand the test of use—as our divorce records, our unguessably large abortion figures, and the lives of "ruined" girls and "illegitimate" babies, testify. If the existing practices are right, why don't they produce the right kind of fruit? Why do they bring hell into so many lives? The burden of proof is on those who defend the existing order and condemn all efforts to change it by the use of a little horse-sense.

And there is still more to be said about "the wave of looseness that has hit our country." What does Mr. Schuler mean by the "wave of looseness?" Does he mean the temporary and admittedly unwise extremes of reckless conduct on the part of ignorant, crude, unenlightened and therefore irresponsible young people—extremes for which the arbitrary methods of restraint and prudish secrecy used by our conservative majority are responsible; or does he mean simply the deliberate departure from certain conventional standards which he and those who see eye to eye with him, happen to believe to be valid and permanent and final standards? Does Mr. Schuler not know that he himself accepts, as a matter of course in his daily life, customs which, when they first established themselves, were opposed by the Mr. Schulers of that day, righteous men who were "tremendously concerned" about the contemporary "wave of looseness"? We've always had a "wave of looseness" in that sense. It is the wave of change and growth; it is the pulse beat of the Living God,—concerning whose purposes our clergy profess, apparently without warrant, to know a great deal.

Does Mr. Schuler think the ability of the human race to find God depends on its conformity to a traditional, received, second-hand code which happens to have his approval and the approval of his generation, on the ground that it is a sacred legacy bequeathed by our fathers, who got it from their fathers? I deny that such a lineage is any test of Twentieth Century authenticity or authority. I deny that we are bound, on pain of any sort of theological damnation, to accept anybody else's thoughts, second hand, regardless of whether "Anybody" be living or dead. But it is the view, particularly among many of our clergy, that we are so bound, and that the past has over us a divinely conferred authority. I hold this to be as flat a superstition as the Divine Right of Kings; and I predict that it is going to be yet flatter. Also, I deny that it is even remotely related to Religion, or to Christianity as it was taught by Jesus, violator of the Sabbath and rebel against the established order of his day.

"No," Mr. Schuler would probably say, "I think nothing so monstrous. You are attributing to me opinions I don't hold. We certainly have a right to think for ourselves in most matters. *But* the things I maintain with respect to marriage are laid down in black and white in the Bible. Jesus said thus and so concerning marriage, which he plainly regarded as a divinely instituted and sanctioned thing.—Besides which it is an obvious social and economic necessity, as every sensible person knows."

As to the last I agree. It does appear to be necessary under our present social order. But that doesn't mean that we can't revise it to meet our changing needs. As to the question of Biblical authority, that's something else again.

Jesus also said to turn the other cheek to him who smites you; and to him who steals your coat give your cloak also; and give all that thou hast to the poor and follow me; and *judge not,* a vice to which many "religious" people seem particularly prone. Why do the people who have so much to say about the pronouncements of Jesus on marriage have so little to say about these other things; and why do they ostracize adulterers while they treat envy, hatred, malice, slander, and the like as venial sins? Since these things are quite as bad as adultery, and since their total actual effect on society is considerably more devastating than all the adultery ever committed, it would seem that these moralists need to introduce some sense of proportion, and perhaps a little more sanity, into their rather preferential system of morality.

I feel sure that whatever Jesus really said about Marriage and Divorce was intended to protect women and children. Women were in that day the slaves of men, and were often put away without the slightest cause. Women lacked economic opportunity; and their only chance against being turned out into the street with the dogs was the respect of the man for his marital obligations. It is true that the Jews had divorce by mutual consent, an arrangement I advocate; but it is also true that men could get rid of their wives when the consent was not mutual; and that the irresponsible tyranny they were able to exercise in this connection was a terrible thing. In an order where women were economically independent many of these possibilities for evil and for helpless misery among women and children would be removed. This is measurably true today in our civilization, even though our women have, as yet, only a partial economic independence. It will be even truer as more changes come.

Jesus, then, was dealing with conditions as they were in his day. He was concerned with what kinds of conduct were expedient and right under the order of society that he saw around him. He would have been the first to readjust his views under a different order; for he had a vigorous independence of thought and a clarity of insight from which many of his followers have taken no lesson. I think nothing could have grieved him more than to have foreseen how millions of our superstitious and intellectually enslaved race would later bind themselves cravenly to the letter of his teaching and ignore the spirit of it; and how they would make mere magic formulas of his golden words,—reported as they were by men, who, as the record itself tells, frequently failed to grasp his meaning, and read their own conventional way of thought into it. Time and again he tried, sometimes with ill-concealed impatience, to drive home to his generation and to all that should follow, that the letter killeth but the spirit giveth life. Why don't we act on this? Why do we learn nothing from his contempt for the rigid formulas that strangled society then as now? Why do we make insane formulas of the very words in which he denounced formulas? Will we never learn? Are we to live forever in this inferno of fear?—Sometimes when I consider these matters I despair; but in more lucid and less emotional moments I know that the

race is winning through; that the leaven is slowly leaven-
ing the loaf; that the Kingdom of Heaven within us
is in truth like the grain of mustard seed, and that it
is growing today, here in this "materialistic" age, with
amazing speed. This is an age of speed, even in matters of the spirit.

Let me repeat, then, that Jesus would probably have
been the last person, had the matter come to an issue
in his day, to have maintained that conventional, legal
marriage was rock-ribbed, like the everlasting hills, or
eternal, like Kindness. Far less would he have maintained
that it must not be modified to meet those great necessities of human life which it was devised to serve in the
first place. He didn't lay down the *formula* for marriage.
It took Paul, the master theologian, to do that. It
also took Paul to lay down formulas about such conventional minutiæ as that women must have their heads
covered in church, a solemn acceptance on his part of
a convention founded, like the use of the veil in Tur-
key, on the not exclusively oriental idea that women are
property and their sex a commodity.

Jesus didn't bother his head about such customs; or
if he did he attacked them at their source rather than
in their superficial manifestations. Jesus had a fine sense
of proportion. But Paul, with his more limited notion
of values, and the flaming zeal which made him one
of the greatest and most gallant figures in history, could
talk at one moment in words like great bells about the
true fundamentals of Life—Faith, Hope, and Love; and
in the next about some question of conventional conduct,
as if it were the equal of these. It is worth noting that
Paul was, by implication, against bobbed hair. In fact,
I don't think Paul would have liked our little flappers;

but I think Jesus would have smiled upon them, as he
did on all children.

To put it bluntly, I think that the Christian Church
had its choice between Paul and Jesus, and that it chose
to follow Paul, that being the easier way. I think, too,
that it is time for a change. I can hardly put the issue
now before our civilization more flatly than that; and
if I shock my theological friends, I challenge them to
show cause.

The application of this choice between Paul and Jesus
in the matter of marriage involves the rooting out of
formulas and a facing of facts. For instance, by the
standards of Jesus, the man who makes his wife and
family unhappy by forever snarling at them is, *ipso facto,*
morally as bad as, and perhaps worse than, the secret
adulterer in whose life hatred and spite play a less conspicuous part. This is the obvious truth, even if you
reckon the effects of hatred on society as compared with
the effects of adultery. For hatred is as common about
us as the air we breathe; and we are so used to contact
with it that we have ceased to notice what it does to us.

Unlike Mr. Schuler, therefore, I am not concerned so
much about the "wave of looseness"—really a wave of
natural economic and social change—"which has hit our
country"; rather I am concerned with the wave of loose
thinking about fundamental matters which has always
hit it—has, indeed, nearly drowned the human race ever
since the Flood. Loose thinking is worse than any form
of "loose living" ever practiced for the simple reason
that it is the cause of it. If the human race could think
straight it could not possibly be guilty of loose living;
though possibly it might elect to live with a freedom which
the loose thinkers of this day would *call* loose, with a

great rattling of loose ancestral skeletons, and loud talk
about what our fathers did.

There is much wailing in pulpit and press about our
"materialism" and our energetic habit of making money.
Here again we love to talk nonsense and ignore the truth,
which is that brick, mortar, and money are legitimate
instruments of living when they are in the hands of people who have the good sense to control them; and that
the way to make them beneficent is to produce in our
children the ability to think straight and be honest with
themselves,—an ability which *our* parents, as good and
regular members of Society, caused to atrophy in us,
by binding our minds the way the Chinese bind the feet
of their children.

And speaking of our parents, the precise nature of
the debt we owe to them is, like our theories about marriage, one of our favorite and most completely standardized lines of bunk, fished out of the necessities of an
oriental, pastoral civilization and transplanted without
qualification into a civilization completely different. It
is obvious that children owe their parents no sentimental
debt whatever; that the parents did not "give them life";
and that in begetting them, the parents simply fulfilled
their own nature and their own desires and—in some
cases—their natural liking for babies. There are parents who make a point of dinning into their children's
ears this talk about the "debt" they owe them. What
they owe, as members of society, is an *obligation*, the
sort of obligation that inheres in family life because
of its personal intimacies, its close and difficult contacts,
and its natural necessity for social coöperation. This
is simply the duty every man owes to his neighbor; it
is a special and intensified form of it, and every man
should take joy in meeting such an obligation. But it

is not the obligation to be a slave bound forever by a debt that he cannot pay; it is not the obligation of conformity in vital matters of the inner life; and it is not a debt of sentimental slush. It is not a tribal formula. *Life* is not a debt; it is a *right*. If there be any conceivable debt, the parents usually cancel it by the almost criminal stupidity with which they rear their offspring. On the whole I think the obligation is on the other side.—Jesus struck a death blow at this old superstition at least twice—once when as a boy he deserted his parents to talk with the learned men in the Temple, and again in this remarkable and stern passage:

"Then one said unto him, Behold, thy mother and thy brethren stand without, desiring to speak with Thee.

"But he answered and said unto Him who told Him, Who is my mother? and who are my brethren?

"And he stretched forth his hand toward his disciples and said, Behold my mother and my brethren! For whosoever shall do the will of my Father which is in Heaven, the same is my brother and sister and mother."

CHAPTER 28

So much for some of the futilities of thought that we habitually impart to our children. But the pity of it is that however much they may rebel, as this younger generation is now rebelling, yet they never wholly recover from so evil an inoculation. It is as if we infected them with an unclean disease while they were very young children, and before they were old enough to resist and resent the outrage.

A child may be likened, indeed, to a naturally sane person set down in a lunatic asylum run by adults for adults. From infancy he gets educated in the prevailing, age-old insanities; and he is counted worthy of stripes if he put them to the test of his naturally excellent reasoning powers, and so fail to accept them and conform.

The effect at first, especially through the period of adolescence, is an enormous confusion of mind, dissatisfaction with standards which all the "sane" people in the asylum regard as fundamental, and possibly a fiery and ill-considered rebellion against every rule of the place, the good rules and the bad rules together. And in such revolts many court their own destruction. I get hold of some of them and save them; but the criminal courts get others, and these victims there encounter treatment which, for them, is often the conclusive end of all things lovely and good.

I shall not attempt to list the manias of the asylum here. Merely to name them would be to fill a catalogue, and I am trying not to write a catalogue.

I may, however, mention one which appears to be the

312

cause of many others. I think the most awful mania we have is the ancient and idolatrous conception of God as an irritable old man with two arms, two legs, a long beard, a thunderous brow, an unstable nervous system, very erratic methods of thought, a nasty temper, and a summary way of torturing through eternity persons who do not conform to certain rules *of the asylum*—which asylum he planned, invented, builded, and organized,— not as a foot-stool but as a door-mat, on lines which must on no account be changed, and which could not possibly be improved on. And, speaking of door-mats, perhaps it couldn't. Certainly it is hard to see how, under their theory, it could be of much use in any other capacity.

I am not talking generalities. An anthropomorphic conception of God is objectionable enough on philosophic grounds, but it is still more objectionable in the light of much that I have seen actually happen as a result of it.

Most of us accept it; and it leads us, as a nation, into an ethical code of a particularly mean sort; a code of rewards and punishments; the identical code by which we bring up children in most American homes. This perversion of the teachings of Jesus we call Christianity. Under it we instruct the young that they are to do right because they will be punished if they don't—by an earthly father now, and by an heavenly father later.

We are all to do right on the same plan all our lives. By giving up our natural impulses and desires now, and by accepting as right or wrong what somebody else tells us is right or wrong, we not only escape hell fire, but are headed for a heaven where there will be plenty of physical comforts later; a heaven where people will be bored to extinction by an eternity of effortless rest,—in plain English, where they can wallow in laziness much as they would do here if they should inherit a million dollars.

This view of God, and of His plan for running the Asylum Earth, is losing some ground in the godless cities, particularly among the younger inmates, most of whom are vigorously interested in the job of living, are as little given to brooding about their immortal souls as they are about their stomachs. They think, quite rightly, in my judgment, that God will look after these matters far better than they can. But in the rural districts the old notion is still swallowed, hook, line, and sinker, and they still sing that horrible thing about there being a fountain filled with blood, the quintessence, I often think, of everything ugly in puritanism, and a travesty on everything Jesus ever stood for. I don't know what ten more years of radio broadcasting will do to this way of thought in the country, but between the radio and the Ford I should say its doom is in sight, or at least just over the rim of the horizon "where the blue begins."

But the idea of a wrathful God still does untold harm; even at the moment of its passing it acts on the human race like a poison gas pouring in clouds from out the Nether Pit. Though some of us are waking up to the notion that God probably isn't anything like as stupid or as dull a person as some merchants in Dogma would have him, still even the freest of us cling to early habits of conduct modeled on that tradition. A mean idea of life, once absorbed in childhood, clings to one like an incubus; the vile smell remains even though one wash in living water. We are like children of a King who have been reared in degradation by incompetent servants.

Ask the ordinary boy why one should do right, and he will hazard many guesses, all of them based on a degraded Fear, and with an eye on the returns. "The

cop will get me.—I'll get a lickin'.—I'll get caught.—
I'll be disgraced.—I'll lose money.—I'll go to jail.—I'll
go to hell later." Such are the answers they give. I
have tried them many times. The thing is lodged in
their very marrow. They absorbed it with their mother's
milk. Almost it seems as if they learned it in the womb.

And yet there is a certain crude power that comes from
a point of view so simple. The old New England puri-
tans had it; and the brooding Fear of God that it created pent-up and restrained within them mighty spiritual
and mystical forces which later sought a permitted and
righteous outlet in the settling of a continent and the
building of a nation.

Times and ways of thought are fortunately changing;
and yet it will be an evil day if this nation shall ever fail
to accord to the brave and simple men who stamped their
heroic image on this continent a reverent love and respect. If I had my way Governor Bradford's "History
of the Plymouth Settlement," a contemporary diary written in the heat of action, would be read by every American. There is a moral grandeur in that great document
which should be a precious heritage, consciously valued
by us. And yet I suppose there are few Americans who
so much as know such a book exists.

All this we should cling to, reverently, as an essential thing in our Americanism. But it is quite as true that
we must nevertheless build independently and in our own
fashion on the foundations that they laid.

But let us have no illusions about their views, nor
about the views of those of us who, today, cling to their
bigoted way of thought. There are many such. These
people find life and all its issue a simple matter of double-
entry bookkeeping, both as to the Here and the Hereafter.
They see it as a business proposition. Goodness has a

price. The Reward of the righteous is not a thing to be kept subjectively in the background, it is frankly in the foreground; it isn't an incidental stone in the arch, it is the keystone.

In this philosophy you take the record of the Bible literally; you admit no middle ground between your two sets of Absolutes, Heaven on the one hand and Hell on the other—not even a purgatory. On the one side are the Church Goers and Observers of God's Sabbath Blue Laws,—on the other the Monkey Man and People Who Fish on Sunday; on the one hand the Sheep, on the other the Goats; on the one hand the Grape Juicers, on the other the Wine Bibbers; Heaven for those the Lord predestined to it on the plan mapped out for Him by John Calvin, and Hell for those He created awry for the sake of the contrast. Isn't that lamentable? Believe me, I set it down with no thought of ridicule and with no wish to hurt the feelings of persons who accept such views and interpretations of the teachings of Jesus. But these are the facts; and they are the fruit of that old, old conception of a bearded deity, a conception Jesus tried to destroy—a conception which is stubbornly clung to to this day by many orthodox Protestants, orthodox Catholics and orthodox Jews.

The Black and White people of this world are those whom William McFee, in his "Casuals of the Sea," calls the Browns—thereby proving that he has a remarkable eye for color. Things are right or wrong, black or white, for the Browns. Often the Browns have a simple sincerity and candor and courage about them which makes them lovable, admirable, and dependable in certain of the less involved, routine, conventional relationships of life. One pleasant thing about the Browns, when they are of the genuine Black and White variety, is that you can always tell what they will do.

But heaven save us from the Browns the minute the affairs of life become involved and complex. They have a devilish consistency about them that makes them judge others, and punish the "sins" of others. I am rescuing "Wayward" girls from their clutches constantly. Their "righteous" way of thought, applied with unflinching and idiotic logic, makes them in certain instances dangerous, bigoted, stupid, fanatical, dishonest, insincere, tolerant of hypocrisy, and intolerant of the Truth—*all under the cloak of solid Morality*. At such times they become wolves in sheeps' clothing. I encounter many of this stripe among social workers, teachers, and others who ought to know better. Most reformers with cut-and-dried programs and panaceas are also of this kind; and most of them are utterly unscrupulous in gaining their ends.

Such persons have a profoundly immoral point of view. They are immoral for the fundamental and sufficient reason that they mulishly refuse to give the undoctored Truth the right of way. The Truth must conform to their preconceptions or they will have none of it.

Their vision, blunted by their formulas, by their jealous fears for the permanence of those formulas, and by their general hatred of being made uncomfortable, has not cut deep enough to tell them that even if Truth should seemingly wipe God from the Universe, as some of the rash ones among our men of science think it some day will, *still* it would merit the right of way; for the Truth would then *be* God, the Great Spirit in whose conscious and perceiving Personality it surely inheres anyway.

They have not perceived that an atheist, clinging to the sharp-edged and terrible Truth, as he sees it, is still bleakly worshiping his God whether he knows and ad-

mits it or not. Sincerely to believe anything is an act
of worship. No man can escape God, not even in what
he may stupidly believe to be a Godless universe. He
cannot even blaspheme save in the name of a God whose
existence he affirms in his very act of denying or flouting it; and the fool who says in his heart "There is no
God," is suffering from a suppressed conviction that God
Is;—what a witty friend of mine felicitously calls "the
God complex." Belief is the natural and instinctive
thing; the religious instinct is as deep rooted and valid
as the sex instinct.

It is because I believe this that I stand ready to adventure with Life, to take chances with people, and to
stop worrying about what will happen to the human race
if a "wave of looseness" hits it. Its life is a progression.
The Force that makes it so is stronger than our follies
can ever be; and it turns even these to account.

This is optimism, but I would not have it interpreted
as a fatuous optimism. The race, as a race, survives
its own follies; but many an individual nation has destroyed itself in the past, and many a civilization has gone
to wreck because of its blindness. The same thing can
happen to us; and it possibly will if we persist indefinitely in our present national dietary, combined with our
present habit of breeding most largely from our moron
stock while the best of our racial strains die out.

The remedy for this situation is real Education and
real Religion in the light of the truth of science. The
Truth, if we will but spread it over the face of the world,
can save us. Not a blind clinging to minor conventions,
not a clinging to the sterile Past, but the free spread,
chiefly through the schools, of scientific information that
would give every young person going out into the world
a comprehension of the laws on which the life of the

race and the life of the individual are founded. Give us *that*, and the race will surely achieve a great destiny. But fail to give it, keep us in the bonds of superstitious ignorance, afraid of a lot of hell-born shadows, and we shall tread the path of racial deterioration on which our feet may even now be perilously set. Albert E. Wiggam in his remarkable book, "The New Decalogue of Science," holds that the race is even now slowly dying, and that nothing but a change to the right about can save it; and that instead of using its newly acquired scientific knowledge to save itself, it is rather ignorantly using it for its own destruction, like a child playing with a great machine of which it knows nothing and cares less. And it is on this ground that he pleads for education of the right sort and for statesmanship in Government that will be concerned with these perils and their avoidance.

I am unable to go the whole distance with Mr. Wiggam. I find in his view what seems to me a mechanistic determinism with which I can't agree. I don't believe Natural Selection is the final thing he thinks it is; and I believe there is, *a priori*, in the human mind, an underived creative energy which must be reckoned with as a force in evolution—creative evolution.

But I do agree with his thesis that ignorance of the laws of racial and individual life, together with consequent failure to obey them, can destroy this nation. And from that I deduce, First, that Adults who insist that Youth must follow no new thing are themselves doing their best to destroy our nation with the bludgeon of Ignorance and Superstition; and Secondly, that the Revolt of Youth against this bludgeoning bespeaks on the part of our race a native ability to find its soul and to live in harmony with God; and that this ineffable urge will in time be victorious.

One thing that has made this possible, as I have already tried to show, is the economic independence, and the subsequent independence of thought and action, which the conditions of this age have conferred on young people. It leaves them free to follow impulses, thoughts, and aspirations which formerly they would have had to forego because of their dependence on their tyrannous elders. The only reason the elders of today are less tyrannous than formerly is that they don't find tyranny so practicable as it once was. Then too, the spirit of the age has reached even their stiffer minds and encrusted hearts; and in a measure they have yielded to it.

The acceptance of such views as these makes Tolerance an easy thing; for it leaves no room for Fear which is the cause of Intolerance. Intolerance is founded on our conviction that *we* are running things, that our decisions and opinions are important, and that ruin will follow if somebody else who thinks less correctly be permitted to make a few mistakes.

Back of this attitude lies a monstrous presumption, a monstrous egoism; and this leads us in turn to the very wrong conclusion that there are two classes of people in the world, good people and bad people—whereas there are only people,—individuals, that is, who aspire toward the happiness that is their right, and who reach toward it as they may, according to their lights.

Each individual of us has every kind of possibility within him. The benignant old lady in lavender and old lace, for instance, the soul all her life of virtue and rectitude, takes on an added interest the instant you stop to think that old ladies just like her have on occasion lost patience with their husbands to the extent of sticking the invaluable carving knife into them just before the Golden Wedding. What course will *this* old

lady take? You may cite the probabilities, and show
that such suspicions are, in her case, unwarranted; but
you can never tell. She *might*. It is largely a question
of bringing the right stimulus to bear. For she *isn't* a
good old lady, nor yet a bad old lady, but just an old
lady.

There is no man, woman, or child in whose nature
there do not exist abysses and unguessable depths of
lawless possibility, and unguessable heights of heroism as
well. During the war we released criminals from our
prisons and sent them to the trenches, where many of
them performed acts of self-sacrifice and self-forgetful-
ness *which proved conclusively that the Law had made
some kind of mistake in dealing with them before*, a mistake which, in the ordinary course of events would never
have been discovered. In each of those "bad" people
there was a spring waiting to be released. I find that
there are no exceptions, though it is often difficult to find
the spring.

Unsuspected depths, unguessable heights—it's all one.
Height and depth are the same thing; in Latin the same
word, *altus*, denotes them both. The only difference is
in your point of view. In our phenomenal world, all
things are relative.

All things are possible to all of us. Let us therefore
see ourselves as we are, strange children of God, who,
for reasons we do not know but which God knows, deny
and affirm their God by turns; and who thus, on an endless ladder of Yea and Nay, climb heavenward and find
Him. I would not go so far as to say that there is a
utility in error. Still, the paradox is there to be reckoned with. Let us at least be honest and admit that
it is there, even though our logic cannot justify it, and

though within the compass of our thought the problem of evil apparently has no solution.

Unfortunately this passion for Intolerance, which, by reason of its bigotry is the cause of so many social aberrations,—does not fully sate itself when directed toward other persons. So all-consuming is this lust for judgment that it turns inward and feeds upon the heart of him who harbors it. We don't stop with passing judgment on others, we judge ourselves—which is far worse. It is worse for the same reason that the man who considers himself physically incapacitated, weak, or crippled, is likely to hold a spiteful envy toward those who do not share his weakness. He wants to hold others down to his level. The attitude of him who produces incapacity in himself by his doubts and his fears, and adverse judgments of himself, is similar. He puts his personality in chains. As a result he wants to see the same chains on others. Whereas if he were himself free and happy and well he would not grudge a like freedom to others. His intolerance toward himself therefore is a more basically destructive thing than intolerance toward others.

We have an instinct which gives us a greater horror of suicide than of ordinary murder. By the same token, the man who judges himself unreasonably murders himself through fear. It is against nature, though it is in accord with many accepted theologies, where it goes too often by the name of "repentance." It all depends on what you mean by "repentance." If it means fresh courage and effort in the face of failure, well and good. If not, not.

The man who can't tolerate himself and his own shortcomings, and, while humbly recognizing his limitations, yet go forward with fresh courage, will play the game badly. The man who can't forgive himself his own sins because he has a "conviction of sin" will be a poor hand at forgiving others.   If you doubt this, watch these thin-lipped, hard-faced ascetic people who have gone through life fighting themselves and their natural inclinations on the theory that whatever is is wrong,—believing what they have been told at second-hand instead of what the heart tells them, and see if the fight has softened them or given them a Christian gentleness toward anybody else.

CHAPTER 29

One reason why I have always been exceedingly fond of boys is that the so-called "incorrigible" boy presents more of this instinctive tolerance toward himself, and consequently toward the rest of the world, than any animal that walks. His incorrigibility usually proceeds from the way society has of treating him when he does things which, to him, are the natural and logical thing to do, and which do, in fact, flow quite naturally from his independent and first-hand way of thinking about things when such a mode of thought is linked with insufficient experience or education. The whole of the Younger Generation has much of that attitude also; but it compromises with Society As Is much more than any independent small boy will deign to do. As an example of the way the human mind tends to act before it becomes "civilized," therefore, the "incorrigible" boy forms the best possible example; and I propose to say something about him here.

A young boy is quite a different animal from anything else in the world on two legs or four. He is unique, both in his independence of mind and in his rather hostile sensitiveness to whatever contacts come his way. Young girls, by comparison, are immensely more stable and complaisant in matters of social conduct. A girl of twelve, for instance, is a social being, already living in outward, tactful, skillful conformity to the world around her. She acquires social graces readily, she can talk with grown women with something of a grown woman's glibness and volubility, and she is sure of herself to an extent that makes one question whether there really is such a thing as an Awkward Age.

Young girls, in their relations with each other, as well as in the restraints they place upon themselves, have already developed something of that attitude of Intolerance, and that bigoted instinct for passing judgment, which is unhappily so characteristic of the adult world into which they fit so readily. They are likely to be spiteful, gossipy, and uncharitable toward each other; and they persecute or ostracize any of their number who fail to keep up with the prevailing mode, whatever it may be. They put shackles on themselves, and they put shackles on each other.

But boys are remarkably free from this adult taint. Boys are not interested in adult standards, and however much they may fear them they have no respect for them. The standards boys impose on each other are natural, primitive, fundamentally valid standards, involving physical and mental strength and skill, and the social quality of minding one's own business, and of not minding even that too particularly—all of which involves the virtue of Tolerance. Some call it Indifference, but I do not agree. It grows rather from a very definite standard of values which rates some things high and others low, and does it very well, on the whole.

A boy's reluctance to wash behind his ears is symbolic of his whole state of mind. His sense of values is his own; it is at variance with that of the world he lives in; he thinks it better than that of the world he lives in; and he is a rebel from his birth.

I remember one boy brought before me to answer for some rascality, who for a time vigorously denied all charges.

"But, Peter," I observed at last, "there's at least one

thing you *can't* deny, and that is that you don't wash your ears. Isn't that so?"

"Naw!" said Peter indignantly. "The reason my ears is dirty is dat a guy threw water on 'em, and the durt settled in 'em before dey got dry."

Only when a boy passes puberty and becomes aware that girls are something other than a nuisance, and begins to wet down his hair when he combs it, and finds his voice shooting off into queer falsetto squeaks, does he become tractable, simply as a means to getting something that he wants, and which he can obtain only by conformity to the ways and the point of view of girls. What he wants he doesn't yet know; but in finding out he walks right into the trap.

Through the whole course of his development as a social being he lags far behind any girl of his own age; and in this respect he never does catch up. All his life he is destined to remain diffident, bashful, and prone to sit in the back pew at church, till he marries, as it were, into the front pew, where other women can see his wife's hat.

But up to the time he is fourteen or fifteen he is a queer and fascinating study, provided you have the energy and the courage to deal with him. He remains so more or less till he is twenty-one; but from puberty on he steadily drifts toward that *conformity*, that intolerance of himself and of others, which finally merges him permanently into the multitude of timid males, just one more standardized man with a brown derby, just one more member of an intolerant mob that stands ready to lynch on sight any one whose derby isn't brown,—the reason being that each and every one of them would wear some other kind of derby or none at all, *if he dared*. Intolerance is a dog-in-the-manger type of revenge.

Boys suit my taste best when they are between twelve and fourteen, though I like them all, regardless of age, and have several of them daily as an *entrée* in my human-nature menu.

Some of them steal automobiles, some steal automobile accessories, others run away from school, still others run away from home. Some defy the cop just to see what he'll do about it; some upset some fruit stand and harvest the reddest of the apples while the owner shrieks in resounding Neapolitan what Judge Lindsey will do to them when he gets them into court. On the other hand, I regret to say that some of them wiggle their fingers at victims who threaten them with my vengeance; and angry citizens have come many times to my court bitterly reproaching me that I "stand back of the young rascals." For here, even as in the case of flappers and flippers, I am famous as an "encourager of immorality."

But I am not an encourager of immorality nor of antisocial conduct of any sort. What I understand first of all is that I must find means to keep these boys from repeating their offenses, and that any punishment which fails to get that result is likely to present society with a dangerous criminal. Reform can come about only through a change in the boy's way of thinking. He doesn't wilfully think wrong; he does it because the premises of his logic are incorrect. Change that and you change the boy; for direct, logical, free, and vigorous thinking, independent of adult conventions, is a peculiar gift of boyhood. A boy has a way of thought which is as deadly direct in its logic from an accepted premise as the path of the bullet from a rifle. If the boy misses it simply means that the rifle is sighted wrong, that's all; there is nothing wrong with the rifle itself.

It is this that makes some of my boy cases almost appallingly funny; for humor is often nothing but a form of logic so honest and remorseless that it follows through to the bitter end.

Take, for example, the case of a certain little "Mickey." Mickey was one of the most conspicuous instances of original sin that I ever had to deal with; and in his dealings with society he seemed born to trouble as the sparks fly upward. His age was eleven; and the police had long since formed the habit of arresting Mickey on general principles whenever anything went wrong in the street where he lived. Sometimes Mickey's hard little pipe-stem legs would carry him to my chambers ahead of time when he felt, as he used to say, "Judge, I dun got in trouble again; en I thought I better git here before de cops do"; and his squinty blue eyes and his shock of Irish red hair were a familiar sight in the court house.

It came to pass, therefore, that whenever there was mischief afoot, and the local cop had gone ahunting, Mickey would run the instant he spied him; and this he would do even if he was innocent, as sometimes happened. Flight naturally drew suspicion and pursuit, and Mickey would then be confronted by the difficulty of explaining why he had run if he "hadn't done nuthin'."

"Mickey," I said to him on one occasion, "when you are innocent, why not stand your ground?"

A pained expression came into his face. "Judge," he said, "don't you know that you can't tell a cop nothin'. Judge, *when a cop is after yuh, he's agin yuh;* and there's only one thing t'do—Ditch and Skidoo. If yuh don't yuh just naturally gits pinched."

"But, Mickey," I protested, "that's no reason why you should lie to the cop."

To my surprise he said, "Judge, I never lies to the cop."

"I don't know what you call it, then," I said, "when you knocked the props out from under that fruit stand, and you skedadled with the cop after you; and when he caught you you told him you didn't do it. Just now you told me you did do it. You told me the truth, and you lied to the cop."

Again he put on the air of injured innocence that he could assume to perfection when he wished, and then came back at me with this:

"Judge, dat ain't lyin' to the cop; dat's *stringin'* de cop. For yuh see, Judge, it's like dis. Dat guy had pinched me so much when I hadn't done nothin' dat when he pinches me for somethin' I done I says I didn't do it, so as to make up fer *one* of the times when he says I done it when I didn't. Dat's stringin' de cop. An' he's still got a lot o' string comin' to 'im!"

I defy anybody to show that Mickey did not there make an effective appeal to the elemental right of self-defense, or to show that the policeman had any right to expect the truth from his lips.

The attitude of injustice on the part of the police—like the attitude of injustice and revenge on the part of parents, forced Mickey to seek an avenue of escape. He lied, not because he was a liar but because he had encountered injustice; also because he was an ingenuous and independent thinker, not afraid of himself or of his own judgments, or of a God fashioned for him, like an idol, by somebody else.

I recall another case that brings out this same streak of undeviating and almost comic independent thought, and unconventional tolerance in the boy mind. I had to send Jerry Saunders to the Industrial School at Golden. It was necessary that he learn a trade and be taught to work; for I have always believed strongly in the saying from the Talmud, "He that teacheth not his child a trade is the same as if he taught him to be a thief."

Parenthetically, and *à propos* that bit of ancient wisdom, let me pause for the space of a paragraph to say that one of the greatest women in the West is Mrs. Emily Griffith of Denver, founder of the Opportunity School. This institution has become nationally famous and I know of no keener satisfaction that I ever felt in my ideas about education than to have them in a large part confirmed by Mrs. Griffith. She told me that the case of four boys who many years ago came to my court from her school which was then the old 24th Street grammar school, interested her. These four boys appeared in court one morning without any charge against them. They said that they wished to learn a trade but that there was no part of the curriculum in our schools at that time that gave them any such opportunity. They wanted me to send them to the reform school where there was such a thing as vocational education. I was so impressed with this case that I wrote an article for the *Rocky Mountain News* entitled, "Is the Public School Just to the Boy," quoting that passage of the Talmud wherein it has said that "he that faileth to teach his child a trade teacheth him to be a thief." Mrs. Griffith told me that this circumstance and that article had much to do with her inspiration and determination to establish the Opportunity School of Denver where children may now have the opportunity that was then denied them.

But to return to Jerry.—Jerry agreed with me that a trade was what he needed; so I gave him the money for his railroad fare, and he started on his 20-mile trip to the so-called reform school near the little town at the foot of the mountains called Golden, from which town that boy-dreaded institution has come to be called Golden instead of by the official name given it by the law of the State. Jerry went alone as most of such boys do.

It happened the next day that one of the Trustees of the Industrial School was driving along the road to that institution when he saw a diminutive and very tired little boy trudging along just ahead of him. He carried a bundle which he evidently found heavy.

"Kid," the Trustee said, "can I give you a lift?"

"Sure, Mister," said the boy. "I didn't ask because I was afraid you'd turn me down like the others."

"Where are you going," asked the Trustee as the lad climbed into the car.

"I'll tell you, private," replied the boy. "I'm goin' to the Reform School. Y'see, it's this way. Judge Lindsey, he gimme a square deal, an' put me on my honor, and put up the money for my ticket. Then I figured I'd have one good feed before leaving town; an' that took all my ticket money. But a kid can't throw the Judge down, y'see; so I'm hoofing it."

The Trustee then admitted that he was going to the reform school too—though for a somewhat different reason; since he already had a "trade." He had no diffi-culty in confirming in the boy's mind the impression I had tried to create, that he would profit by going there, and that he ought not to regard his stay there as a pun-ishment, but as an education.

In due time they reached the school and parted on very cordial terms.

Months later the Trustee had occasion to visit the school again, and this time he spied Jerry on the campus.

The instant the boy saw him he ran to him with all his might. "Well, it isn't so bad, is it!" said the Trustee as they shook hands.

"You bet it ain't," cried Jerry. "Say, I've got a garden.

It's all mine. I always wanted a garden. My garden's mostly onions. Don't you want to see it?"

To this the Trustee assented, and they started for the garden. It was quite a walk, because the grounds at Golden occupy hundreds of acres; but finally they arrived there.

"Say," said Jerry, "I'm gonna trust you. I come out here to make some onion sandwiches. D'you want one?" Then he pulled from his pocket two large hunks of bread. "I know you won't snitch. I stole this bread out o' the refectory. Some other kids is comin', and they'll have some bread too. Before they come I'll show you how to make an onion sandwich."

With that he began carving the bread with his jackknife, and having done that, he pulled several of the choicest of his onions and began to peel them.

"Won't they smell your breath when you get back?" asked the Trustee.

"Yes," said Jerry; "I've got some peppermints. Anyway," he added, "it ain't the onions they'd kick about. I don't have to steal the onions."

Pretty soon a group of other boys arrived, and were instantly thrown into awe and consternation at the sight of the enemy in their midst.

"This is a real guy," said Jerry nodding reassuringly toward the Trustee, "an' I'll answer for him. He's goin' to eat a sandwich too. Come on, you fellers; get busy."

That put everybody, including the Trustee, at ease. They all fell to; in due time the sandwiches were made and spread on a board which one of the gang had dug up from a hiding place. Around it they now gathered with due ceremony, with Jerry at the head, and the Trustee at his right as a guest of honor.

One grimy paw started to reach for refreshment; but

Jerry put out a forbidding hand. "Hol' on, you," he said sternly to the abashed owner of the paw; "We gotta say the blessin' first."

Every head ducked, including that of the Trustee, who was so devout that he had to double up so as not to show his face; and Jerry said grace. It was short and to the point.—After which the stolen bread and the fresh onions were duly consumed. The Trustee ate two. At any rate that's what he said when he told me the story on his return to Denver. "I've listened to a lot of mechanical blessings that nobody meant," he observed; "but that was the first time I ever listened to a real one; and at many a communion service I have eaten bread that has seemed to me less effectively consecrated."

But what consecrated it? Boy logic! the logic and the tolerance and the instinct for free thought that cuts through to essentials, knows no hypocrisy, and seeks an inward and spiritual rather than an outward and visible consistency.

CHAPTER 30

When I first started my work in the Juvenile Court of Denver I began, to the wrath and consternation of all sensible and sane persons, including the sheriff, who missed numerous fat fees because of my peculiarities, to send boys, when I had to send them, to prisons or State institutions on their own responsibility. Formerly they had generally been taken to such places handcuffed to an officer, the handcuffs being necessary because young boys are as slippery as eels and a lot quicker. All officers of the law, including the sheriff, were a unit in calling me a crack-brained fanatic, and in predicting that since it was necessary to handcuff these boys to an officer to keep them from getting away, they would obviously fly to the ends of the earth if the handcuffs and the officer were both omitted. This, said they, was the only thing that could logically happen. Any sensible man could see it, just as any sane person could see that two and two make four, or that there are only three dimensions, length, breadth, and thickness.

Unfortunately for this method of reasoning, a lot of hard-headed mathematicians have long since shown that there are at least four dimensions, and possibly an infinite number of them. In like manner, these worthies discovered that their logic about boys was just logic, and therefore quite silly. The boys didn't run. The minute the handcuffs and the officers were out of the way they didn't feel any desire to run. In fact they couldn't be persuaded to run. I gave them their railroad fare, explained the idea, and they always arrived. They didn't

334

arrive only occasionally. They kept it up, in spite of a certain newspaper, which scolded, threatened, and ridiculed by turns. If a boy didn't have any other motive for going through, he would do it in order to put one over on the newspapers and police and the district attorney's office, and show them that they didn't know what they were talking about.

So far the record is 100 per cent. I've never lost one. Four or five out of all those hundreds did once, at first, run away, but they returned and apologized for their lack of sense and loyalty.

Back in the days when I was beginning my work among juveniles, I had one boy who was among the first I sent to Golden. It took some nerve to stand by my guns, for the tradition was not yet established, and I had to break new ground with every boy; also this youngster was considered by the police to be the worst rapscallion that ever rapscalled; and I guess he was. He was more than just a ten-minute egg; he was, to all appearances, petrified. His name, let us say, was Skinny Moran.—And speaking of names, the really enterprising ones are usually Irish or Scotch or both. I'm of Scotch-Irish descent myself. I've had them that were a cross between an Irish stew and a Scotch broth, whose talents were almost incredible. —But to my story. Skinny was always running away from the cops. He had served time in the reform school, and had been the terror of that institution. He was the leader of several gangs, and had within him the imagination, the fire, the courage, and the talents for roguery that, in other walks of life, make Captains of Industry— the kind whose exploits in millions are so magnificent that nobody has the heart to put them in jail.

I shall never forget the day when two six-foot policemen, both of them breathing hard and both of them evidently more or less under a nervous strain, came into my chambers with the diminutive form of Skinny between them, each of them with a big hand firmly encircling his lean little arms. Skinny clearly resented the familiarity, and yet I think he took a kind of pride in their evident respect for his resourcefulness.

One of these officers I knew to be very hostile to my methods; and, as I learned, he had just tipped off a reporter that the Judge was going to try sending Skinny to Golden alone, and that it was going to result in a good laugh on the Judge.

I told Skinny flat that I was going to have to send him to Golden. This brought from him a storm of tears and violent pleadings for "one more chance." But as I had given him "one more chance" on former occasions, I now had to point out that he was at the end of his rope. I tried in vain to calm him, but he wouldn't be consoled. And yet I just had to get hold of him somehow; and make some appeal that would win him.

I looked into the face of the policeman, who wasn't taking the trouble to conceal a sneer; and I looked at the interested and expectant face of the reporter who was there on the policeman's tip. And the thought came to me that I might shell them with their own guns.

"Skinny," I said, "do you know what this officer has told this reporter? He has told him that there is going to be a good story in this because Skinny can't be trusted; and that when I try to send you to Golden by yourself, and you run away, it will be a fine joke on the Judge. Now what do you think of that?"

Skinny's tears dried so fast that I seemed to see them sizzle into steam; and he turned on the policeman with flashing eyes. "So dat's what yuh told de guy, did yuh! Yuh thinks yuh knows a lot; but yuh don't know nothin' at all." Then he turned to me. "Judge, gimme that writ an' watch me fool dis cop."

I handed him the writ and some money, and the last I saw of him he was tearing across the court-house yard, regardless of keep-off-the-grass signs.

The policeman laughed as he saw him go. "Judge," he said, "that's the Grand Throw Down for you."

But at Police Headquarters there was another policeman who, even in those early days, had a faith in my methods which is common enough among our Denver police now. This man took up the cudgels in my behalf, and offered the cynic a substantial wager that Skinny would go through. The bet was made, and the stakes were placed in the hands of a stake-holder, who in due time called the Industrial School on the telephone. It appeared that Skinny was there. It appeared, moreover, that he was following a line of good behavior which was astounding to those who had had official dealings with him before.

Months later I made a trip to Golden; and out from a crowd of boys darted Skinny, his face all smiles, the pinched look gone from it, and a different expression about the eyes. "Say, Judge," he shouted the instant he was within earshot, "didn't we put one over on dat cop?"

Skinny is a prosperous Denverite today instead of an inmate of the penitentiary. He has a happy wife and a thriving family. Occasionally he drops in to watch me deal with other Skinnys; he always votes for me.

In the boy world you find no Conservatism for its own Sacred Sake. The laws of that world have a clearly defined use, and they derive from it. It's a pragmatic world. The only question asked of any code whatever is, "Does it work?"

In the boy world there is a freedom of experimentation, joy in discovery, and a "mind-your-own-business" spirit which denotes true democracy, as contrasted with the sham democracy whose tyrannies rest with such crushing weight on all of us.

Some thinkers have denounced democracy on the ground that it puts a premium on mediocrity, rewards conformity, standardizes clothes, thought, and conduct, reduces all men to a dead level, and cuts off the heads of any who dare to rise above that level. That is quite true of our leaderless civilization; but it would not be true of a *democracy*. The gentlemen have their terms mixed.

"Do not think," says Emerson, "that the youth has no force because he cannot speak to you and me. Hark! in the next room, who spoke so clear and emphatic? Good heaven! It is he! It is that very lump of bashfulness and phlegm which for weeks has done nothing but eat when you were by, that now rolls out those words like bell-strokes. It seems he knows how to speak to his contemporaries. Bashful or bold, then, he will know how to make us seniors very unnecessary.

"The nonchalance of boys who are sure of dinner, and would disdain as much as a lord to say aught to conciliate one, is the healthy attitude of human nature. How is the boy the master of society!—independent, irresponsible, looking out from his corner on such people and facts as pass by, he tries and sentences them on their merits, in the swift, summary way of boys, as good, bad, interesting, silly, eloquent, troublesome. He cumbers himself never about consequences, about interests; he gives an independent and genuine verdict. You must court him; he does not court you. But the man is, as it were, clapped into jail by his consciousness. As soon as he has once acted or spoken with *éclat*, he is a committed person, watched by the sympathy or the hatred of hundreds whose affections must now enter into his account. There is no Lethe for this. Ah, that he could pass again into his neutral, god-like independence! Who can thus lose all pledge, and having observed, observe again from the same unaffected, unbiased, unbribable, unaffrighted innocence, must always be formidable, must always engage the poet's and the man's regards. Of such an immortal youth the force would be felt. He would utter opinions on all passing affairs, which being not private but necessary, would sink like darts into the ears of men, and put them in fear. . . .

"Whoso would be a man must be a nonconformist. He who would gather immortal palms must not be hindered by the name of goodness, but must explore if it be goodness. Nothing at the last is sacred but the integrity of your own mind. Absolve you to yourself, and you shall have the suffrage of the world. I remember an answer which when quite young I was prompted to make to a valued adviser who was wont to importune me with the dear old doctrines of the church. On my saying, What have I to do with the sacredness of traditions, if I live wholly from within? my friend suggested—But these impulses may be from below, not from above. I replied, They do not seem to me to be such; but if I am the devil's child, I will live then from the devil."

I commend that passage from Emerson to the consideration of anybody who finds an incongruity in Jerry Saunders' grace before meat over sandwiches made with stolen bread.

I commend it to others who would fain know which traits in our younger generation we should be encouraging rather than strangling in this convention-ridden country.

A large part of my work, whether I deal with boys,

girls, or adults, consists in getting people to tell me the whole truth about what they think, what they want, and why they do things.

They are thankful for an opportunity to do this so soon as they are satisfied that they will not be judged, reproached, or ridiculed. Usually I find that I am the first person who has ever afforded them this essential relief, —unless they happen to be Roman Catholics, in which event the Confessional, which is in many respects one of the most profoundly wise of human institutions, has helped them.

When they deal with me they get it all off their chests. Then, with all the cards on the table, we take stock, and find out just how bankrupt they are, as if I were a receiver arbitrating between them and Society, which, though their creditor, is more often than not the real swindler and the real villain in the plot. Between us we decide which cards need to go into the discard, and which can be retained, as the Trumps of Life, so to speak. Sometimes the hand that's left is pitifully poor; but by slipping in an Ace now and then when they aren't looking, I often contrive to pull them through. Since this way of dealing with sin cuts Revenge out of the situation, a good many who would have been members of that crowd that wanted to stone to death the woman taken in adultery, hate me. They can't conceive of a Court of Justice that administers equity rather than "Justice." They can't conceive of a Court where hunted people can cry "Sanctuary," as wrong-doers fled to the Altar during the Middle Ages, and be safe. They can't conceive of a Court that looks upon Society as a ravening wolf from which the weak must be protected and against whose attacks they must be made strong. They can't conceive of a Court that can look upon the State as a criminally negligent parent, which neglects its children and leads them into temptation.—And so, as I say, they hate me.

Consequently I often find myself and my methods in sharp collision with various disapproving and hostile powers that be; and this sometimes sadly impairs the efficiency of the Juvenile Court. The story of what happened to me in connection with the famous Wright murder case, for instance, is typical; and it traveled all over the country at the time.

Mrs. Wright was on trial charged with killing her husband. Her twelve-year-old son came forward and alleged that he was the one who had killed his father; and that the thing happened by accident while he was trying to wrest from his mother's hand the revolver with which, driven to despair by her husband's treatment, she was threatening to kill herself.

The boy made this statement before the trial. I immediately went to the jail to see him. From there I took him to the Wright home, where I had a two-hour talk with him of an intensely intimate kind. There he told me the whole story, going into all that had led up to the tragedy through many years. He even reënacted what had happened at the shooting of his father. He was a very remarkable boy; and for the way in which he was trying to stand between his mother and the assaults of the prosecution my heart went out to him.

What he told me was told in confidence; and beyond saying that his mother did not know who killed his father, I can't reveal his story even now.

When the mother's case came to trial the prosecution contended that the boy was not telling the truth, and surmised that the story he had told to me in private was different from that which he had related on the witness stand.

I had, of course, gotten my information from the boy because he was not afraid of me; and it should have been patent to the District Attorney that he could have gotten the same information by using the same brand of common sense that I did. But no; having terrorized the boy into dumbness, he must put me on the witness stand and call on me to relate to the jury what the boy had told to me.

I refused, on the ground that the information had been imparted in confidence, that it was privileged just as much as information imparted to a doctor by a patient, and that for me to betray this boy would be to repudiate one of the fundamental principles on which the Juvenile Court of Denver depended for its very existence.

As a result of this refusal I was sentenced for contempt of court, and required to pay a fine of $500, with an additional $500 in costs, bringing the total to a thousand dollars. I appealed the case to the Supreme Court of Colorado, which sustained the contempt verdict, and held that, technically, I should have betrayed the boy's confidence. The Supreme Court came to this conclusion by a vote of 4 to 3. The difference of opinion was a sharp one, and the minority wrote an opinion on the case that makes very caustic reading.

In the meantime, apparently as a result of the boy's testimony, the jury acquitted Mrs. Wright.

Before I paid my fine a remarkable thing happened. Letters poured in from all over the country. They came from children to "de Kids' Judge" as my newsboy friends call me, contributing pennies and stamps toward the paying of my fine. By the time the letters stopped coming I literally had a basketful of money. It totaled several hundred dollars. I turned it over to be used for charitable purposes.

I have pointed out that the District Attorney could

have gotten the truth from the Wright boy had he used the methods of dealing with children that I use, and had he thus lifted from the boy's mind the weight of fear which caused him, quite rightly in this case, to regard society as his enemy. But that is never easy; it was much simpler for the District Attorney to go after my scalp, and to attempt to minimize the value of what I had done in my dealings with the boy.

CHAPTER 31

My first and important work, then, is in sharp contrast to what is ordinarily undertaken by courts; it is to draw the truth from people much as I drew it from the Wright boy when he so gallantly came to his mother's defense. This is always a delicate process. Many things contribute to its success—my experience, my reputation for tolerance, and whatever natural gift for the work I, and those who labor with me, may have. We are specialists in this field, and often we get results we could not get if we did not know every step of the game. A man who is experienced in dealing with animals knows beforehand, with fair certainty, what an animal is going to do in a given situation. It is much the same with people, with the difference that they are complex and fine, and correspondingly uncertain.

It is not easy to get the truth from people. This is due in part to their fears, and in part to the fact that most of them are novices when they attempt, by introspection, to come at their own motives. Always I know before I begin with them that whatever I can reveal to them about themselves and their own errors they will absorb very slowly; and that they will in most cases complete and practice what I teach them only at the cost of many mistakes and lapses. They have to be taught, line upon line, precept upon precept, here a little and there a little.

Such teaching requires of the teacher that he exercise as well as he can, certain qualities that are not easily acquired; and that he have a habit of mind which is

344

learned only by use and discipline. What this is I have already indicated. It includes tolerance, pity, sympathy, understanding, and abstention from judgment *combined with certain uncompromising demands for a free and willing change of conduct on the part of the culprit.*

In this matter Authority—an authority greater than that of any natural parent—must often play its part. A court is able to accomplish many things by fiat which agencies not vested with judicial authority would find impossible. In this sense the court is simply the State acting as a super-parent, much as the school is the state acting as a super-parent. It isn't paternalism, as the word is usually understood; but, whatever name you call it by, we have got to have vastly more of it as time goes on.

I may sum up the matter by saying that the work of this court calls for a love for human beings which is not a personal love, and which becomes catholic in its applications in proportion as it is impersonal. Faith, Hope, Love, these three—and the greatest of these is Love. It has always seemed to me that Love which St. Paul meant by those words derives its values in part from the absence of the Personal Equation.

In this court of human adjustment these virtues, Faith, Hope, and Love, are the only possible tools. We use them without sentimentality; we are entirely free from the mist of maudlin tears with which ill-informed persons connect these stern yet delicate instruments of regeneration. We use them because they are sound means of producing given psychological effects. We use them because they work. And we joy to use them because the process is life-giving to him who uses them. "It blesses him that gives and him that takes."

I do not mean that the application of such principles in the lives of people can ever be mechanical or that it is ever twice the same. What I do mean is that such work is a nice and difficult art; and that its instruments can be used with precision and certainty by human artists who are trained to do creative work in the field of human relations. It is at once a scientific and an artistic task. It calls for psychologic technique which is exact and scientific; and it calls also for an exquisite, almost subconscious *touch faculty*, a gift of adaptability, which is creative and original. These are the two things that enter into every art—they are its Form and its Spirit.

By such methods, so applied, we successfully reach people and change their lives. I do not mean that we reach all of the people who come before us, for there are some whose biological inheritance makes them apparently incapable of enduring the discipline of sustained social conduct, even with the best that science can do to strengthen their physical mechanisms. Also, there are still others who, though they may be brought to a fair degree of social efficiency, yet lack that inherited strength of mind and body which is fundamentally necessary. People in these two classes should be cared for; but it is one of the monstrous crimes of our civilization that they are allowed, without let or hindrance, to marry and reproduce their kind. If, through Birth Control, Education, and in some instances sterilization voluntarily accepted, as I believe it would be, they are not prevented from doing this, this moron class is quite capable of throwing us back into barbarism in the course of time.— I know of few tragedies more awful, and more repulsive, than the tragedy I see daily—helpless children, babies in arms, who are in the power of parents who should have been sterilized before they could contract this awful responsibility, and commit against society what, in their case, is the *awful crime of marriage*. Leave them their sex life—yes. Sterilization is possible without depriving them of that. But for God's sake don't let them sin against the unborn. I should never ask for forcible sterilization of any individual. Except in extreme cases of admitted feeble-mindedness, I only ask the right of education and appeal to such defectives; because I find from experience that they gladly accept a solution so merciful and so reasonable.

But a goodly part of those who come to my attention, I am happy to say, have qualities of the highest value, and are in need of enlightenment and instruction rather than reformation. Indeed, I find that waywardness in young persons is much more likely to be the result of superabundant energy and worth than it is of the degenerate weakness which predestines some unfortunates to crime. The line between these two classes of offenders needs to be sharply drawn. Better a child born of biologically competent parents out of wedlock than one born of degenerate morons "respectably" married!— And yet we permit laws which forbid Birth Control and which class contraception with lewdness, in the name of Anthony Comstock!

With persons whose inheritance is good, then, I have proof, in the way of consistent success through many years, that the application of the virtues I have named works like magic. I know by experience that these virtues, once in action, are capable of giving health, not to people's minds only but to their bodies as well. I have seen their application restore people to physical health as by a miracle, simply because the heart, the source of the sickness, had found peace.

Let me again insist that there is no maudlin sentimentality in this. What I have just said is in strict accord with what, in the field of psychology, are scientific truisms.

And nowhere in the world, in no psychological laboratory, have they ever had the thorough-going try-out that
they have received in this court of human relationships
through its twenty-five years of high pressure work, in
the handling of thousands of cases yearly.

I have, as I have already said, sent men to prison
for life. When there is stern work to be done I can do
it. It is not I that deal with "abstractions and theories."
The persons who do that are the so-called "practical"
people who, having had no experience in the application
of such methods, necessarily have to do their talking
through their hats. *Their* record is a record of consistent failure. This is true in most of the cases with
the criminal courts, the district-attorneys' offices, jails,
prisons, and the whole damnable machinery by which
perfectly sane and sound human beings, instead of being
salvaged, are turned into confirmed criminals as the inevitable sequence to their first trifling mistakes of conduct. Let these *anti-social forces,* many of whose methods
are far worse than the crime they fight, stack their facts
beside my "theories" and see what happens.

Such methods of "justice" don't belong on the Junk
Heap, for there they might be gathered in by some of
our professional Junk Men. Rather let them be loaded
onto an iceberg together, and then towed by a fleet of
battleships to the equator. It would, incidentally, be a
fine last use to make of the battleships before *they* were
junked—or sunk. Tug Boats of the Lord!

But is the Ocean deep enough? I think so. God
made it.

The Christian virtues which we so consistently apply
in the Juvenile Court of Denver are, then, the higher,
the more powerful, practical, and effective forces of life.
Their opposites, namely hate, intolerance, hypocrisy,

violence, revenge, ignorance, and fear, *are the weak and ineffective forces of life,* strong only as a means to death. They are dangerous in the sense that the molecular weakness and instability of dynamite is dangerous. We all find it hard to believe this and act upon it; for Life is a thing of Four Dimensions, and its fundamental paradoxes, therefore, are absurd to the reason though they are plain to the intuitions.

Dynamite is unstable, yet it presents an illusion of strength. So it is with all violence. The violent is the unstable; violent persons are violent because they are weak and afraid; bluff is a cloak for fear; bombast the emptiness of a drum; "virtuous" intolerance a confession of hid repressions and of the secret and opposite desires of the heart. Contrawise, it is as little children that men enter the Kingdom of Heaven; it is the meek who inherit the earth; he that loseth his life shall find it. And these are the paradoxes of Life, absurd to the wisdom of the wise, but plain to the heart.

The positive virtues, which have about them the calm of eternity, and are part of the Being of God, have a perfectly resistless force when once they become operative. Not only that but they form those natural and stable internal restraints of conduct, whereby human beings learn the inwardness of the words, "He hath showed thee, O man, what is good; and what doth the Lord require of thee, but to do justly, and to love mercy, and to walk humbly with thy God!"

When Jesus prescribed these virtues two thousand years ago, he said positively that they are the *only* means by which the human spirit can be controlled. He also pronounced then a practicable way of life, and not an impossible counsel of perfection.

But the illusion that spiritual instability is strength,

that violence is power, that force is efficacious, stays with us. The man in the story who spends the night in a haunted house always loads a futile revolver and tries to shoot the ghost when it appears.

First efforts to deal with these exalted forces of the spirit are like any other attempt to walk in high places when one is not accustomed to seeing an abyss of menacing possibilities at one's feet. One has to *learn* to do it.

I never see a window washer, fearlessly plying his trade ten stories up from the street, without nervousness, even when I know he is strapped by law to the window casing. I suppose persons who are not used to taking chances with human nature feel somewhat the same way when they see me, in the Juvenile Court, washing windows they consider difficult to reach.

I never see an iron worker carelessly strolling along a steel girder near the top of some skyscraper he is helping to build, without wishing—really, you know,—that he would get down on his hands and knees and crawl. I suppose people who see me strolling apparently at ease over the frame of what O. Henry might have called our psychic pskyscraper, feel a similar nervousness about seeing such liberties taken with the law of psychic gravitation in the name of Faith, Hope, and Charity. They may be intellectually convinced that there is no more reason for a tumble than there would be five feet above the ground; but the subconscious mind, trained by tradition and habit in terms of Fear, won't be quiet. It is the plank in mid-air, made famous by Monsieur Coué, right over again.—Or, as I prefer to think, it is the magic Flying Carpet right out of Arabian Nights, from which nobody ever tumbled that had the nerve to ride it.

I have been taking these chances with people for so long that I'm used to it. I know, by my constant failure to take tumbles, that there is nothing to it. The angels, or something, bear you up. You're as stable as a pyramid so long as you believe other people are the same way. In this Faith resides a magic that sees you through.

It goes without saying that it is more difficult to appeal to human beings by the methods used in the Juvenile Court than it is to hit them with a club or put them in jail. But if results be the important thing, then the gentler method, however difficult, and whatever skill it takes, does restore offenders permanently to society, while the method of force and violence permanently alienates them from it. Ninety per cent of my boys and girls become good citizens in spite of their bad start. Ninety per cent of those treated by the other method, the punishment method, become criminals for life. Society tells them they are criminals and treats them as such, and they accept the suggestion. This is a matter of record.—The same is even more true of girls than of boys, particularly those who get into sex difficulties. I put them straight and they stay straight: Society, by its usual methods of social ostracism and mental torture, and of jail in some cases, puts them crooked, and they stay crooked.

What it all means is that *if* the purpose of our system of criminal jurisprudence and of our prisons and other penal institutions is *punishment,* then they are admirable successes, and lack for nothing save the rack, the boot, the thumb-screw and the boiling oil. They have the whipping post, the solitary confinement, the brutality of keepers, the practically unpaid labor, and nameless ways of torture which "punish" fully and completely— to such an extent that if the whole thing could be exhibited to the public by putting glass walls—of unbreakable glass —on our prisons, our mobs could sit and watch and smack their lips, and, being sated, refrain from violence themselves. I suggest this as possibly the most effective way to put an end to our national institution of lynching. Mobs lynch offenders partly because they like the sport and partly because they are afraid the law won't punish them hard enough. But under this plan they would have their sport, long drawn out—and the punishment is of a kind that would meet their every desire.

A further argument in favor of this plan is that it would be inexpensive, save for the cost of glass. It would involve no change whatever in our prison system as it exists right now. Not a warden nor a keeper—nor a prisoner—would have to vary his daily routine in the slightest. I recommend it to the consideration of the "law enforcement" fiends who don't believe in making imprisonment "easy and pleasant" for the prisoner.

A still further improvement on our present out-of-date system of doing justice would be to have an annual drawing of lots by all citizens of this free country to determine who should go to jail and who shouldn't. This would result in quite as much even-handed justice as we now have, and would, besides, give every one a chance to be punished and redeemed from being a miserable sinner. The method should be especially welcomed by the Jonah-and-the-whale school, since the Lord would undoubtedly oversee the outcome, and attend to it that those not elected got what was coming to them. All told, the lottery system for keeping our prisons going deserves serious consideration by the American people.

CHAPTER 32

If, on the other hand, the real purpose of our system of criminal justice is to make people over, cure their defects, and normalize their point of view, to the end that they may be restored to society as useful citizens, then we are not within sight of it—save in the case of a few prisons that are managed by men of vision and imagination.

It is not merely brutalized wardens and keepers with low foreheads, fat jowls, and walrus mustaches that are responsible for this condition. These Simon Legrees are responsible for it only to the extent that they are the kind of men willing to be employed to destroy and degrade other men. There is nothing surprising or astounding about that. What *is* surprising and astounding is that supposedly intelligent persons, men high in public life, and men of fine feeling and judgment in other matters, approve of such methods, just as they approve of so unthinkable a barbarism as capital punishment.

For instance, I recently read in one of the very biggest and most widely circulated of our national magazines a series of articles by several eminent judges on the subject of crime and its prevention. These gentlemen wrote with about as much insight and evidence of thought as you would expect from a bunch of gossipy old women discussing what ought to be done to some pretty girl in the village who can't satisfactorily account for the dimensions of her waistband. They were unanimously of the opinion that the way to stop crime is to have "law enforcement."

"Arrest and try and convict more people," said they

353

in effect. "Put more offenders in jail with maximum sentences. Make them be good. Terrorize them into virtue."

There's constructive imagination and original thinking for you. If there be any method—*in view of the present nature of our prison system*—more certain than that to turn human beings into devils, I don't know what it is. Any chimpanzee in the jungle could think out *that* solution.

Don't misunderstand me, however. *Corrective* punishment is often necessary; and the fear of such punishment is undoubtedly an effective deterrent to many a would-be offender against society. *I am not advocating the omission of punishment, provided it be corrective and curative rather than vengeful punishment; nor am I advocating a lax enforcement of the laws.* The laws should be enforced with the utmost vigor by officials appointed for that purpose; and offenders, big and little, should be brought to book. What I object to is that we are not interested in *saving* these unfortunates. We merely want to take a brutal crack at them, and make them suffer, without stopping to think that they come out of prison after such treatment ten times worse than when they went in.

Nor do we give serious thought to crime as the result, not of innate cussedness and criminality on the part of individuals but rather as the result of *conditions* which mold some lives to an evil conformation. Many of these conditions could be changed easily; but others of them are rooted so deep in our defective social system that they are exceedingly difficult to come at. Among these latter are Poverty, and the freedom with which persons mentally and physically unfit are permitted to breed without let or hindrance. These, I should say, are the two worst.

One other might be added—Ignorance. But the three evils go hand in hand, they chase each other in a vicious circle, and I don't know that it is possible to say that one of them is more fundamental and basic than the two others. From any one of the group the other two can spring.

It must be remembered, however, that unfavorable economic conditions are not the only cause of crime. Such conditions produce the sordid forms of crime that are peculiar to Poverty and all that goes with it; but favorable economic conditions produce still another class of crime, peculiar to wealth and opportunity. In no country in the world is this so evident as in the United States, with its crimes of big and little business, and its crimes of special privilege.

Relatively, considering our opportunities and temptations to wrongdoing, and our exceedingly limited education in matters of ethical conduct, I think our national morals compare favorably with those of any nation in the world—by which I in no sense intimate that they are what they might be. This is just as true of our industrial conduct as it is of the conduct of American youth, whose temptations and opportunities toward wrongdoing are relatively greater than those of any Youth in the world.

We need not reproach ourselves too greatly for our sins; but we should face them and intelligently correct them. Our wrongdoing is a beneficent social energy which lacks intelligent direction and control, of the kind which education alone will make possible.

It is not putting it too strongly, indeed, to say that freedom from our characteristic national faults would in the circumstances argue, not that we were righteous but that we lacked spirit, energy, and enterprise. That we have had the energy to do wrong is a hopeful sign; it argues that with a little education we shall have an even greater energy to do right.

Education—that is our hope. It is the remedy, not merely for crimes of privilege committed by those quick-witted, half-baked intelligences, but for the crimes of poverty and blank ignorance, committed by those who simply lack the mental and physical mechanism for ef-fective action of any kind.

These people should be our real anxiety. They come from the hordes of morons, who are at present spawning, unchecked, like herring in the sea, filling our insane asy-lums and prisons at such a rate that we can't build fast enough to keep up with them. Relative to these hordes of degenerates, that part of our racial stock which ought to survive is dwindling. In my judgment this is the most serious and basic social problem we have today; and it is one to which, as a nation, we are giving no thought at all.

Our present laws forbidding contraception have done much to bring this about; for they put knowledge of contraception out of reach of the poor and the ignorant who most need it, and who should be encouraged not to breed other social incompetents like themselves, while it is easily within the reach of the educated, the alert, and the competent who should, by all means, be multiplying their numbers at least as rapidly as those whose ignorance causes them to breed unchecked. Certainly the *first* step should be to teach these teeming masses to have as few children as possible, or at any rate so few that they would be able to rear them properly. An opening up to the public of contraceptive knowledge would automatically place a limit on the rate at which we are producing people whose inherited weaknesses and biological inadequacy causes them to adopt crime as the easiest way of coping with a harsh and difficult world. That would be a long step ahead, for it would tend to restore the balance. At the same time it would *not* have the effect of further reducing the birth rate among the fit because they already practice contraception, and would continue to have children at least the same rate as at present; and would undoubtedly have more in the course of time, as changed conditions made it economically practicable.—

As general social and economic conditions improved the fit would deliberately increase the size of their families, and the balance would tip more and more in the direction of race improvement, biological adequacy, and an automatic lessening of those forms of crime which are the fruit of weakness.

I don't mean that this change would come in a day; but it would be unmistakable in the course of fifty years, and tremendous within a century.

This result would be very greatly hastened and intensified if every school child in this country could be given a thorough knowledge of the whole problem of eugenics; and of the duty which he, or she, individually owes to the race; a duty either to have *no* children in case of biological unfitness, or else, with biological fitness, to have children by a mate capable of transmitting desirable qualities to offspring.

At present what do we do? Why we limit our efforts to teaching school children what we are pleased to call One Hundred Per Cent Americanism. Our notion of One Hundred Per Cent Americanism includes the singing of such songs as America the Beautiful, which gives a picture of our civilization that, thanks to our follies, has little existence in fact, and which feeds a half-truth into the mind of every child that sings it; and we teach them to salute the Flag—which is perfectly all right if at the same time we teach them to preserve that Flag by introducing into their lives the sanities it might well symbolize.

If with the saluting of the Flag, we gave more solid consideration to those lines of social conduct that would *be* a salute to it, we should be getting somewhere. We need something more than a ritual and a loud noise.

The channel through which such changes as I have described could most readily come is the school. If the schools of the country should forthwith begin sending out into the world a younger generation scientifically grounded in a knowledge of its eugenic duty, a sufficient proportion of them would do that duty, and would in time change the whole aspect and meaning of our present civilization. Not only would they produce descendants with an intelligent idea of what it was all about, but they would, on reaching adulthood, be hospitable to forms of socially remedial legislation which are at present exceedingly difficult either to pass or to enforce.

Thus in time we should produce in this country a dominant racial strain, that would be new, improved, and thoroughly fit for survival; a strain which would have within it an inherited bent and vigor of mind and body which would cause it, as by birthright, to make certain demands on life, and to execute these demands by vigorous performance in the art of living.

The puritan strain that settled New England was of this kind; and that handful of Englishmen, only 23 of whom left descendants, settled a continent, and left a mark on human history such as can be attributed, I believe, to no other group of similar size in history. It was a great inheritance; and one of the greatest crimes ever committed against God and Man is that we are today heedlessly throwing it away.

There would, I say, rise up again in this country a

dominant strain, dominant by reason of its natural fitness; and along with it would go at least a partial crowding out, through birth control and other eugenic agencies, of the thousands of unfit and the decadent bipeds who now swarm over this country like noxious insects.

From that dominant class I exclude no European racial strain. Quite possibly it would contain the cream of many racial strains. I merely want to make clear the point that such a class would survive, rule, and increase by virtue of its inherent and inherited qualities; that it would increase and foster those qualities by education; and that it would intensify them always by its intelligent control of *all* the factors which science today recognizes as being active eugenic agents.

About this process there would be nothing arbitrary, forced, or tyrannical. I am not advocating human stud farms nor any other such nonsense. I am advocating freedom and the education that will enable people to use it aright. The change that would result from such a combination would be natural, organic, and slow. It would also be self-conscious, deliberate, and sure of itself.

CHAPTER 33

I believe in the destinies of America. Even as it is the glorious privilege of this present generation to make of its body a bridge whereby the children of the Future may reach to new levels of achievement, so it may be the privilege of America, not to call its civilization the final Social Polity, but rather to be one of the longest single steps the human race has ever taken toward those counsels of perfection to which it forever aspires. We are a bridge toward far-off futures, toward ideal destinies, toward grandeurs of the spirit that are millenniums distant, perhaps, and yet certain in Time to arrive. How if, without ourselves attaining to the full light of these things, we might bring them nearer by thousands of years, near enough to be predicted as sure within the course of immediate centuries! What a legacy to leave! What a glorious function to have filled in the workshop of our God! "Better fifty years of Europe," said Tennyson, "than a cycle of Cathay." Speed is the word; speed is the keynote to which our every national harmony is set; and within these last fifty years, truly, we have set a pace of material achievement that cannot fail to be an enormous stimulus to spiritual life in our children, and which has already produced in our present madcap younger generation conscious reachings out which are as godlike and courageous as they are young.

Peril? Yes, there is peril in it. So was there peril in the Spirit of '76. So was there peril in the guns of Fort Sumter. So was there peril on those trails toward the sunset where the Buffalo and the Indian trod and the Covered Wagon of the White Man followed. So is there peril in what the microscope, the retort, the test tube, and all other eyes of the probing mind of science bring to view. So is there peril in every spark of fire that Prometheus brings from heaven,—Prometheus chained to the Cliff of Time, with what vultures of conservatism tearing at his vitals! In all discovery and in every new thing there is peril. But it were better for the race that it ride the chariot of the sun across the heavens, and plunge to death at high noon from the pinnacle of its daring, than that it rest at ease on the lowlands in the State of As Is.

How hard it is to look at a near thing, and yet see a far thing; how hard to draw one's mortal breath in pain here in the Valley of the Shadow and yet remember the Hills from whence cometh our help; how hard to believe in God more and in Man less,—and yet, as by a divine paradox, a very gift of Grace, find in that choice the ground for unbounded faith in Man.

We are back where we started. I continue my life traveling, with what skill and care I may, these hidden regions of the Human spirit, through landscapes never twice the same. The work must go on. It is my hope that many will in time engage in it; for the world today is ripe for a new profession, the profession of Human Artistry, a royal priesthood, if you like, made up of those with such gifts of eye and hand that they can work on men and women as a sculptor works on marble, amending the flaws and making straight that which was crooked. Part of my thought in the preparation of this book has been that perhaps it would crystallize, in the minds of many, convictions which they may long unconsciously have held,—in solution, as it were,—convictions needing but a touch to give them form, even as a freezing solution in the laboratory needs but a touch to turn it instantly from fluidity to ice.

Particularly do I hope that this book will put heart and hope and understanding of self into many of our bewildered Youth, especially those who have run afoul of certain of our conventions with no clear understanding of how they are and why. To these I say, lose your "conviction of sin," order your lives sanely and courageously, and fear nothing; finally, try to impart to *your* children that gift of rational freedom which carries with it its own valid restraints, its sane and cultured preferences, and legitimate and healthful aspirations. Let *them* march into the Future over *your* bodies, to the end that your mistakes may be their ladder of ascent, and your darkness a light upon their ways. Thus your lives, in humble imitation of the life of the Master, may become a ransom for many.

I come to the end of my theme. It is too big for any book. Always in the background of my mind swirls and changes and shifts a rich kaleidoscopic bewilderment of memories, from which, with or without my bidding, troop thousands of experiences.

I have gleaned a handful from these at random, selecting from the welter what seemed best for the purpose. I have tried to avoid abstractions; rather I have dealt as much as I might in images and pictures of the realities I see. Yet I do it with a sense of despair. How can it be possible, though one spake like a sword or wrote with a pen of fire, to carry over at second-hand that sense of vivid conviction which comes only through immediate contact with the Fact itself. It is not enough that one's words be written, or that they be printed in a book.

I have tried to be honest, and yet to present the truth of recorded fact in a way that would not be needlessly shocking to persons who find such departures from their routine way of thought disturbing; who think there is comfort and security in Habit, safety in Conservative Tradition, and nothing but an unreasonable, foolish, and fruitless peril in the Radicalism that, true to its name, digs and explores amid the Roots of Things. In Life as in Mathematics, a Radical is the Root. From it springs other Life, luxuriant, spawning rankly abundant in the sun. Yet while it spawns it dreams—and dreams—and dreams of those illimitable things toward which it so awfully and mysteriously reaches. To me the whole meaning of Radicalism is these first and last things; and the notion that it is merely a superficial and reckless extremism is itself a superficial reasoning that is unfortunately peculiar to most conservative thought. For conservative thought deals with the surfaces of things, not with their insides. It is interested in preserving the World As Is.

What concerns me, what concerns all Mankind, is the nature of the true and deep Radicals of Human Life, there where they branch and extend themselves endlessly in the dark and silent places of the soil. We are wont to scorn the kindly earth from which the Tree Igdrasil, towering toward Heaven, draws half its nutriment; we call it "dirt"; we tread upon our brother the worm; we find in all this hidden, subtle flow of Life nothing dim, dreaming, and lovely, but only primitive slime and mud. We refuse to dream dreams or to have visions. And herein is our death—Save that in these days we Children of Men have at least *begun* to dream; and may yet, like Moses looking out upon the Promised Land he could not enter, obtain for our descendants, the Children of the Future, this happiness denied to us,—a Dream Come True. Thus in strife and aspiration do we die daily— the Death that passeth into Life.

THE END

AMERICANA LIBRARY

The City: The Hope of Democracy
By Frederic C. Howe
With a new introduction by Otis A. Pease

Bourbon Democracy of the Middle West, 1865–1896
By Horace Samuel Merrill
With a new introduction by the author

*The Deflation of American Ideals: An Ethical Guide
for New Dealers*
By Edgar Kemler
With a new introduction by Otis L. Graham, Jr.

Borah of Idaho
By Claudius O. Johnson
With a new introduction by the author

The Fight for Conservation
By Gifford Pinchot
With a new introduction by Gerald D. Nash

Upbuilders
By Lincoln Steffens
With a new introduction by Earl Pomeroy

The Progressive Movement
By Benjamin Parke De Witt
With a new introduction by Arthur Mann

*Coxey's Army: A Study of the
Industrial Army Movement of 1894*
By Donald L. McMurry
With a new introduction by John D. Hicks

*Jack London and His Times: An Unconventional
Biography*
By Joan London
With a new introduction by the author

San Francisco's Literary Frontier
By Franklin Walker
With a new introduction by the author

Men of Destiny
By Walter Lippmann
With a new introduction by Richard Lowitt

Woman Suffrage and Politics:
The Inner Story of the Suffrage Movement
By Carrie Chapman Catt and Nettie H. Shuler
With a new introduction by T. A. Larson

The Dry Decade
By Charles Merz
With a new introduction by the author

The Conquest of Arid America
By William E. Smythe
With a new introduction by Lawrence B. Lee

The Territories and the United States, 1861-1890:
Studies in Colonial Administration
By Earl S. Pomeroy
With a new introduction by the author

Why War
By Frederic C. Howe
With a new introduction by W. B. Fowler

Sons of the Wild Jackass
By Ray Tucker and Frederick R. Barkley
With a new introduction by Robert S. Maxwell

My Story
By Tom L. Johnson
With a new introduction by Melvin G. Holli

The Beast
By Ben B. Lindsey and Harvey J. O'Higgins
With a new introduction by Charles E. Larsen

The Liberal Republican Movement
By Earle D. Ross
With a new introduction by John G. Sproat

Growth and Decadence of Constitutional Government
By J. Allen Smith
With a new introduction by Dennis L Thompson

Breaking New Ground
By Gifford Pinchot
With a new introduction by James Penick, Jr.

Spending to Save: The Complete Story of Relief
By Harry L. Hopkins
With a new introduction by Roger Daniels

A Victorian in the Modern World
By Hutchins Hapgood
With a new introduction by Robert Allen Skotheim

The Casual Laborer and Other Essays
By Carleton H. Parker
With a new introduction by Harold M. Hyman

Revolt on the Campus
By James Wechsler
With a new introduction by the author

American World Policies
By Walter E. Weyl
With a new introduction by Wilton B. Fowler

The Revolt of Modern Youth
By Ben B. Lindsey and Wainwright Evans
With a new introduction by Charles E. Larsen